THE

EYE

OF THE

I

ALSO BY DAVID R. HAWKINS, M.D., PH.D.

Dissolving the Ego, Realizing the Self

Along the Path to Enlightenment

Letting Go

Healing and Recovery

Reality, Spirituality, and Modern Man

Discovery of the Presence of God: Devotional Nonduality

*Transcending the Levels of Consciousness:
The Stairway to Enlightenment*

Truth vs. Falsehood: How to Tell the Difference

I: Reality and Subjectivity

*Power vs. Force: The Hidden Determinants
of Human Behavior*

Dialogues on Consciousness and Spirituality

*Qualitative and Quantitative Analysis and Calibration of
the Levels of Human Consciousness*

Orthomolecular Psychiatry (with Linus Pauling)

Please visit:

Hay House USA: www.hayhouse.com®
Hay House Australia: www.hayhouse.com.au
Hay House UK: www.hayhouse.co.uk
Hay House India: www.hayhouse.co.in

THE
EYE
OF THE
I

FROM
WHICH
NOTHING
IS HIDDEN

David R. Hawkins, M.D., Ph.D.

HAY HOUSE, INC.
Carlsbad, California • New York City
London • Sydney • New Delhi

Previously published by Veritas Publishing (ISBN 978-096432615-6)

Library of Congress Control Number: 2013946874

Tradepaper ISBN: 978-1-4019-4504-6

13 12 11 10 9
1st Hay House edition, February 2014

Printed in the United States of America

SUSTAINABLE
FORESTRY
INITIATIVE

Certified Chain of Custody
Promoting Sustainable Forestry

www.forests.org
SFI-01268

SFI label applies to the text stock

Straight and narrow is the path ...
Waste no time.
Gloria in Excelsis Deo!

DEDICATION

At a young age, the totality and immensity of man's suffering revealed itself spontaneously as a massive, limitless comprehension. It was a shocking experience that resulted in a dedication to the relief of human suffering by all the means available—science, philosophy, spirituality, neurochemistry, medicine, psychoanalysis, humor, psychiatry, teaching, and healing. The greatest modality of all, however, was given as a gift, and it is this understanding that is capable of healing the very basis of human suffering.

By grace, it is shared with the world with the hope that it will be the catalyst that dissolves some of the sources of human pain and suffering.

This endeavor is dedicated to being a servant of the Lord and therefore, of all mankind. It is with gratitude that the fit that was given is shared. The inspiration to write of what is contained herein came from the joy on the faces of those who heard the speaking of these things. It is by these writings and conversations that their love is returned.

TABLE OF CONTENTS

PREFACE

The scope of this work is immense. It includes not only a detailed, subjective report of very advanced states of spiritual consciousness traditionally called enlightenment, but, for the first time, it correlates and recontextualizes spiritual information in such a manner as to make it comprehensible to reason and the intellect.

This correlation between science and spirituality represents a cohesive integration between the linear and the nonlinear dimensions. By "transcending the opposites," the author resolves the ages-old, seemingly irresolvable conflict and impasse between science and religion, between materiality and spirituality, and between ego and spirit. This resolution then clarifies unresolved mysteries and dilemmas that have been with mankind throughout history. With the expansion of consciousness afforded by this work, questions answer themselves and truth becomes self-evident.

The style of presentation takes the reader back and forth from the linear to the nonlinear domains until, to one's surprise, the incomprehensible becomes not only comprehensible but also actually obvious.

The calibrated level of consciousness of those who have been exposed to this material has been experimentally documented and has shown considerable elevation and advancement. Power accomplishes without effort what force cannot do for it goes where force cannot follow.

This book is written for both the self and the Self of the reader. Although the traditional great obstacle to enlightenment called "transcending the opposites of duality and nonduality" may sound obscure, by the time one has finished the book, this critical awareness is self-resolving.

———

The material is presented in four main sections:
  I.   Description of the Subjective States of Spiritual Awareness
  II. The Spiritual Pathway
  III. The Pathway to Enlightenment Through Understanding the Nature of Consciousness.
  IV. Lectures, dialogues, interviews, and group discussions with a great variety of spiritual students and groups in various countries.

Because of the multiplicity of groups and presentations, at first glance some of the material in the book seems repetitious. However, it is re-presented deliberately because each time it is presented in a different context and in a different sequence of questions and answers. Each re-presentation reveals additional subtleties.

Whereas, in 1985, eighty-five percent of the world's population calibrated below the level of Integrity (200), that has now dropped significantly to seventy-eight percent. Research indicates that this is due to an overall advance in spiritual awareness.

———

The reported material is unique in that the author is neither an ecclesiastic, nor a religionist, nor a theologian but instead has been a clinician with extensive experience in education and science, medicine, psychiatry, psychoanalysis, and research, as well as clinical and scientific writing. He is described as having been accomplished, successful, and talented in many fields. At the time of the advent of his sudden enlightenment, he had the largest psychiatric clinical practice in New York City.

Also unique were the intense spiritual experiences that began in early childhood, recurred in adolescence, and burst forth overwhelmingly during middle life. This caused his retreat to seclusion for a period of years and the final research into the nature of consciousness, which led to *Power versus Force* and this treatise.

Another seeming curiosity is that despite the overwhelming nature of his spiritual experience, he never mentioned it for over thirty years, until the publication of *Power versus Force*. When asked why this was so, he merely commented that "there was nothing you could say about it."

This more advanced work succeeds with the mighty task of making the incomprehensible comprehensible. With adequate description and explanation, the obscure becomes clear and obvious. It was this gift for communication and writing that occasioned Mother Teresa's comments.

The actual author of the book is Consciousness itself.

—The Editor

ACKNOWLEDGEMENTS

Gratitude is due to the many spiritual students for their pertinent questions and enthusiasm and to:

Lynn Johnson for research and preparation of materials.

Susan Hawkins for endless hours of research, critical participation, and inspirational intuition.

Dr. Moon Jin Hee, Radha Soami Meditation Center, General Kyong-Suk Jahng and their spiritual communities for their concordance with the purpose of the work, and to Dr. Moon for the Korean translation.

The gracious members of the National Assembly of the Republic of Korea for their hospitality and generosity of spirit.

Sonia Martin for the diligence required to prepare and edit the manuscript.

CAVEAT

The traditional religionist or the spiritually timid is forewarned that the material herein presented may be disturbing and therefore better bypassed.

The teachings are presented for the seriously committed spiritual student who is seeking God as Enlightenment.

The pathway to Enlightenment via radical truth is demanding and requires surrender of belief systems. Only then does the ultimate reality reveal itself as the sought-after 'I' of the Supreme.

The material presented therefore is from the perspective of the Eye of the I.

INTRODUCTION

Throughout history, descriptions of enlightened states of consciousness have been of great interest to many people, and the reporting of these states has had an impact on individuals and society. The statistical rarity of the occurrence stimulates curiosity and underscores the value of such information.

Although there is already spiritual literature in all languages that describes such states, many of these reports are sketchy and incomplete. Some include errors in translation, and there are many errors in transmission over generations until they finally acquired written form. Some scriptures have therefore included errors that have brought down the level of truth from the original as stated by the enlightened teacher.

An articulate restatement of the evolution of consciousness to advanced states in current language is therefore of value. In addition, many spiritual treatises lack explanation and the reporting of subtle details that are of considerable importance to the advanced seeker. The purpose of *The Eye of the I* is to convey information that can be verified and whose level of truth can be calibrated in order to provide, for the first time, a body of useful information which can withstand the tests of certainty. Until now, spiritual students relied on faith, belief, or hearsay, as well as the reputation and standing of the spiritual teacher.

The complaint of the doubter was that verification of the truth was the very ingredient they were lacking. The great 'doubt block' had to be overcome. As in *Power versus Force*, the truth of every page, paragraph, sentence, and statement in this book has been calibrated and is verifiable. To doubt is to become educated, and the purpose of writing this present book is to share totally that which has been experienced.

Power versus Force ended with "Gloria in Excelsis Deo!" This book begins with that statement by referring to what is the ultimate, final spiritual experience. It is, of course, not an experience at all but instead an eternal state. The condition is its own authority. It speaks for itself; it presents itself as an actuality. There is no speaker. Truth is self-revealing. It stands on its own and is complete, total, profoundly obvious, and overwhelming by virtue of its innate magnificence.

Section One

The Presence of God

An account of Enlightenment in recent times:
Its sudden onset, the replacement of ordinary
consciousness by an Infinite Awareness,
and the transformation of the self to the Self
by the Grace of the Divine Presence.

CHAPTER 1

The Presence

Prologue

Years of inner struggle, suffering, and seemingly futile
spiritual striving had eventually culminated in a state of
black despair. Even a retreat into atheism had not
brought relief from the ceaseless quest. Reason and
intellect were too frail for the formidable task of finding the ultimate truth. The mind itself had been led to
a final, agonizing, crushing defeat. Even the will had
been stilled. Then an inner voice cried out, "If there is a
God, I ask Him for help."

Then all ceased and disappeared into oblivion. The
mind and all sense of a personal self disappeared. In a
stunning moment, it had been replaced by an infinite,
all-encompassing awareness that was radiant, complete, total, silent, and still as the promised essence of
All That Is. The exquisite splendor, beauty, and peace of
Divinity shone forth. It was autonomous, final, timeless,
perfect, the Self of the manifest and the unmanifest, the
Supreme Godhead, and thus was set forth . . .

The Presence

A hushed silence pervades the surroundings, and
motion itself slows and becomes still. All things radiate
forth an intense aliveness. Each is aware of every other.
The luminous quality of the radiance is overwhelmingly
Divine in nature. It completely includes everything in
its total Oneness so that all things are interconnected
and in communication and harmony by means of
awareness and by sharing the basic quality of the
essence of existence itself.

The Presence is a continuum that completely occupies what had appeared previously to ordinary perception as vacant, empty space. That inner Awareness is not different from the Self; it pervades the essence of everything. Awareness is aware of its own awareness and omnipresence. Existence and its expression as both form and formlessness is God and prevail equally in all objects, persons, plants, and animals. Everything is united by the Divinity of existence.

The pervasive Essence includes everything without exception. The furnishings in the room are equal to rocks or plants in their importance or significance. Nothing is excluded from the Allness, which is all encompassing, total, complete, and lacking in nothing. All is of equal value because the only real value is the Divinity of existence.

That which is the Self is total and complete. It is equally present everywhere. There are no needs, desires, or lack. Neither imperfection nor discord is possible, and every object stands forth like a work of art, a piece of sculpture in perfect beauty and harmony. The Holiness of all Creation is the reverence held by everything for everything else. All is imbued with a great splendor, and everything is silenced in awe and reverence. The Revelation instills an infinite Peace and stillness.

A glance at the body reveals it to be the same as everything else—unowned, unpossessed by an individual, equal to the furniture or other objects, and merely part of All That Is. There is nothing personal about the body, and there is no identification with it. It moves about spontaneously, correctly executes its bodily functions, and effortlessly walks and breathes. It is self-propelled, and its actions are determined and activated by the Presence. The body is merely an 'it', equal to any other 'thing' in the room.

When addressed by other persons, the body's voice responds appropriately, but what is heard in the discussion resonates at a higher level of meaning. The deeper and more profound meaning is revealed in every sentence. All communication is now understood at a deeper level, almost as though each simple-sounding question is actually an existential question and statement about mankind itself. On the surface, the wording sounds superficial, but on the deeper level, there are profound spiritual implications.

Appropriate responses are given by the body, which everyone assumes is a 'me' that they are talking to. This in itself is strange because there is no actual 'me' associated with this body at all. The real Self is invisible and has no locality. The body speaks and answers questions simultaneously in parallel ways, on two levels at the same time.

Stilled by the Silence of the Presence, the mind is silent and wordless. No images, concepts, or thoughts occur. There is no one to think them. With no person present, there is neither thinker nor doer. All is happening of itself as an aspect of the Presence.

In ordinary states of consciousness, sound prevails over a background of silence and replaces it. In contrast, in the Presence, the opposite occurs. Although sound is perceptible, it is in the background. The Silence prevails so that the silence is actually not interrupted or displaced by the sound. Nothing disturbs the stillness or interferes with its peace. Although movement occurs, it does not disturb the motionless stillness that is beyond, yet inclusive of, motion. Everything appears to move as though in slow motion because time is absent. There is only a continuous state of Now. There are neither events nor happenings because all starts and stops, all beginnings and endings, occur only in the dualistic consciousness of an observer. In their absence, there is no succession of events to be described or explained.

Instead of thinkingness, there is a self-revealing knowingness that imparts complete understanding and is self-explanatory by its self-effulgent essence. It is as though everything speaks silently and presents itself in its entirety in the absolute beauty of its perfection. In so doing, it manifests its glory and reveals its intrinsic Divinity.

The suffusion of the Presence throughout the totality and essence of all that exists is exquisite in its gentleness, and its touch is like a meltingness. The inner Self is its very core. In the ordinary world, only the surfaces of things can be touched, but in the Presence, it is the innermost essence of everything that is interspersed with every other thing. This touch, which is the Hand of God in its soft gentleness, is at the same time an expression and the abode of infinite power. In its contact with the inner essence of everything, one is aware that the Presence is being felt by every other thing, object, or person.

The power of this gentleness is unlimited, and because it is total and all present, no opposition is possible. It pervades All That Is, and out of its power arises existence itself, which is both created by the power and, at the same time, held together by it. That power is an intrinsic quality of the Presence, and its presence is the essence of existence itself. It is equally present in all objects. There is no emptiness anywhere as the Presence fills all of space and the objects in it. Every leaf shares in the joy of the Divine Presence.

All things are in a state of silent rejoicing that their consciousness is an experience of Divinity. Unique to all things is a still, ever-present gratitude that it has been granted the gift of experiencing the presence of God. This gratitude is the form in which worship is expressed. All that is created and has existence shares in reflecting the glory of God.

Human appearance has taken on a whole new aura. The One Self shines forth through everyone's eyes. A radiance shines forth from everyone's face; everyone is equally beautiful.

Most difficult to describe is the interaction among people that moves onto a different level of communication. There is obvious love among everyone. Their speech, however, has changed so that all conversation has become loving and peaceful. The meaning of the words that are heard is not the same as others hear. It is as though there are two different levels of consciousness going on, coming out of the same scenario of form and movement; two different scripts are being spoken via the same words. The meanings of words themselves have been transformed onto a different plane by the higher selves of the people involved with each other, and the communication of understanding is on a higher plane. At the same time, it is clear that the lower selves of the people are unaware of the communication simultaneously going on with their higher selves. People are as though hypnotized into believing the reality of the ordinary selves, which is merely the unwitting acting out of scenarios or roles, as in a movie.

By ignoring the lesser selves, the higher selves address each other directly, and the persons' ordinary selves appear to be unaware of this ongoing higher level of conversation. At the same time, people are sensing intuitively that something different from the ordinary is happening. The conscious presence of the Self creates an energy field that people find extremely pleasurable. It is this energy field that performs the miraculous and brings occurrences into harmony, along with a sense of peace to all who experience it.

Visitors who had traveled many miles to ask questions suddenly knew in the presence of that aura the answers that came about through an inner understanding that made the original question irrelevant. This occurred because the Presence recontextualized the illusion of a 'problem' and thus caused it to disappear.

The body continued in its operation and reflected the intentions transmitted through consciousness. The continuance of the body was not of any great interest, and it was clear that the body is actually the property of the universe. The bodies and objects in the world reflect endless variation and are without imperfection. Nothing is better or worse than anything else, nor is it of different value or significance. The quality of perfect self-identity defines the intrinsic worth of all that exists as equal expressions of innate Divinity. Inasmuch as 'relationship' is a concept of dualistic mental observation, in Reality there are no relationships. Everything merely 'is' and exhibits the beingness of existence.

Similarly, without the interposition of a functioning observer with its innate categorization of thought, there is neither change nor movement to be explained or described. Each 'thing' is merely evolving as an expression of its divine essence. Evolution therefore takes place as a manifestation of consciousness, and it takes expression from higher-energy abstract levels to lesser but more specific forms, and finally into physical materiality. Thus, creation manifests from the abstract formless through progressive form into a final energy pattern, and then into concrete materiality. The power to become manifest is the expression of divine omnipotence as continuous creation.

Creation is the Present and the Now. This Now is continuous so that neither beginnings nor endings are possible. Visibility, or materiality itself, is merely a sensory phenomenon and not a necessary condition for existence, which is in itself formless yet intrinsic to all form.

Because everything is always in the process of creation, it means that everything is an expression of Divinity, or it would not have the capacity to exist at all. The realization that everything which exists reflects the Divinity of Creation is why it is worthy of respect and reverence. This accounts for the reverence for the spirit within all living beings and nature, which is characteristic of many cultures.

All sentient beings are equal. Only material manifestation is subject to cessation, and essence is unaffected and retains the potentiality of reappearing in material form. Essence is affected only by the forces of evolution itself. The emergence of material form from essence is influenced by the presence of that which is already in form. The content of material manifestation may therefore facilitate essence manifesting as form, or it may not be favorable, depending on conditions. One might say that Creation fulfills its own inner divine

instructions or tendencies. Traditionally this tendency
has been called destiny, which is the unfolding of the
potentiality and the reflection of preexisting conditions (the classical Sanskrit 'gunas' of *rajas, sattva,* and
tamas, or action, awareness, and resistance). Thus, man
can influence conditions in order to potentiate the
manifestation of desired eventualities. Through choices
human consciousness can influence outcomes, but the
power of creation is the province of God.

The nature of creation, which is beyond time,
space, and causality, is self-revealing and presents itself
to the consciousness of Awareness as a gift of the
Presence. All things are intrinsically holy in the divinity
of their creation. When the criticalness and discrimination of dualistic perception are set aside, the absolute
perfection and beauty of everything stands revealed.

Art seeks to abstract this awareness when it takes
one moment in time and freezes it in photographic art
or sculpture. Each stop frame depicts the perfection
that can be appreciated only when a single view is
isolated from the distortion of the superimposed story.
The drama of every moment of existence lends itself to
preservation when art saves it from the extinction of
transformation of material form called history. The
innocence intrinsic to any given moment is apparent
when that moment is taken out of the context projected
onto a sequence of selected moments that then
become a 'story'. Once converted into a story by the
dualistic mind, the terms 'good' or 'bad' are then
applied. One can readily see that even the terms 'good'
or 'bad' refer in their origination to what is really merely
human desire. If something is desired, it becomes a
'good', and if undesired, it becomes a 'bad'. If human

judgmentalism is removed from observation, all that can be seen is that form is in constant evolution as 'change', which is neither intrinsically desirable nor undesirable.

Everything is manifesting its inherent potentiality as determined by its essence and prevailing conditions. The splendor of all things is that by their very existence, they manifest the glory of God's creation as existence itself. By virtue of merely 'being', each and every sentient and insentient thing that exists is fulfilling the will of God. It is because of divine intention that the unmanifest becomes manifest; creation is the name of the process that we witness.

Because the nature of Creation is not apparent to ordinary consciousness, the mind manufactures conundrums that have no answers, e.g., how can a 'good' God allow so much that is 'bad'? Beyond dualistic perception and arbitrary categories of manifestation, there is neither good nor bad to be explained, and it can be seen that the universe itself is harmless. The human mind constructs its scenarios of goals and desires, and events are either concordant with them or not. Both tragedy and victory occur only within the limitations of the dualistic mind and have no independent reality. Everything in this world seems to arise and then dissolve within the limitations of perception. Inasmuch as Reality is beyond time, space, and form, it is immaterial whether a 'thing' or a 'person' exists for a split second or for a thousand years. Thus the struggle to live a few more years or even a few more moments appears to be an empty illusion because existence is not experienced within time at all. This moment is the only reality that is being experienced; all else is an abstraction and a mental construct. Therefore, one cannot actually live seventy years at all; only this exact, fleeting moment is possible.

In the reality of nonduality, everything is complete, and desire is replaced by appreciation. As life evolves, each living thing is the total expression of its potentiality at any given moment. Motivation as such disappears, and action takes place as a phase in the process of potentiality actualizing. There is, therefore, no actor behind the action. There is, instead, a sense of completeness and total fulfillment in every moment. Enjoyment of physical needs is the product of action itself. The appetite for eating, for example, arises out of the act of eating, with no prior desire for the next bite. If eating is stopped by an interruption, there is no feeling of loss. The joy of life originates out of one's existence at any given moment, and the awareness of continuous completion is an aspect of the joy of existence. The totality of the Oneness of the All cannot be 'experienced'. Instead, it is known by virtue of being it. The 'I' of the Self is the Eye of God witnessing the unfolding of Creation as Now. Sequence is an illusion created by the perception of the 'I' of the ego, which is the point of observation of the processing of the nonlocal to the local, of the nonlinear to the linear, of Allness to 'this-ness'. Perception is the eye of the ego that, as it translates the inexperienceable Infinite to the experienceable finite, produces the perception of time, place, duration, dimension, position, form, limitation, and singularity.

CHAPTER 2

The Resumption of Earthly Life

The perceptual world had been replaced. Identity had shifted from being a limited subject (a personal 'I') to unlimited context. Everything was transformed and revealed beauty, perfection, love, and innocence. Everyone's face shone forth with the glow of inner beauty. Every plant revealed itself as an art form. Each object was a perfect sculpture.

All exists effortlessly in its own place, and everything is sequenced in synchronicity. The miraculous is continuous. The details of life mysteriously accommodate themselves spontaneously. The energy of the Presence effortlessly accomplishes the seemingly impossible and brings about phenomena that the ordinary world would consider miraculous.

There was a period of several years during which what are ordinarily called psychic phenomena (the classical *siddhis*) occurred spontaneously with regularity. Such phenomena as clairvoyance, distant viewing (the ability to see what is ahead), telepathy, and psychometry were common. There was an automatic knowing of what people were thinking and feeling before they spoke. Divine love prevailed as the organizing power and was the all-present stage upon which all phenomena occurred.

The Physical Body

An extremely powerful energy ran up the spine and the back and into the brain where it would center, depending on where attention was focused. The energy then passed down over the face and into the region of the heart. This energy was exquisite and would sometimes flow out into the world where there was human distress.

One time, while driving down a remote highway, the energy began to pour out from the heart and go down the highway and around the next bend. From there the energy poured into the site of an automobile accident that had just occurred. The energy had a healing effect on everyone that it enveloped. After a short while, the energy seemed to have accomplished its purpose, and suddenly, it came to a stop. A few miles farther down the same highway, the same phenomenon began to recur. Again, a delicious, exquisite energy poured forth from the heart region and again went down the road about a mile and around another bend. There, another accident had just occurred. In fact, the wheels of the car were still spinning. The energy was pouring into the passengers. It was as if a channel for some angelic energy was transmitting to the people in distress who were praying.

Another time, the healing presence occurred during a walk down a street in Chicago. This time, the energy poured into a group of young men who were about to get into a fight. As the energy enveloped them, they slowly fell back and started to relax and laugh. They began to disband, at which point the energy flow stopped.

The energy aura that emanated from the Presence had infinite capacity. People wanted to sit near it because in that energy field, they automatically went into a state of bliss or a higher state of consciousness and experienced that feeling of divine love, joy, and healing. In it, disturbed people became calm and self-healed.

The body, which I had previously considered as

'mine', now healed itself of a variety of illnesses. Astonishingly, sight occurred without wearing glasses. The impaired vision had required trifocal glasses since the age of twelve. The capacity to be able to see without glasses, even at a distance, came on suddenly without warning and was a pleasant surprise. When it occurred, there was a realization that sensory faculties were a function of consciousness itself and not the body. Then the memory came back of an experience of being 'out of the body' during which the capacity to see and hear went with the 'etheric' body and was not connected at all with the physical body, which was some distance away in a different location.

It appeared that physical illness was really the result of negative belief systems and that the body could actually literally change as a result of the shift of a belief pattern. One is really subject only to what is held in mind. (It is a common observation that many people have recovered from almost every illness known to mankind by following spiritual pathways.)

The seemingly miraculous properties and capacity of the divine energy and the phenomena it brought about were intrinsic to that energy field and were in no way personal. They occurred spontaneously and seemed to be occasioned by some need somewhere in the world.

It was also interesting that many of the ordinary people who witnessed these phenomena handled it by going into denial and actually blanking out what they had just witnessed as it seemed to be completely outside the ego's perceptual systems and belief of what was possible. If asked about the phenomena, the people quickly manufactured some rationalization, similar to patients who have been hypnotized and fabricate a plausible answer when asked to explain a post-hypnotic behavior. In contrast, people who were quite spiritually evolved accepted the occurrence of miraculous phenomena without comment as though it was a natural part of life.

After the major transformation of consciousness, the Presence determines all actions and events. A permanent alteration of consciousness establishes itself and is constantly present in its stillness and silence, even though the body talks and functions in the world. Over the years, with effort, there develops the capacity to focus on various levels as is required at the time to be able to function within the world. If allowed to, the silent Peace takes over completely and brings on a state of quiet, infinite joy. By withdrawing interest from the external world and the ordinary functions of perception, the infinite bliss state prevails and can only be curtailed by intense focus on the ordinary world. The Self is beyond time and form, and within it, the ordinary consciousness is potentially able to simultaneously function in a worldly manner.

There was a difficulty in considering the world of ordinary perception to be real and taking it seriously. This led to a sort of permanent capacity to see the world from a humorous viewpoint. Ordinary life seemed to be an endless comedy so that even seriousness itself was humorous. It became necessary to quell expressions of the sense of humor that some people were unable to accept because they were so deeply involved in the perceptual world of negativity.

Most people seem to have a vested interest in the negativity of their perceptual world and resist leaving it for awarenesses on a higher level. People seem to derive sufficient satisfaction from their endless anger, resentment, remorse, and self-pity to actively resist moving on to such levels as understanding, forgiveness, or compassion. There seems to be sufficient gain in negativity so as to perpetuate ways of thinking that are obviously illogical and self-serving, much as politicians distort the truth in order to gain votes, or criminal prosecutors suppress evidence of the innocence of the accused in order to obtain a conviction.

When these negative 'gains' are relinquished, the world becomes an endless presence of intense beauty and perfection, and love dominates all of life. Everything is self-luminous, and the joy of its divine essence shines forth, radiating through its all-present formlessness, which is expressed in the perceptual world as form. There is no further need to 'know' anything because there is no further need to know when one is actually all that exists. The mind in its ordinary state merely knows 'about'. That is no longer necessary when one is everything that can be. The Identity, which replaced the former sense of 'I', has no parts or divisions. Nothing is excluded from its totality and its Allness. The Self has become the Essence, not different from the essence of everything. In nonduality, there is neither a knower nor that which is known because they have become one and the same. Nothing is incomplete. Omniscience is self-completion. There is no desire for the next second of experiencing that propels the ordinary mind, which, from moment to moment, always feels incomplete.

The sense of completeness prevails with the physical senses. Desire and anticipation disappear, and pleasure arises out of the activity itself. Because the experience of time has stopped, there is no experience of a succession of events to be anticipated or regretted. Each moment is total and complete within itself. The condition of beingness replaces all sense of past, present, or future so that there is nothing to anticipate or try to control. This is part and parcel of the profound state of peace and stillness. All needs and wants stop with the cessation of any sense of time. The Presence, with its infinite stillness, has displaced all mental and emotional activity. The body becomes self-propagating and merely another property of nature that functions by responding to the flow of conditions. Nothing moves or acts independently of the entire universe. In absolute concordance, all lives, moves, and has its existence in the absolute perfection, beauty, and harmony of All That Is.

Motivation as the basis for action disappeared. The phenomena of life were now of a different dimension and were observed as though one were in a different realm. Everything occurs of its own in the state of inner stillness and silence, activated by the love that expresses itself as the universe and everything in it. The beauty of life shines forth as infinite joy and happiness, infinitely peaceful and beyond emotion. The peace of God is so complete and total that there is nothing left to desire or want. Even 'experiencing' has ceased. In duality, there is an experiencer and, separately, that which is experienced. In nonduality, this is replaced by having become All That Is so there is no separation in time, space, or subjective experience between the experiencer and that which is experienced.

In the nonduality of awareness, even sequence no longer occurs, and awareness replaces experiencing.

There is no longer the experience of 'moments', as there is only a continuous Now. Movement appears as slow motion, as though suspended outside of time. Nothing is imperfect. Nothing actually moves or changes; no events actually take place. Instead of sequence, there is the observation that everything is in a stage of unfolding, and that all form is only a transitional epiphenomenon created by perception and the observational habits of mentation. In reality, all comes into being as an expression of the infinite potentiality of the universe. Evolving states are the consequences of conditions but are not caused by them. Conditions account for appearances, and the phenomena as change are really the result of an arbitrary point of observation.

From the viewpoint of singularity, there appears to be multiplicity, but from the omnipresence of simultaneous multiplicity, there is only the singularity of oneness. Omnipresence obliterates any perceptual artifact of either singularity or multiplicity. In reality, neither condition exists. There is neither 'here' nor 'there'; there is neither 'now' nor 'then'; there is neither 'past' nor 'future'; there is neither 'complete' nor 'incomplete', nor is there 'becoming' in that which is already and totally self-existent. Time itself is an arbitrary point of observation as is the speed of light. Our customary attempts to describe the universe can be seen not as a description of the universe but instead as a description of arbitrary points of observation and really as a map of how the ordinary mind works.

What is actually being described is not an objective, self-existent universe but merely the categories of mentation of the mind and the structures and forms of its sequential processing. The limitation of science, then, is preordained by the limitations imposed by the perceptual world of duality. Perception itself is self-limiting in that it can only know 'about' rather than know. Science is not expected to reach beyond the limits of perception nor should it be faulted for failing to do so. It can only take us to the threshold of awareness, which does not depend on perception at all. In actuality, science progresses by scientific intuition, with the logic and the proof coming afterwards. We customarily call these intuitive leaps creativity, which supersede logic and energize progress. Thus, discovery is the real mainspring of the evolution of society.

In the state of Awareness, the mind has become silent. Logical or sequential thought has stopped, and instead, there is silence and stillness, and a continuous, effortless unfolding and presentation as revelation. Knowingness unfolds of itself and the divinity of All That Is silently shines forth as self-evident and self-effulgent. All stands forth in complete and continuous revelation. There is no need to seek or get for everything already is in its totality and completeness. All seeming action takes place on its own.

There is no doer behind action in that the mythical entity that one had always assumed was the wellspring of experience had disappeared and dissolved into the absolute oneness of the universe. The Self, in its totality and completeness, is beyond and before all worlds, universes, or time, dependent on nothing and caused by nothing. The Self is beyond existence, neither subject to existence nor nonexistence, beginning nor ending, time nor space. It cannot even be included in the concepts of 'is' or 'is not'. The Self is neither manifest nor unmanifest and is beyond any dimensions implied by such categorization of concepts.

The capacity to operate cogently in the world of ordinary experience required some major adjustments. There is a continuity and oneness between the 'realms' of duality and nonduality, and nonduality pervades all duality. The limitation within duality is really one of awareness. This limitation of awareness appears to be the consequence of focus.

Human beings are seen to be innocent due to their extreme unawareness and unconsciousness of their reality. In this state, they are run by programming and illusory belief systems. At the same time, the purity of spirit shines forth as their intrinsic beauty.

It might be said in modern terms that people are run by their 'software programs' of which they are unconscious. Each person is in the process of the evolution of consciousness, with some more evolved than others. Each one represents the unfolding of consciousness under different conditions and therefore has different levels of appearance. It is as though each person is caught in a certain level and cannot proceed to another level without the consent, decision, and agreement of the will. The intrinsic innocence is because, comparably, the person is like the hardware, and their actions and beliefs are like the software. The hardware is unaffected by the software programs that they are following blindly without awareness of significance or consequence of these actions. Classically, the unconscious software programs are called 'karma'.

The state in which ordinary people operate does not imply any moral fault or defect but merely represents the possibilities of the fields of consciousness as they express themselves through each living entity. Although, in reality, there is neither 'good' nor 'bad', it is obvious that all actions have consequences. Behind the apparent differences, there is actually only the reality of the one Self shining forth as the source of life in all that lives; each entity lives in the stop frame of this instant, which is all there actually is beyond their awareness.

In nonduality, in no one instant can any such thing as a 'problem', 'conflict', or 'suffering' occur. These all arise in anticipation of the next instant or recall of the past. The ego appears to be the product of fear, and its purpose is to control the next instant of experience and ensure its survival. It seems to vacillate between fear of the future and regret over the past, and the desire and sense of time that repel action stems from the illusion of lack. With a sense of completion, desire ceases. That which believes it is finite fears for its survival for it is subject to time and the illusions of causality.

When the usual motivations of life disappeared, it became effortless. What had been the personality was now only a vague propensity that seemed to know how to mimic ordinary behavior from a recollection of those patterns, but its ongoingness stemmed from a different source. What had previously been considered to be personal was now obviously impersonal. For one thing, the real Self could not really explain itself to others. What to this Self was reality, rocklike, and substantial, when expressed in words, it sounded abstract or philosophical to ordinary people who were run by concepts and sequential thought patterns; what seemed mystical to the average person was merely concrete, subjective reality. It took effort to reenergize ordinary thought patterns in order to facilitate verbal communication. The real 'I' is beyond consciousness itself but can radiate down as the capacity to move out of bliss into worldly activity. Love becomes the sole motivator of the continuance of physical existence.

During the transition, the body felt a considerable strain as though the nervous system was having to handle more energy than it was originally designed to do. The body's nerves often felt as though they were high-tension wires burning with high-voltage energy and current. This eventually required moving away from the big city and the life that went with it to a small town in the West that had, over the years, attracted people who were dedicated to a nonmaterialistic, spiritually oriented life. Now meditation could take the place of activity and the bliss state would return, resulting in what appeared to be an ascetic lifestyle only because there were neither needs nor wants. There was a time of even forgetting to eat, as though the body were very peripheral or perhaps not even in existence. One could pass a mirror and be surprised that there was even a body image there. There was no interest in the events of the world, a condition that lasted for some ten years of withdrawal from ordinary functioning in order to become adjusted to the spiritual state that had replaced the former consciousness.

One aspect of this state of awareness was the capacity to discern greater significances within phenomena than were ordinarily observed. Thus, the interesting clinical technique of muscle testing revealed the missing link and bridge between the mind and the body, and between the manifest and the unmanifest. That which is invisible could now easily be made visible. This clinical phenomenon transcended the autonomic nervous system or the acupuncture system as an explanation of the link between psyche and soma. It was obvious that the muscle-test response originated from the nonlocality of consciousness, and that its former limitation to the investigation of local phenomena was an expression of the limitation of perception of the clinicians or experimenters.

Although it is only because of nonduality that duality can be said to exist, muscle testing was the easiest and most practical phenomenon by which to take advantage of that reality. It became obvious that one could actually calibrate the different energy fields within consciousness and arrange them in a hierarchical scale, and when calibrated numerically, literally demonstrate the classical levels of consciousness as described since the beginning of time.

The most astonishing aspect of the phenomenon was its capacity to instantly register the difference between truth and falsehood. This quality was beyond time and space and bypassed the human psyche and the minds of the individuals involved. It was a universal quality of consciousness, just as protoplasm has the universal qualities of reactivity to stimuli. Protoplasm reacts involuntarily to noxious or beneficial stimuli and differentiates between the two. It withdraws from that which is antithetical to life and is attracted to that which supports it. With lightning-like speed, the muscles of the body go instantly weak in the absence of truth; they go strong in the presence of truth or that which supports life.

Everything in the world, including thoughts, concepts, substances, and images, calls forth a response that can be demonstrated as positive or negative. The response is not limited by time, space, distance, or personal opinion.

With this simple tool, the exact nature of everything in the universe, anywhere in time, could be explained and documented. All that ever is or was, without exception, radiates forth a frequency and a vibration as a permanent imprint in the impersonal field of consciousness and can be retrieved by this test through consciousness itself.

The universe stood revealed; secrets were no longer possible. It was apparent that "every hair on one's head" could indeed and in fact be counted and that no sparrow could fall unnoticed. That "all will be revealed" had become a fact.

Power Versus Force

A testing procedure was tried on literally thousands of test subjects, both individually and in groups. The results were universally concordant, irrespective of the age or mental state of the test subjects. The applications of the discovery were obvious in the fields of clinical activity, research, and spiritual teaching.

The discoveries that ensued were recorded in the book, *Power versus Force*, as well as in a Ph.D. dissertation published as "Qualitative and Quantitative Analysis and Calibration of the Levels of Human Consciousness." The purpose of the latter endeavor was to give additional credibility and scientific validation to the discoveries that were not explicable by ordinary human logic or the restrictions of Newtonian causality.

Although the numerical scale of consciousness is logarithmic and numerically presented, the fields of consciousness that are referenced are nonlinear and beyond the Newtonian paradigm of reality. The scale provides a link between the known and the unknown, between the manifest and the unmanifest, between duality and nonduality. The value of such a tool was so immense that many people went into paradigm shock when they first discovered this work. That anyone anywhere can instantly tell the truth about anyone, anything, or everything anywhere in time or space is a giant leap and can be disturbing at first to one's sense of reality. Everyone thinks they are completely separate and that their thoughts are private.

One value of the research tool was that it could be used to check the truth and validity of its own research and experimental work. Thus, in *Power versus Force*, as in this book, every chapter was calibrated. The book as a whole was also calibrated and found to be in the 800s, so the inference was that the energy of the book itself would accomplish its own spread and communication. And, as such, it did, all by itself, with no advertising or promotion. It spread to other countries and continents and into other translations. It eventuated into widespread interest and distribution and is used by study groups in colleges, universities, and research departments.

On the Map of the Scale of Consciousness (see Appendix B), the level 600 indicates the crossing over from the perceptual world of duality to the nonperceptual world of nonduality. Interestingly enough, the muscle test and response itself calibrate at 600. This means that its true nature cannot really be comprehended by most people, although everyone can learn to use it in a practical manner.

Interest in the book, *Power versus Force*, came

primarily from spiritually interested people and groups as well as from healers and those interested in studying consciousness itself. Although the book defines very profound benefits from applying the technique to many areas of ordinary human life, thus far there has been very little interest from those areas of society that could benefit instantly and to a great degree by the use of the technique. Society has yet to discover its profound benefits.

Section Two

The Spiritual Process

CHAPTER 3

The Nature of the Quest

Nonlinear learning takes place more as a result of familiarity than by logically sequenced, processed intellection. Consciousness tends to advance as an automatic consequence of having acquired new information. On review, then, it is capable of integrating information that may have been missed or not understood. Each exposure advances integration and therefore new insights.

It was discovered that a clinically useful diagnostic muscle test had a much higher potentiality than had been previously suspected. Much as the telescope is found to be capable of revealing the planets of the universe and not just the goings-on in the woods or the neighbors' back yards, the muscle test was found to be based on a nonlocal, universal quality of consciousness that was impersonal and that transcended the personality or the particulars of the test subject.

It was found that the response of the body's muscles to a test stimulus was determined by an essential quality of consciousness itself that is able to instantly react to the presence of truth by going strong, thereby giving a 'yes' or positive response. The absence of truth is indicated by weakness, a 'no' response. Investigation of this reproducible phenomenon was conducted with thousands of test subjects from all walks of life over a twenty-year period and confirmed by teams of investigators.

By clinical trial and error, research established that the muscle-test response differentiated between that which was beneficial and that which was destructive. It had diagnostic value for discerning physical disease and identifying beneficial treatments. These events occurred in the 1970s, leading to the development of the whole clinical body of information, and clinicians established colleges of kinesiology and applied kinesiology. These primarily attracted general physicians and holistic health practitioners. It also attracted the interest of a psychiatrist, Dr. John Diamond, who took the research to a new level and began to use the muscle response to investigate attitudes, emotions, belief systems, music, sounds, and symbols. This heralded the advent of Behavioral Kinesiology, which had much broader implications.

The next step was the use of the muscle-test response to categorize and eventually numerically calibrate the levels of consciousness. These had been classically stratified in philosophical and spiritual traditions, as the well-recognized levels of spiritual advancement accepted in all cultures. It was found that these stratified levels could be calibrated (logarithmically). A useful scale of consciousness emerged that correlated and, in fact, illustrated man's entire history. It was found that on an arbitrary scale of 1 to 1,000, anything that calibrated below the level of 200 was negative, anti-life, false, and universally experienced as destructive. Consciousness, then, could differentiate truth from falsehood, which was a major discovery.

The next leap in awareness was the discovery that the level 200 differentiated between power and force, which enabled an investigation into the different qualities of these two contrasting realms. Force is temporary, consumes energy, and moves from one location to another. Power, in contrast, is self-sustaining, permanent, stationary, and invincible. The result of these investigations led to the emergence of the Calibrated Scale of Consciousness and the publication of *Power versus Force*. The different levels were correlated with social phenomena and also with the prevailing levels of consciousness that were found to dominate human consciousness.

Although the calibrations of these levels can be denoted numerically for easy recognition and understanding, it was discovered that they actually refer to realms beyond the reach of traditional science. This had, in the interim, become termed "chaos theory" or "nonlinear dynamics." The realm of nonduality is not describable in terms of traditional mathematics, such as differential calculus. The realm of nondualistic, nonlinear reality turned out to be the realm traditionally described as spiritual. The power behind human affairs stemmed from these indefinable, indescribable, and immeasurable realities that constituted human motivation, significance, and meaning.

Life itself had been beyond scientific investigation because life is nonlinear and dynamic. Thus, the descriptive terminology and conceptualization of linear Newtonian physics and its paradigm of reality had to be transcended.

The measurable, observable, physical world turned out to be a world of effects, with no intrinsic power. Real power resides in the infinitely powerful domains of the unseen and the nonlinear. Reality was not describable in terms of time, dimension, location, or measurement but existed independently in the infinite potentiality beyond space and time, traditionally called 'Reality'. These are the infinite 'domains' that had never been described except by exceptionally gifted individuals deemed to be enlightened.

Investigation of the higher calibrated levels of consciousness correlated exactly with the degree of enlightenment of the great spiritual teachers of human history. It was found that no human had ever lived who calibrated at a consciousness level beyond 1,000, and those who did calibrate in such high numbers had been accorded the status of great teacher, Christ, Buddha, Krishna, Avatar, Savior, the teachers of Divinity, or the windows of God. For thousands of years their teachings had shaped mankind's context of reality and contextualized the total human experience.

Of exceptional value is the discovery that inasmuch as everything in the universe, even the smallest thought, gives off a calibratable energy or vibratory track, these vibratory events were recorded permanently in the energy field of consciousness, which was beyond time and space.

Outside time or space, there is no 'then' or 'now', no 'here' or 'there'. All that ever transpired had laid down a permanent record that was calibratable and retraceable. 'All that ever was' in the universe still is and is identifiable, discernible, and trackable by anyone anywhere, at any time.

All supposedly 'unrecorded history' had, in fact, been precisely recorded forever with identifying details. With this realization, scripture now actually became verifiable. The capacity to discern, discriminate, and differentiate between truth and falsehood revealed itself for the first time in human history. This led to a massive amount of research. The accuracy of the ensuing observations was subjected to academic standards of research and published as the dissertation,

"Qualitative and Quantitative Analysis and Calibration of the Levels of Human Consciousness."

The necessary preconditions, background, and basis for the evolution of this progressive understanding of human consciousness had been the emergence of a transformative, enlightening state of consciousness in 1965. The brilliance, peace, love, and profound compassion and understanding of the Divine Presence revealed the infinite nature of reality as the awareness/Self and source of all existence beyond all time, form, conditions, or description.

Innate to the Presence is an Infinite, Timeless Knowingness that illuminates all possibility, beyond all opposites or causality. Revelation presents itself as self-explanatory and obvious, the essence of all truth. The totality and completeness of the knowingness prevails beyond time and is therefore always present. One reflection of its presence is the capacity to comprehend the incomprehensible by its self-revelation of its essence. Therefore, all stands revealed. The unmanifest and the manifest are one and the same.

The essence of truth is subjectivity, which transcends duality and yet provides a bridge between. It took years to perfect the bridge so that communication of the ineffable to the world of form was made possible. The book, *Power versus Force*, was the result.

The discoveries thus far described had profound implications and evolved into years of research by peers and then teams of co-investigators by whom hundreds of thousands of calibrations were made of every aspect of human life, events, and personages of history. These included spiritual teachings, literature, and teachers.

Out of all this emerged lengthy calibrations of human attitudes, ideas, concepts, and belief systems. The sheer mass of data took years to correlate and abstract the essentials in order to be able to provide a comprehensive presentation of the information. The data had obvious potential value to mankind as a research technique for obtaining heretofore inaccessible knowledge.

The leap from the Newtonian paradigm of linear causality, perception, and duality to the nonlinear reality that transcends perception is not easily made in our society. However, it is of value to those who work towards spiritual evolution or the progression of science to understanding the nature of life itself.

The discovery of the distribution of the levels of consciousness throughout society was also quite significant and explained much of human behavior in history. How millions of people, whole generations and whole cultures, even whole continents, could be so easily manipulated to their own destruction was explained by the discovery that seventy-eight percent of the world's population calibrates below the level of Integrity at 200. In addition to this limitation, the consciousness level of mankind as a whole remained at only 190 and was unchanged for centuries until, suddenly, in 1986, it jumped across the critical line from falsehood to Integrity and Truth at 200, and on to its current level at 207, which indicates progressive integrity and truth. The calibrated Scale of Consciousness, together with the capacity of the muscle test, thus provided a reliable map and compass for anyone desiring to evolve spiritually or advance their level of consciousness.

The heavy programming of man's consciousness by negativity has meant that not only is seventy-eight percent of the population below the level of Integrity at 200, but only four percent of the world's population ever reaches the level of Love at 500, and only 0.4 percent reaches the level of 540, or Unconditional Love. The consciousness level of Enlightenment at 600, which is the crossover from duality to nonduality, is reached by approximately one in ten million persons (0.000001 percent). Also of importance is the realization of the enormously different levels of power between the calibrated levels. Because they are logarithmic, even a few points are very significant. If the muscle-testing method and the Scale of Consciousness are used to elucidate the underpinnings of the great barrier of duality that arises from perception, which, in turn, arises from positionality, the veil that hides the light of truth falls away. Divinity is present everywhere but obscured by identification with the mind and the body.

The Eye of the I is the Self of Divinity expressed as Awareness. The unmanifest, transcendental divinity of Allah/God/Brahman/Krishna becomes manifest as the Self/Atman—the immanent divinity.

Spiritual evolution occurs as the result of removing obstacles and not actually acquiring anything new. Devotion enables surrender of the mind's vanities and cherished illusions so that it progressively becomes freer and more open to the light of Truth.

Illumination refers to those spiritual states where sufficient barriers have been dropped, either deliberately or unconsciously, so that a greater context suddenly presents itself, and in so doing, illuminates, clarifies, and reveals an expanded field of consciousness actually experienced as inner light. This is the light of awareness, the radiance of the Self that emanates as a profound lovingness. Although, for many people, the experience may not last (as in near-death experiences), the residual effect is permanent and transformative. In due time, the light is likely to return again for periods of infinite bliss, peace, and silence, followed by a profound gratitude for the gift.

The unforgettable event tends to set up a yearning to return to that state, which may result in the willingness to give up everything in this world to do so. Curiosity is replaced by dedication, surrender, and devotion. Spiritual inspiration strengthens and becomes the guiding light of one's life. All human desires fade away in comparison to what is now realized as the ultimately possible state. One then has become truly a devotee and a servant of God for whom one is willing to surrender all that this life has to offer.

The next obstacle that is likely to arise is impatience, which sometimes reaches the level of desperation. Having once experienced Shangri-la, the explorer will risk life itself and make any sacrifice in order to return. The search and the journey can become a powerful, driving obsession. There is, therefore, sometimes the awful grief at the disappearance of that illumined state, or the guilt that perhaps one has done something to deserve being separated from it. One beseeches God in heaven for assistance.

Despair can set in, as well as periods of despondency and self-blame. These are followed, however, by even more powerful rededication and commitment to the journey. The soul is unwilling and now perhaps even unable to settle for anything less than the presence of God. Surrender occurs at greater and greater depths until there is finally the willingness to let even one's very self as 'I' disappear. That 'self' goes deeper and is stronger than one had suspected. Its hold seems tenacious and fierce.

Then, by the greatest surrender, which is accomplished not by one's own will but by the grace of God, the agony of the death of the ego/self occurs and seems almost unbearable. It then disappears into eternity, and into the vacancy swells the All-encompassing Presence in stunning glory and radiance. That one ever experienced oneself as separate or not identical with that Presence is unthinkable and incomprehensible. There is no explanation.

There then arose the potentiality for the one to know and experience itself as One. It is simultaneously both and yet neither. That is the present state or condition—all potentiality, all possibility, all states—all of them, yet none of them. It is not verbally explicable.

Preliminaries

One difficulty with spiritual writings is that they often do not present a context of familiarity so that a seeker can approach the subject with comfort. For instance, it is often stated that the personal life of the writer or speaker is of no consequence, which, although true in an absolute sense, ignores the level of consciousness of most of humanity that has a natural curiosity and expectation about the style in which information needs to be presented. To say that one's personal life is of no significance has no meaning to most people.

There is a natural tendency to be curious about what kind of person experiences unusual spiritual revelations. There is curiosity about the personality traits or lifestyle. There is also the intuitive awareness that to understand it is to discover that perhaps those traits or characteristics tend to eventuate in spiritual awareness. Perhaps there are certain personality styles or characteristics that are common to those who become dedicated to spiritual discovery or who realize certain states of consciousness.

The spiritual pathway is facilitated by certain characteristics that become reinforced and more powerful with practice, experience, and success. These include the capacity to focus unswervingly on a goal and to concentrate fixedly on a technique or spiritual exercise with commitment and dedication. Thus, there is a resolution of purpose and a willingness to let go of everything or anything based upon one's profound belief and faith in a spiritual teaching or truth. In general, there is a willingness to forgive and love rather than to hate and condemn. There is a willingness to forsake the lesser for the greater and a desire to understand rather than to judge. The reason people with spiritual interests seem to congregate is because they have a preference for peace and tranquility over stimulation and excitement. Perhaps the most useful tool is the capacity for humility and the realization of the limitations of ordinary consciousness and their consequences. To ensure the validity of one's direction of endeavor, it is crucial to calibrate the level of truth of every teaching, teacher, guru, or spiritual group.

Historically, it can be seen that mankind stumbles

on blindly, much like ships did in the unmarked oceans, without a compass or maps. Literally hundreds of millions of people throughout time have been destroyed for lack of a simple technique to overcome the mind's incapacity to tell a sheep from a wolf in sheep's clothing. Whole nations have gone down; whole civilizations have died from following propaganda, slogans, and belief systems that, when muscle tested, make one go weak. Although the muscle-testing technique may sound simple and crude, so was the discovery of the lodestone for use as a compass.

Most people on the planet today owe their survival to things that were once thought unscientific and crude, such as the dirty-looking growth of mold on a petri dish that was observed to be able to kill bacteria. This little discovery led to antibiotics and thereby increased mankind's quality of health and expected longevity.

The naïve seeker is fair game for any and all would-be captors via various ideologies through the sheer influence of numbers, persuasion, and charisma. Peer pressure for the gullible is also prevalent so that finding one's way through the thickets of profuse religious and purportedly spiritual teachings becomes hazardous and problematic. It requires some inner conviction and means of guidance to not follow the throngs of worshippers because the herd instinct is strong. Surely, one's mind says to itself, "All those millions of people could not be wrong or be misled by error." To find the answer to this paradox, we merely need to examine the makeup of those throngs of often-zealous believers. That human error is not only possible but also certain and probable becomes evident from the fact that seventy-eight percent of the world's population calibrates below the level of 200, the level of Truth and Integrity.

The muscle-testing response is determined solely by the response of universal consciousness to either truth or falseness. On an arbitrary scale (see Appendix B), that which makes one go strong is calibrated at the level of 200. That which is false or destructive calibrates below 200. (From zero to 200, one discovers the levels of Shame, Guilt, Remorse, Fear, Hate, Greed, Pride, Avarice, Anger, etc.)

At the level of Truth and Integrity, the body goes strong, and these levels go up through Courage, Neutrality, Willingness, Capability, Lovingness, Joy, and Peace. The positive levels are then calibrated from 200 up to a possible 1,000. Love is at 500, the Intellect is in the 400s, and Capability and Willingness are in the 300s. That seventy-eight percent of mankind calibrates below the level of 200 means that most of society assumes that falsehood is truth. Only twenty-two percent of the world's population is even capable of understanding what truth is, and of that, only four percent of the world's population calibrates at 500 or over, which is the level of Love. Farther up the scale, the number of people at the top of this pyramid of humanity dwindles rapidly. Enlightenment calibrates at 600, where duality dissolves into nonduality. The 700s are the realm of the great spiritual teachers, gurus, and saints. Few can be identified in the 800s or 900s. The energy field at 1,000 is the maximum that can be tolerated by the human body and nervous system, and it is the rare level of the great avatars of history. No human has ever existed who calibrated beyond 1,000.

The value of all these realizations is merely to describe a means of discernment because human consciousness lacks the innate capacity to tell truth from falsehood. It is therefore imperative to know the calibrated level of truth of any teaching or teacher.

With this awareness, we begin to understand the great myths of mankind, which are always about the vicissitudes of the seeker who, in the classic story, becomes besieged by challenges, seductions, snares, traps, beguilements, and savage beasts. There are always dragons, fires, swamps, bodies of water, and other hazards to be overcome. In the legends, success depends on knowing a single secret or a mystical bit of information, which becomes the key to progress. Without help from on high or 'high helpers', the hero or heroine becomes lost and is finally saved by divine goodness in some disguised form, such as a bird that signals or shows the way. Muscle testing then is such a bird and prevents the painful stumbling into a morass from which it is often difficult or impossible to escape.

The spiritual quest is classically likened to a pathway, a journey, or a venture. Unfortunately, the naïve seeker often goes unprepared on a difficult journey without the necessary tools. In the ordinary world, we depend on many safety measures. We wear seatbelts, get inoculated against epidemic diseases, and accept that there are hazards to be guarded against and overcome. Thus, caution comes from wisdom, not from fear. Prudence requires awareness of the pitfalls to be avoided. If enlightenment were easy to come by, it would be a common phenomenon. However, statistically, the chances are less than one in ten million.

There is also the common thought held by seekers

that there are only two alternatives, either enlightenment or painful entrapment by the ego. Actually, each step forward brings new joys and a jump in consciousness that calibrates at even only a few points higher on the Scale of Consciousness. Because it is a logarithmic jump, however, it can bring about much greater happiness and accord. As one progresses, confidence replaces fear, emotional comfort replaces distress, and the ease and quality of life improves.

The Desire for Enlightenment

Unless one has fallen unbidden and without previous effort into an enlightened state of consciousness, as happened to such saints as Ramana Maharshi during adolescence, the more common route is to begin to desire to reach an enlightened state. The Buddha said that those who hear and learn of enlightenment will never be satisfied with anything else and, therefore, the end is certain.

Sometimes the seeker puts forth great effort and patience, and discouragement follows. At this stage, the ego assumes there is an 'I' that is seeking an 'it' (the state of enlightenment), and it therefore seeks to redouble its efforts.

Traditionally, the pathways to God have been through the heart (love, devotion, selfless service, surrender, worship, and adoration) or through the mind (advaita, or the pathway of nonduality). Each way may seem more comfortable at one stage or another, or they may alternate in emphasis. Either way, it is a hindrance to consider that there is a personal self, or an 'I', or an ego that is doing the striving or seeking or that will become enlightened. It is much easier to realize there is no such thing as the ego or an 'I' identity that is doing any seeking, but instead, it is an impersonal aspect of consciousness that is doing the exploring and seeking.

A useful approach is to let the love for God replace the willfulness that is driving the seeking. One can release all desire to seek and realize that the thought that there is anything else but God is a baseless vanity. This is the same vanity that claims authorship for one's experiences, thoughts, and actions. With reflection, it can be seen that both the body and the mind are the result of the innumerable conditions of the universe, and that one is at best the witness of this concordance. Out of an unrestricted love for God arises the willingness to surrender all motives except to serve God completely. To be the servant of God becomes one's goal rather than enlightenment. To be a perfect channel for God's love is to surrender completely and to eliminate the goal seeking of the spiritual ego. Joy itself becomes the initiator of further spiritual work.

From joy and humility, the rest of the process is certain. One becomes aware that the whole spiritual-seeking process is being activated by the attraction of the ultimate destiny to realize the Self rather than being propelled by the limited ego. It could be said in ordinary language that one is being pulled along by the future rather than being propelled by the past. It is obvious that unless one was destined for enlightenment, one would not even be interested in the subject. To even aspire to such a state is actually quite rare. In an entire lifetime, the average person does not meet even one other person who is primarily interested in reaching enlightenment. The path can be arduous and demanding.

In the Western world, there is really no accepted or traditional role for the spiritual seeker. It is not expected that one will finish up one's worldly business and then, at retirement, spend the rest of life spiritually seeking the truth to the exclusion of all else. In some countries such as India, there is such a cultural path traditionally accepted as a normal development. In the West, a serious spiritual student most often joins dedicated, like-minded persons who are often viewed somewhat suspiciously as dropouts from society unless they enter a monastery or theological seminary.

The Teacher

Spiritual groups are often organizations with their own agendas. Here again is a pitfall for the unwary, for the spiritual world, as well as the ordinary world, contains charlatans whose purpose is to capture the naïve initiate for purposes of control, domination, power, money, or prestige, such as having 'lots of followers'.

The true teachers can be seen to have no interest in fame or in having followers, prestige, or trappings. If we calibrate them, they usually calibrate from the high 500s on up or, more rarely, to the 700s. The teachings and not the teacher are what are important. Inasmuch as the teachings do not come from the personage of the teacher at all, it does not make sense to idolize or worship that personage. The information is transmitted as a gift because it was received as such. There is, therefore, nothing to sell, to enforce, to control, or to charge for inasmuch as the information was free and a gift from God. A valid spiritual organization may make nominal charges to cover ordinary expenses in that everyone contributes for the common good.

The spiritual teacher transmits a benefit due not just to the words themselves but to the high energy of consciousness that accompanies the words. The teacher's level of consciousness creates what might be likened to a carrier wave that accompanies and empowers the words.

As was cited in the research done in *Power versus Force*, one single avatar at a consciousness level of 1,000 totally counterbalances the collective negativity of all mankind. An individual at level 700 counterbalances the negativity of 70 million individuals below the level of 200. One individual at 600 counterbalances ten million people below 200; one at 500 counterbalances 750,000 below 200. One individual at consciousness level 300 counterbalances the negativity of 90,000 individuals below 200.

There are currently approximately twenty-two sages on the planet who calibrate at 700 or above. Of these, there are twenty at 800 or more, of whom there are ten at or over 900, and one sage is over 990. These figures have changed since 1995 when *Power versus Force* was published. (Only ten were over 700.) The negativity of the entire human population would self-destruct were it not for the counteracting effect of these higher energy fields.

It would seem then that there is some truth to the saying that the infinite power of God transmits itself down to beings on earth as though through a series of step-down transformers. Although the actual number of persons on the planet who calibrate negatively far exceeds those who calibrate positively, their actual individual power is very small by comparison so that at the present time, the calibrated energy of mankind as a whole since the 1980s is on the positive side. As previously mentioned, for many centuries prior to 1986, the consciousness level of mankind stood at 190, and then, rather suddenly, it jumped to the level of 207.

The power of the teachings of the original avatars then influences and contextualizes the significance of the life of mankind through centuries and even thousands of years. It is very informative, however, to calibrate the level of consciousness of a great teacher and then calibrate the level of institutionalized teachings that are then brought down through the centuries. Some teachings have survived almost totally unscathed while others have seriously deteriorated. Some have even fallen to such low levels that they calibrate below the critical level of Truth altogether, resulting in negative cults and becoming sources of conflict and negativity in the world. It is well to remember that popularity is not a sign of truth. It is not surprising then that the great majority of the population of mankind falls below the level of 200, and that multimillions are following 'religions' that are basically negative.

What Is Spiritual?

It is common for people to confuse 'spiritual' with 'religious,' and even with the supernatural, or 'astral' domains. They are, in fact, quite different, and this confusion often results in social strife and uncertainty.

In the United States Declaration of Independence, for instance, it was stated with great clarity by the originators that the rights of man stem from the divinity of their creation, and thus was established the principle of spirituality. However, they differentiated this from religion by saying that citizens are to be free from the establishment of any religion. The founders were aware that religion divides and is based on secular power, whereas, spirituality unites and has no worldly organization. The Declaration of Independence (which calibrates at 705) spells out that this is a nation whose government derives its authority from the spiritual principles of the Creator, and that it is to be guided by spiritual principles that see everyone as equal, with justice and freedom for all. This obvious position has great power and needs no defense.

Religion, on the other hand, can be sectarian and divide people into conflicting groups, often with dire consequences to civilization and to life itself, as history reveals. The sole power of truly spiritual groups originates only from the truth of their teachings, and they have no significant earthly power, edifices, wealth, or reigning officers. Generally in spirituality, the central ideas that hold the group together are commonly those of love, forgiveness, peace, gratitude, thankfulness, kindness, nonmateriality, and nonjudgmentalism. Usually, religion, in essence, originally has a core of spirituality that, however, becomes submerged and often lost from sight. Otherwise, war, for example, would have little chance to even occur. Spiritual truth, then, is universally true and without variation through time or place. It always brings peace, harmony, accord, love, compassion, and mercy. Truth can be identified by these qualities. All else is the invention of the ego.

CHAPTER 4

The Basics

Religion As A Source of Spiritual Error

There are two sources of error stemming from traditional 'true' religions. The first is simply misunderstanding
or misinterpretation of the specific teachings of the
original great teacher. Because the original listeners, or
followers, were not themselves enlightened, the original
teachings were contaminated by their egos. This then
became magnified by subsequent translators and
scribes down through the generations. The warp often
is due to the fact that the ego has a tendency to be
literal in its hearing of the word rather than the spirit
or essence of a teaching. Any translation that teaches
anything other than peace or love is in error. This is
a basic rule and easy to spot.

The second and more prevalent gross distortions
are spiritual teachings that arise from what is usually
referred to as 'church doctrine.' These regulations, often
in the form of guilt-provoking prohibitions, were actually totally made up by church officials and supposed
authorities who, in reality, had no claim to authority at
all but instead had acquired political power in the
structure of the institutions at the time.

There is no authentic or plausible reason to modify
the precise teaching of an original great teacher for
some ostensible gain. As obvious as it may seem, it has
not been clear through the centuries that to be a
Christian, for example, means simply to exactly follow
Christ's teachings.

All the great teachers teach nonviolence, noncon-
demnation, and unconditional love. It is hard to see

how any alleged ecclesiastical authority could violate these basic truisms supposedly for 'the good of the faith', or 'the good of the church', or the 'elimination of infidelities,' or 'just' wars.

There are many subjects not addressed in original spiritual teachings, thus creating the opportunity for fallacious religious elaborations. All kinds of 'sins' have been invented over the centuries, with elaborate explanations and rationalizations that can only be described clinically as rather sick manipulations of natural human affairs. The harm that resulted was not only spiritual error but also psychological cruelty and the blanket guilt of humanity. This focus on guilt and sin further condemns human consciousness by reinforcing the dilemma of the opposites and the duality of perception. This latter destructive effect on human consciousness takes man farther away from God and creates a barrier that is transcended only by the very few who have to be almost spiritual geniuses in order to succeed in escaping the coercive trap of elaborate fallacies.

A further destructive effect of the promulgations of some religious doctrine is that it creates the very basis for terrible wars and persecutions. These are always based on religious differences that are exaggerated in importance in order to justify religiously sanctioned mayhem. These misinterpretations and deviations are especially notable in the murky religious meddlings with sexuality, procreation, child rearing, diet, details of daily living, customs, dress, and political power.

Wearing different kinds of clothing, hats, or facial hair is enough to fuel religious persecution or war. Circumcision, not eating meat on Fridays, saying grace before meals, and dates and details of religious holidays all become ammunition. Whether the Sabbath is Saturday or Sunday becomes more important than the truth. Whether wearing a hat or no hat shows respect for God becomes a hoary issue.

By exploiting trivialities at the cost of ignoring the main thrust of spiritual truth, religions contribute to their own downfall and that of all humanity. Much that is revered as church doctrine is really the product of the ego. If it is true, as Jesus said, that evil is in the eye of the beholder, then those who see sin and evil everywhere are themselves the problem. In Victorian times, even the leg of a table was considered to be a temptation and had to be discretely covered with a drape.

Much of what has traditionally been described as sin is really the guilt-ridden exaggerations held in the mind of some emotionally disturbed church authority. Adherence to the admonition, "Let he who is without sin cast the first stone," would silence all these misappropriations of spiritual truth.

Collectively, these distortions of spiritual truth have paradoxically condemned both God and human nature in the name of 'Divinity'. To usurp that authority and make pronouncements in the name of God seems rather grandiose and delusional. No one who had ever experienced the absolute reality of the presence of God could ever make such distorted statements.

The Emancipation of Humanity

Before a new direction is sought, it is necessary to discern the error of the old and awaken a desire to transcend that error. This requires courage and fearless honesty. The recovery from many serious and incurable, potentially fatal disorders is based on the willing-

ness and capacity to face the truth and choose a different pathway. To break down denial and admit the truth
takes one above the critical line of Integrity (at 200).

The phoenix of spiritual awakening is birthed out
of the ashes of human despair. As Mother Teresa said,
the beautiful flower, the lotus, arises from its roots in
the slime and mud at the bottom of the pond.

Early in this writer's life, there occurred the revelation of the totality of the suffering of all mankind. It
was staggering and overwhelming in its sheer immensity. As stated elsewhere, this led, unfortunately, to the
mistake of blaming all that suffering of humanity on
the god of religion who had 'allowed all that to take
place'. However, it did reinforce the drive and desire to
relieve human suffering.

Many years later, the resultant atheist, without
warning and at the depth of despair, surrendered to
God and had a profound spiritual awakening that transformed all understanding of God, Truth, and Reality. Yet,
some years later came the vision and comprehension
of the profound ignorance and limitation of human
consciousness that revealed itself as the very foundation and source of all human suffering. The realization
of the immensity of the hold of ignorance on and its
terrible price to humanity was profound and resulted
in a shifting of endeavor from relieving physical and
mental sickness and suffering to the spiritual error that
accounted for all of it.

The collective human ego as expressed by society
is blind to the basic problem that underlies its own
suffering. Typical of the ego is its belief that the
problems to be addressed are 'out there', and therefore
all the social programs, including wars, are devoted to

fixing 'them' or fixing 'out there'.

The basic problem with humanity is that the human mind is incapable of discerning truth from falsehood. It cannot tell 'good' from 'evil'. With no means of self-protection, humans are at the mercy of falsehood in all its beguiling disguises that parade as patriotism, religion, the social good, harmless entertainment, etc.

With a simple, at-home test of true/false, all the dictators, emperors, and demagogues of history would have fallen. If one simply places a picture of Hitler in a manila envelope and has a child hold it over their solar plexus, the child's arm goes weak. The same telltale weakness reveals the true nature of Stalin, Lenin, the Arab zealot leaders, communism and the lethal leaders of Cambodia and African countries, and dictators who hide behind the name of Allah.

All the slaughters of mankind down through the centuries have been the result of force, to which the only antidote is Power. Force is based on falsehood; power is based solely on truth. 'Evil' loses its hold when it is revealed; that is, its vulnerable weak side, its Achilles' heal, which is exposed to everyone.

Falsity collapses when it is exposed for what it is. It does not take the U.S. government, the CIA, the FBI, spy satellites, or computers to discern the obvious—the arm of an innocent, five-year-old child has the only real might on Earth—the power of truth itself is invincible and requires no sacrifice.

The Arm of The Child

It is the arm of innocence that the dark legions of the world fear most of all for it unmasks the disguises by which they hold sway over *seventy-eight percent* of the world's population.

If one drops denial, one will see that falsehood, manipulation, and distortion of truth cater prevalently to man's lowest propensities and pervade all society. The popular computer games are neither innocent nor harmless; they are calculated killing training machines to deaden the spiritual sensitivity by conditioning the mind to thoughtless maiming and killing. The deliberate killing of prairie dogs is not 'sport' but callous mayhem. Drugs are not 'cool', but enslaving. Heavy-metal rock and rap music are neither liberating nor amusing; they are a deliberate mode by which to entrain the consciousness of youth. The media pretend innocence as they rake in the huge profits that stem from catering to man's lowest weaknesses and vulnerabilities.

The innocent child's arm is frightening to the vast establishments that draw their attraction from ignorance. The fallacious 'war on drugs' is revealed to be the very cause of the problem and the bulwark of the whole drug trade that it created, empowered, and enriched. Communism was not defeated by war but by the nonviolence of Gorbachev.

The rebirth of Christ—the great, heralded Second Coming—from a spiritual viewpoint, means the displacement of falsehood by truth, of darkness by light, of ignorance by awareness.

The significance of Krishna, Buddha, Christ, and Allah was not their personal presence on the planet but the truths they revealed and espoused, and the calibratable high energy that accompanied the teachings. All enlightened beings tell the populace to ignore their personality or personhood, but, instead, to focus on the teachings. Typical of the misunderstandings and distortions that prevail in religion, mankind does just the opposite and worships the personages, the dates, the times, and the places they visited and ignores the teachings.

The prevalence of the teachings of the Christ/Buddha/Krishna/Avatar seems to have been signaled recently by the transition of the consciousness level of mankind from the negative realm at 190 to cross over the line of Truth and Integrity of 200 to its present level of 207. The significance of this major event, which has happened for the first time in the history of mankind, cannot be understated. By analogy, we know that just on the physical level, a change of only a few degrees in the prevailing global temperature has profound effects on the entire planet and all life on it. In contrast, the shift in man's consciousness from 190 to 207 is far more significant and profound in its total and eventual effects than any change in the temperature of the planet.

If the Second Coming of Christ is to be revealed by a sign, then that sign has already, and only very recently, appeared. Unmistakable in its implication and promise for all mankind is that profound shift from falsehoods distorting the consciousness of mankind to that of truth.

It could be that the arm of the child can reveal to us the first light of a new dawn for civilization. It was said that it will be by the innocence of the child that man is led to God and to heaven. It is actually only by the innocence of the child within that the door to truth can be opened.

The innocence of the child remains undisturbed

and unsullied within the consciousness of everyone. It is the very basic 'structure' of consciousness itself. The analogy to current life is that the hardware is unsullied by the software which is processed through the computer, just as the camera is unaffected by the images transmitted through its lens.

Rediscovery of The Pristine State

While we speculate about the limitations of the consciousness of mankind, it is actually the individual who transforms society in a manner that is invisible and unsuspected. Force is vulnerable to an infinite number of oppositions, but power has no possible opposite or enemy. Like space itself, power is immune to attack and forever invulnerable. People think they are ruled by their unruly minds and that they are the victims of circumstances. All this sums up how a person feels from moment to moment. Thus, people see themselves as victims of their stream of consciousness or feeling states and transitory circumstances. The prevailing view is that there are no options to one's current state of mind and feeling tone or emotions.

This succumbing to 'it' (the mind) and 'out there' (the world) is accepted as natural and normal. Few people suspect that there is actually any other option. By self-examination and inward focus, one can discover that all states of consciousness are the result of the execution of an option. They are not unchangeable certainties determined by uncontrollable factors at all. This can be discovered by examining how the mind works.

One is not really ruled by the mind at all. What the mind reveals is an endless stream of options, all disguised as memories, fantasies, fears, concepts, etc. To get free of domination by the mind, it is only necessary to realize that its parade of subjects is merely an arbitrary cafeteria of selections wending their way across the screen of the mind.

One is not 'forced' to feel resentment by a negative memory, nor does one have to buy into a fearful thought about the future. These are only options. The mind is like a television set running its various channels for selection, and one does not have to follow any particular temptation of thought. One can fall into the temptation of feeling sorry for oneself, or angry, or worried. The secret attraction of all these options is that they offer an inner payoff or a secret satisfaction, which is the source of the attraction of the mind's thoughts.

If these payoffs are refused, it will be discovered that, at all times, behind the thought screen, there is a silent, invisible, thought-free space of joy. This is an option that is always available, but to be experienced, it has to be chosen above all other tempting options. The source of joy is always present, always available, and not dependent on circumstances. There are only two obstacles: (1) the ignorance that it is always available and present, and (2) valuing something other than peace and joy above that peace and joy because of the secret pleasure of the payoff.

The experience of the presence of God is available and within at all times, but awaits choice. That choice is made only by surrendering everything other than peace and love to God. In return, the divinity of the Self reveals Itself as ever present but not experienced because it has been ignored or forgotten, or one has chosen otherwise.

When Is The Future?

To choose to experience the presence of God occurs outside time. It is therefore nowhere in the future; it is available only in the present. No other condition is necessary or even possible because the present moment is permanent; it never changes; it never disappears into yesterday or tomorrow. In fact, it is inescapable. Everyone is actually safe in the exact moment of now.

By observation, it will become apparent that the only thing that seems to change is appearance. The now stands still; the screen is permanent. Although a movie script changes and a story unfolds, even then it can do so only within the precise instant of now.

'Now-ness' is the primordial, overreaching, all-powerful, unchangeable, and absolute requirement to experiencing. It is the essence of awareness of being and existence. It is impossible to exist anywhere at all except in the drastic, radical reality of now. This instant is all there is. One's own consciousness as Self is the only Eye by which anything can be experienced or known. The inner sense of reality is bestowed by the Self on the 'outer' surroundings, which is what makes them seem real. The sense of realness is therefore a projection of consciousness by the self, originating from the Self. One is therefore not the witness of a 'real' world; one is actually the source of its seeming reality. The world is actually entertainment. Like amusement, it is meant to be worn lightly. Heaven is within and is revealed by awareness. The world is merely an appearance. Its melodrama is an artifice of the distorted sense of perception. It leads one to think that the world is large, powerful, and permanent and that the Self is small, weak, and transitory; exactly the opposite is true.

Without belief in its appearance as defined by perception, the world we thought was real disappears. When one chooses to be at one with the inner, ever-present potentiality of joy and peace, the world transforms into a humorous amusement park, and all the drama is seen to be just drama.

The option for truth, peace, and joy is always available, although seemingly buried behind an ignorance and nonawareness that results from having chosen other options as a habit of thought. The inner truth reveals itself when all other options are refused by surrender to God.

The Human Condition As An 'Altered State of Consciousness'

A fact or truth is not established by the fact of commonality, as history demonstrates profoundly. Falsehood is most commonly the pervasive human experience. One of the most significant discoveries in consciousness research is that what is commonly understood and accepted as 'normal human experience' in thought, behavior, and feeling is technically merely an altered state of consciousness that prevails in a limited stratum of society for a limited duration. It is actually not man's real state.

Man is so used to worry, fear, anxiety, remorse, guilt, conflict, and distress that they are accepted as normal life, with negative emotions, attitudes, and feelings. Mankind (the patient) is advised to seek a therapist to 'get in touch with their feelings'. Rather than 'getting in touch' with these fermentations of illusion, it would be more beneficial to liquidate them by uncovering their source as perception itself.

A truly 'normal' state of consciousness is one that is free of all negativity and instead filled with joy and love. Anything else is based on illusion and perceptual distortions. Because disease prevails in a society does not mean that disease is a normal condition. Throughout history, such things have prevailed in society and, in fact, have killed off large portions of the population, but that does not mean they are a natural condition. Even the Black Plague eventually disappeared.

By simple means, it can be discovered that seventy-eight percent of the world's population is actually disturbed. That means that only twenty-two percent of the population is out of the extreme danger zone of the calibrated levels of consciousness below 200.

We tend to think of an altered state of consciousness as an artificially produced paranormal state, or something similar to a hypnotic state or trance, or as being programmed or brainwashed. From a study of the pervasive influences that act by the repetitive entrainment of man's levels of consciousness, it becomes obvious that the mind of mankind meets the criteria of having been controlled, influenced, and brainwashed in a systematic and continuous manner that is in accord with the definition of such processes in scientific research.

A child is born with the innocence of an unprogrammed consciousness, but then, like the hardware of a computer, it is systematically programmed with software, which is society's input. This system has one glaring and all-important defect, however. There is no program in place or available to ascertain the truth or falsehood of the new software programs! (It is much like a computer virus.) The child will innocently believe anything it is told. The unprotected consciousness of the child then becomes prey to the collective ignorance, misinformation, and fallacious belief systems that have blighted man's capacity for happiness for the last millennia.

The programming that ensues is actually uncorrectable as there has been no mechanism available to test the authenticity of the material with which the child's mind is programmed. On the surface, it would seem that up to seventy-eight percent of the data will not only be fallacious but destructive and damaging. This is superimposed on a human brain that is already genetically defective to begin with. Over one-third of the population has a brain that does not even supply enough of the neurotransmitter serotonin to keep the individual from being depressed, overeating, addictive, or being out of behavioral control. The capacity for reason itself can be completely destroyed in an instant by uncontrollable bursts of emotion.

Rationality is further undermined by the biological fact that the old reptile and animal brain is still anatomically and functionally present, and its atavistic activity continues to exert a pervasive animal instinct that strengthens predatory tendencies and aggression. All the instincts of the animal persist and influence or even dominate much of the behavioral and feeling states. The emotions of the animal are ever present and close to the surface. These tendencies are themselves vulnerable to training and manipulation by social programming and propaganda.

Man, therefore, starts out with a biologically defective brain with instincts of the animal, and his intelligence and information are then systematically downgraded and programmed with data that is inaccurate, fallacious, destructive, negative, and damaging at least seventy-eight percent of the time. That is just a statistical probability for mankind as a whole, but within society, there are vast populations where the percentage of fallacious material comes close to one hundred percent, e.g., criminal street-gang subcultures, etc. Often, what is most damaging is that the error in programming pertains to very critical behavioral elements. The total productivity of whole nations and cultures can be subverted to destructive ends. The whole economy of entire nations, such as Germany and Japan during World War II, was subverted to mass destruction, not only of innocent victims but also of their very own culture. Whole countries can be reduced to rubble by propaganda that is so ignorant and fallacious that one wonders in retrospect how anyone could have been gullible enough to buy it, much less sacrifice their lives for it.

The simple muscle test instantly reveals the truth. Dictators make everyone go weak, e.g., Hirohito is revealed as not divine, Caesar is not God, etc.

Society has no safeguard other than teaching the population a simple test of truth that anyone can do anywhere in a moment. If this simple test were widely known, it would have a total, uplifting effect on mankind. The very simplicity of the test, along with its wide benefit and availability, puts it in the same class as the inventions of the wheel, the level, electricity, or the computer chip. At a cost of zero, mankind can reap unlimited benefits. Perhaps the realization that the test can also be used to reap great profitability would elicit notice and interest.

Applied to business, research, manufacturing, and industry, the potential benefits do actually guarantee the savings of literally trillions of dollars. On the other hand, large segments of society have a vested interest in maintaining the status quo. As astonishing as it may seem, we live in a society where prosecutors knowingly withhold evidence that would prove the accused innocent in order to get a conviction, even if it means execution. Such incidents are merely symptoms that indicate the degree of severity of the illness of mankind's consciousness.

Like the DNA test, the muscle test instantly reveals the guilt or innocence of any accused. It instantly determines the truth or falsehood of any witness or testimony. It instantly reveals the presence or identities of traitors, defectors, foreign agents, informers, cheats, liars, and all forms of renegades.

The test reveals, in a matter of seconds or minutes, the identities of industrial or political spies, dishonest employees, drug dealers, dangerous persons, and the location of criminals. It does not take hundreds or thousands of hours of criminal investigation to identify a serial killer or their whereabouts. All crimes are easily solvable. Every detail of a crime or past crimes and events is accurately trackable, including, time, date, motive, whereabouts of evidence, identity of perpetrators, etc. The answers to questions, such as where is the body, where is the weapon, and what was the motive, are answerable.

Similarly, as the compass enables navigation, the

telescope enables astronomy, and the microscope enables bacteriology, muscle testing enables one to discover any fact about any subject anywhere in space or history within seconds. Muscle testing is a highly versatile tool whose true value is as yet undiscovered.

Historical Perspective

Throughout history there has been a plentitude of spiritual teachings and established pathways to God. These are the 'yogas' or ways that have been traditionally described. Each has developed its own schools, religions, spiritual literature, scriptures, saints, teachers, and historic figures. Historically, these have also absorbed various degrees of ethnicity and remnants of the culture in which they originated. Most of the world's great spiritual traditions have thus become identified with ethnic influences and customs that can be and often are deterrents to or distractions from the inner purity of the teachings themselves.

This has led to divisiveness among the world's great religions and has even been the basis for terrible religious wars. Perhaps a renewed study of spiritual truth would transcend these superficial differences and cull the critical essence of all spiritual teachings of merit, no matter what their origin or label.

What Is A Pure Spiritual Pathway?

Actually, until the present time, there was no way to ascertain the truth or falsehood of any spiritual teaching or teacher; thus, a spiritual student relied on faith in the spiritual integrity of a teacher as revealed by reputation. The only reliable guideline was that by one's inner grace and karma, one hopefully became involved with an integrous and valid spiritual endeavor.

The limitations of the great pathways that originated thousands of years of ago were the dearth of the original teachings and caused the progressive loss of what was written through word of mouth. There was also a loss of accuracy in translation from one language to another and misinterpretation by the listeners who themselves were unenlightened.

If we use the muscle test to calibrate the level of truth of the world's great religions, we see, as was detailed in the book, *Power versus Force*, that over time there was a general decline in the level of truth of some of those religions. The decline in Buddhism was perhaps the least and relatively small, but in other religions, the loss was very considerable. One can easily do a very informative study by researching and calibrating the level of consciousness of each religion, century by century, as well as that of its various interpreters of the times. It is possible by doing so to even pinpoint during which year and by whose dictates the declines occurred. These can often be identified with specific events in which religious decisions were made by ecclesiastical authorities, resulting in dire consequences. The exact nature of the error can also be clearly defined and understood by elucidation of the cultural and political forces of the particular times. Compromises were made that probably seemed justified at the time and were considered to be temporary for the sake of survival but which had very unfortunate long-term consequences as they were never later corrected.

The most grievous and serious example of this was the great decline in the level of truth of Christianity that occurred at the time of the Council of Nicaea. Christianity, which had been in the 900s, dropped over 400 points due to the inclusion of the Old Testament with the New Testament as 'the Bible', plus the inclusion of the Book of Revelation (which is of astral origin). This was a very devastating error inasmuch as all the books of the Old Testament, with the exception of Genesis, Psalms, and Proverbs, make one go weak with muscle testing, thus indicating that their level of truth is below 200 and therefore untrue. This negativity is due to the anthropomorphic depictions of God as fallible and subject to negative human emotions, such as revenge, hatred, partiality, bargaining, vulnerability, wrath, destruction, pride, and vanity. This angry god of revenge had to be appeased, flattered, assuaged, and bargained with so as not to go on a destructive rampage and cast down storms, floods, fire, and pestilence. This was the exact opposite of the God of truth, mercy, and forgiveness that Christ represented. Christ said the god of revenge was to be replaced by the God of mercy and forgiveness. Enemies were to be prayed for and forgiven for their ignorance. This teaching was repudiated by the ancient Hebraic tradition of the God of Righteousness, Vengeance, and Favoritism. (See Note at end of this chapter.)

The ancient gods of primitive cultures stem from 'astral' levels of consciousness and are the origin of the Scandinavian, German, Greek, Hebraic, Roman, Egyptian, Babylonian, Incan, and Mayan 'gods', with their telltale limitations of human passions, motives, positionalities, hatreds, and demands for sacrifice and jealous, angry destruction. That which is truly God has infinite power and has no need to employ the weak manipulation of force. That which is truly divine has no vulnerabilities, needs, or vested interests. Emotionality, selectivity, and the limitations they reveal are not attributes of God whose Presence is innately revealed by Love and Peace. Negativity originates from the mind of man who manufactures the endless array of false gods, all of whom demand worship and sacrifice. The God of Reality has no 'needs' and is not subject to being pleased or displeased, much less appeased.

The severity of the loss of understanding can be appreciated by realizing that the numerical calibrated values are logarithmic. A loss of one hundred points represents a vast loss of truth and power. In some religions, these errors were so severe that the fundamentalist branches of those religions fell below the critical level of 200, and the resultant falsehoods being misrepresented as truth had serious consequences in massive suffering and destruction by mankind. The levels below 200 represent suffering in all its forms.

One of the main levers that tilted the world in a negative direction was the self-defeating conceptual weapon called 'righteousness', which calibrates as Pride at 190. It has been the primary destructive force and Achilles' heel for the last several thousand years of man's history. It was the great, highest excuse for every form of imaginable savagery and barbarism.

The truly great historical pathways originated from the avatars, or great teachers, whom we have identified as those who calibrate at the level of 1,000, which is the maximum possibility in the earthly domain. Best known in the Western world are the names of Christ, Buddha, Krishna, and Zoroaster. The level of 1,000 is concerned with the salvation of all mankind. Thus, a spiritual teacher who is addressing all mankind is speaking from the level of the avatar.

The great avatars lived before the printed word was available, and thus there is a paucity of reliable data as to exactly what was taught and how it was interpreted. Because there are few explanations of what was originally meant, misinterpretations readily occurred as the original teaching was handed down. We can readily ascertain that error did creep in and distort the original purity. Many of these deviations are quite blatant and readily apparent to anyone with any spiritual intuition or even a basic sense of ethics. The distortions seem to have occurred with the establishment of religions and when authoritative institutions took the name of their ostensible founders in order to give themselves authority and power to attract followers and worldly assets, and to gain control over others.

Spirituality as such has no argument with anyone, and the misinterpretations that split off as dogmatic, ecclesiastical bodies did so to empower themselves and exploit the misinterpretations as spiritual truth in order to gain worldly advantage. By doing so, they forsook power for force and undermined the truth as set forth by the founders who, historically, then became founders in name only.

The status and prestige of the original avatar, the great name, was then stolen and merchandised in order to build great empires. With this short historical perspective, one can see that the original truth remains unsullied to this very day and can be rediscovered.

The word 'spiritual', like 'religion' and 'God', has become so overdescribed as to be misleading. A more comprehensive term, which avoids historical distortions and encompasses all available and possible information about man and God, is 'consciousness'. Spirituality properly refers to those aspects of consciousness that pertain to the awareness of truth and divinity and includes all references to the Absolute and all-present Reality, which is the Source and infinite domain of all that exists as Existence itself.

In that definition, consciousness includes all possibilities and realities in their totality, and it is the very space and matrix in which awareness progresses to its ultimate potentiality. We can safely and accurately validate this pathway, at least up to the calibrated consciousness level of 1,000, at which point the illusion of a separate seeker will have already dissolved.

The teachings of every great spiritual teacher who ever lived are now available for inspection and even detailed calibration and verification. The consciousness level of 600 denotes the level at which duality disappears into nonduality. It is at this point that a bridge between the seen and the unseen, the known and the unknown, the ordinary and the possible, can be approached. At the level of 600, spirit and man meet. The visible and the invisible diffuse into each other. It is a reference point to serve as a guide. It is the level of enlightenment.

Curiously enough, the muscle test of Truth itself calibrates at the level of 600 and therefore is the physical expression of the meeting of the realms of duality and nonduality. The study of the nature of consciousness is perhaps the most powerful and pure of all spiritual pathways because it becomes self-correcting and self-propelling.

The literature about consciousness and spirituality

easily leads to error, and thus, today's serious seeker of enlightenment excludes all teachings whose truth cannot be verified objectively. Consciousness levels from 500 up to 1,000 really denote what could be described as different realms or dimensions.

The spiritual teachers in the high 500s are the ones who have the most contact with significant numbers of people. By the time their spiritually evolved consciousness reaches 700, they become less available and more legendary, and their legacy consists of their recorded teachings.

We could typify human life as various fields and levels of human consciousness talking to each other and seeing people as impersonal spokespersons for these various levels. Thus, the disparaging of religion or spirituality by the hardcore materialistic scientist is not really a personal view but merely an expression of the energy field of the 400s, with their inherent limitations as well as capabilities. In the lower 400s, particularly, there is often an egotism about the intellect, reason, and intellectualization. In the 400s, therefore, God is replaced by science as the font of all knowledge and the hope for the future.

In the 300s, politics becomes the hope for man's salvation, and wars are fought over political ideologies, labels, and slogans, with their degradation of the value of individual human life. 'Bad' people are eliminated by the guillotine and the electric chair or put in prisons. At this level, there is the dualistic preoccupation with the limited realm of 'right' versus 'wrong', with its innate blindness to the positionality that creates such a dichotomy.

The lower levels live in a chaotic world because

definitions of right or wrong vary from moment to moment, from culture to culture, and within the culture itself, depending on education, IQ, social mores, or geography. This level is very vulnerable to the news media, which exploits it to the maximum and milks the public with sentimentality and maudlin emotionality.

This propensity to either/or-ness persists in the 400s as 'scientific' versus 'nonscientific'. Thus science itself is the home of a mechanistic reductionism and determinism that is held with the prevailing dogma which rivals that of the Church in the Middle Ages.

By the consciousness level of the 500s, the tendency to get caught in the innate limitations and ignorance of the opposites diminishes and such fallacies lessen their grip on the mind. In the 500s, spirit in the form of love begins to dissolve these hardened extremes, and humanism and situational ethics that take context into account emerge to bring about greater balance and a sense of ethics to counteract extremism.

The level of the heart (500) becomes the bridge from secularism, hardcore righteousness, and vindictive moralism and opens the door for consideration of alternate views, benevolence, mercy, and forgiveness through understanding and nonjudgment. The great power of the 500s is in the use of the faculty of understanding, and it is understanding that allows for the progression to 540, the level of Unconditional Love.

In these levels there is the capacity to differentiate the act from the actor. Thus, the mother visits her convicted son in prison and continues to love him despite his having committed a horrible crime. In the 500s, also, there is the capacity to realize man's limitations and inability to rise above them. The capacity and the willingness to forgive them "for they know not what they do" becomes a realizable goal as benevolence replaces the desire for retribution, revenge, and counter-aggression. Forgiveness thus becomes the keystone.

In the 500s, the limitations of the capacity of choice become obvious. The child within everyone comes into view, and its innermost primordial innocence becomes more visible and tends to preclude the use of retaliation, which, in our society, often takes the same form or worse than that of the crime which is being punished.

In the 500s, there is also the capacity to see all actions as the result of a multitude of contributing factors so that responsibility is now seen as being present or possible only to varying degrees, depending on context and conditions. Behavior takes on shades of meaning, and knee-jerk oversimplifications are no longer acceptable. Snap judgments cease and the various paradoxes are weighed and considered. It becomes comprehensible that things do not happen against a person's will but only by concurrence of one's own current or prior spiritual positions with the choices one has made. Life in all its expressions is seeing this as opportunity for spiritual growth and appropriate for the participants.

Human life, as ordinarily experienced, is an epic and dramatization of all the possibilities below the level of 600, at which point the context changes dramatically and a whole different set of seeming obstacles now presents itself as principles and challenges to awareness. At 600, perception is replaced by vision. What might have been seen as a misfortune in the world of perception might now be seen as a gift by the more advanced awareness of vision.

Also at 600, identification with the physical body ceases and thus, that great fear above all fears, death itself, disappears as a possible 'reality'. Like a caterpillar emerging from its cocoon, the newly liberated spirit rejoices in its non-physicality since the Self is totally invisible.

The levels over 600 can most accurately be described or referred to as a state or condition that is all prevailing and self-evident as there is neither subject nor object. The knower and the known are self-identical and self-evident as one and the same, without division. There is no inner or outer, no individual versus God, no part outside the whole, and no independent entity to account for. All the dualities have been transcended. The awareness is self-existent so that there remains no individual to whom it has occurred.

For a brief moment, as the self disappears into the Self, there is a transitory amazement and awe of profound proportion and depth. The death of the self is experienced, and then all is stillness and peace. That the body was ever considered to be 'me' seems absurd and must have been due to a passing lapse and forget-fulness. It is as though one had mysteriously forgotten who one really was, and now, with joy, remembered. All the fears and vicissitudes of life disappear, and now, free of even death itself, there is the remembrance that one always has been and always will be, and that sur-vival was never a problem at all. One's innate safety had been guaranteed all along by the reality of the Self, which is all-present and beyond time and space. No beginnings or endings are even possible, and one's reality existed before all worlds or universes. There are neither questions nor answers because no dichotomy exists within identity.

One is neither the one nor the many but instead beyond all positionalities and mentations. It would be more accurate to say that one's Self is the reality out of which 'the one and the many' arise. All is self-complete, autonomous, and not in need of anything outside itself since 'outside itself' is an impossibility. Thus, 'Self' is context whereas 'self' is content.

There is no division between creator and that which is created. All is self-creating as the manifestation of the mind of God. This great awareness characterizes the consciousness level of the 700s where Self is All That Is. Because the universe is self-evolving and self-fulfilling, no intervention is necessary. All is in perfect balance and harmony.

The consciousness levels of the 800s and the 900s represent the highest levels of the potential consciousness of humanity. A sage may occasionally return to the world but the world has now been transformed. It is no longer a world with individuals who need 'saving' but an energy field to lift and reinforce. Each consciousness in the world that calibrates above the level of Integrity serves to counterbalance the negativity of the seventy-eight percent of the population which reflects negativity below the level of 200.

The power of the consciousness level of 1,000 counterbalances the total negativity of all mankind and creates not only the potentiality but also the certainty of the salvation of all humanity. Although this eventuality seems to unfold slowly in the world of time, it already exists in the reality of the absoluteness beyond time.

Spiritual progress is based on acceptance as a

matter of free will and choice, and thus everyone experiences only the world of their own choosing. The universe is totally free of victims, and all eventualities are the unfolding of inner choice and decision.

What accounts for the apparent delay in this inevitable destiny? It appears to be the attraction of the energy fields that we have delineated as 'force', or illusion and falsehood. Central to this attraction is the identification of self as the body and the survival fears that ensue. Death is then feared as the end of life and is perceived as a self-existent, possible reality that has a fearsome, imaginary existence.

To the higher self, human life is composed of games and charades because, unconsciously, everyone knows that death is not an actual possibility. Why else would anybody risk their 'life' for political gain or money? Even at a brief glimpse, the history of mangled bodies convinces any would-be hero that the glory of war is a total absurdity. After a war where seventy million people 'die', the country's borders remain the same, business returns to usual, and the whole charade is a sad joke. Former enemies now shake hands, observe each other's Memorial Days, and visit each other's war memorials.

In a game of chess or checkers, the pieces are not destroyed but merely moved off the board for another day. The ego engages in performances that are utterly convincing to the players and onlookers. On a certain level, each player is providing a spiritual service to others by acting out the lessons that need to be learned for the benefit of all. Acts of courage awaken the soul to its own innate power, which it will need to reach the ultimate awareness.

Beyond the 600s, there is no personal self to makes choices. Progression is an expression of the nature of consciousness itself. The commitment to a specific spiritual task does therefore keep the body running on in the material world until the project is completed. There is, in reality, only one lifetime that has the appearance of successive chapters.

Note on the Christian Holy Bible
(King James Version)

The Old Testament calibrates at 190. However, Genesis is at 660, Psalms is 650 and Proverbs is 350. If these are excluded, then the remaining books collectively calibrate at only 125.

The New Testament calibrates at 640. However, if Revelation were removed (it calibrates at only 70), then the New Testament would calibrate at 790.

The current Bible calibrates at 475. To make it authentically 'holy' as its title implies, it would have to exclude all the books of the Old Testament (except Genesis, Psalms and Proverbs) and Revelation. If that were done, then the Bible would be truly holy and calibrate at 740.

Importantly, the Lamsa version of the Bible (translated from the Aramaic Peshitta) is more accurate than the King James version (translated from the Greek). It calibrates 20 points higher. The King James version has serious errors, for example, on the cross Jesus is misquoted as saying, "My God, why hast Thou forsaken me?" In the Aramaic translation, the quote is, "My God, for this I was spared." Jesus spoke Aramaic, not Greek (see Introduction, Lamsa Bible, p. xi).

If the Lamsa Bible excluded the Old Testament

(except for Genesis, Psalms and Proverbs) and Revelation, it would calibrate at 810. If Revelation were removed from the Lamsa translation of the New Testament, then the Lamsa New Testament would calibrate at 880.

CHAPTER 5

Circumventing the Ego

Simplicity

The core of all the great spiritual teachings and teachers can be surmised in a few simple paragraphs. (Operationally, they all amount to the admonition to avoid that which makes one go weak with muscle testing and pursue that which makes one go strong!)

Choose to be easygoing, benign, forgiving, compassionate, and unconditionally loving towards all life in all its expressions, without exception, including oneself. Focus on unselfish service and the giving of love, consideration, and respect to all creatures.

Avoid negativity and the desire for worldliness and its greed for pleasure and possessions. Forego opinionating, the judgment of right versus wrong, the vanity of being 'right', and the trap of righteousness.

Seek to understand rather than to condemn. Venerate the teachers of these basic principles and ignore all others. Apply these principles to one's view of oneself as well as of others. Trust in the love, mercy, infinite wisdom, and compassion of Divinity that sees through all human error, limitation, and frailty. Place faith and trust in the love of God who is all-forgiving, and understand that condemnation and fear of judgment stem from the ego. Like the sun, the love of God shines equally on all. Avoid negative depictions of God as an anthropomorphic error, i.e., jealous, angry, destructive, partial, favoring, vengeful, insecure, vulnerable, contractual, etc.

Surrender and Sacrifice

These are arbitrary terms that presume that one is looking at spiritual principles from the viewpoint of the ego's vested interests and justifications for negativity. To the ego, spiritual principles represent a possible loss of positionality, but from the viewpoint of spirit, they are gains.

The primary surrenders and sacrifices have to do with the substitution of humility for vanity. In actual practice, one merely relinquishes the vanities of opinionating and judgmentalism. The letting go of positionalities undoes the limitation of the 'error of the polarity of the opposites', which is the dualistic consequence of perception. By letting go of the self-referential term 'I' as a habit of thinking, the hold of the narcissistic core of the ego is lessened. Substitute the habit of expressing ideas in the third person instead of with the subjective pronoun 'I'. The use of impersonal statements about how things seem avoids getting personally embroiled in issues. Dispassionate statements tend to be more balanced and objective because they include many sides of an argument rather than a single-sided, biased view.

What one witnesses in the world of human events is neither right nor wrong but the acting out of the energy fields of consciousness as they impinge and express through particular individuals under specified conditions of time and place. If we avoid the hypothetical positionality that people 'could' be different than they are, we see that, in actuality, people cannot really help being other than they are. If they could be different, they would be. Limitations define possibilities; the hypothetical does not exist; it is not a reality but an imagination. It is irrational to condemn human behavior by comparing it with the hypothetical ideal.

Indignation gives way to compassion through understanding and brings into prominence the truth of the great historical statements, "They know not what they do" (Jesus Christ), or, "The only sin is that of ignorance" (Buddha).

Transcending The Negatives

It is not very efficient or rewarding to 'battle sin' and get into a struggle to use 'will power' to overcome defects. These are already positionalities and traps that bind the mind in the dualistic error of the 'opposites'.

The way out of conflict is not to try to eliminate the negative but instead to choose and adopt the positive. To view that one's mission in life is to understand rather than to judge automatically resolves moral dilemmas. Professionals do this all the time. Doctors and lawyers will actually even tell their patients and clients that their job is to heal or defend and not to judge. The surgeon operates equally on the broken hip of the saint or the criminal. "It is not my position or function to judge in such matters," is a common statement.

Much relief is experienced when we realize that by adopting a spiritual life, righteous condemnation and the hate that ensues from it can be left to others. This pursuit of the spiritual 'good' benefits all mankind, and it could therefore be said to be the most praiseworthy vocation of all.

The spiritual commitment then defines a distinct

role that differs from that of the uncommitted person. It implies a different set of standards and focus of energy and attention from the ordinary seeking of the vanities of the ego and worldly accomplishments. One sacrifices material or egocentric gain for spiritual progress, and in so doing, the transient is subordinated to the permanent, and that which is of true value is chosen over that which is only an illusion. A yardstick that is helpful in making decisions is to project oneself ahead to one's deathbed and ask, Which decisions do I want to be accountable for at that time?

We know with certainty from spiritual research (which anyone can verify) that consciousness does not miss one single iota of life; all is to be counted and taken responsibility for, and nothing goes unnoticed or unrecorded. This is in general agreement with the totality of man's experience and wisdom throughout all cultures and ages and is the common theme of all religions and spiritual teachings.

In practice, then, one transcends the negative by merely choosing the opposite. With the internal discipline that stems from passionate commitment, the negative choices are no longer seen as options. We all then become conscientious objectors when we draw the line and set boundaries. This rather automatically occurs as a consequence of choosing spiritual goals that we value above the goals of the world.

Keeping One's Own Counsel

Spiritual views are not very popular in society in general. It is not necessary to impose one's views on others. Proselytizing is best done by example rather than by coercion and lapel grabbing. We influence others by what we are rather than by what we say or have. To express views that are contrary to public opinion may be sociologically praiseworthy, but to do so leads to conflict and enmeshment in the arguments and discord in the world. The pursuit of 'causes' is the role of the social and political reformer, which is an activity different from that of the seeker of enlightenment. Praiseworthy endeavors can be seen as deserving of sympathetic support, but they are also perceptually defined positionalities with intrinsic limitations and agendas. Embroilment in the issues of society is a luxury that the seeker of spiritual enlightenment needs to forego.

Each person has their own karma or destiny to fulfill, and it is best not to confuse these missions. The spiritually motivated saints of history did indeed uplift mankind, and such was the nature of their missions and the merit of spiritual courage, which often included even the sacrifice of their physical lives. Collectively, these social saints inspire whole nations and cultures, and thus, by their public lives, silently serve all mankind for generations.

The calling of the private-life spiritual aspirant is more socially humble but equally important and of service to the whole of mankind. The social saint uplifts by external action and example. The devotee uplifts by internal progression. Every increase in the level of consciousness affects the consciousness of all mankind in a manner that is unsung but discernible and demonstrable by spiritual research. The calibrated level of the consciousness of mankind is a composite resultant of everyone's stage of evolution, and the higher calibrated levels are immensely more powerful than the negative ones.

The power of love emanated by the consciousness of only a fraction of mankind actually totally counterbalances the negativity of the whole mass of humanity. Seventy-eight percent of the world's population is still in the negative range, below the calibrated level of 200, only four percent even reaches the level of Love, which calibrates at 500, and only 0.4 percent reaches Unconditional Love, which calibrates at 540. Therefore, every loving or compassionate thought outweighs many thousands of negative thoughts held by others. We change the world not by what we say or do but as a consequence of what we have become. Thus, every spiritual aspirant serves the world.

Ordinary Life

Meaning is defined by context, which determines motive. It is the motive that establishes spiritual value. To dedicate one's actions as a service of love to life is to sanctify them and transform them from self-seeking motives to unselfish gifts. We define excellence as dedication to the highest standards. Every act can then be held as an opportunity to glorify God by sheer purity of endeavor. All physical tasks and labor can be ingredients in one's contribution to the world. Even the smallest task can be seen as serving the common good, and if viewed in that light, work becomes ennobled.

How life is contextualized can bring either joy or resentment. Begrudging is replaced by generosity. If others benefit from one's efforts, so much the better. Everyone has the opportunity to contribute to harmony and beauty by kindness to others and thereby support the human spirit. That which is freely given to life flows back to us because we are equally part of that life. Like ripples on the water, every gift returns to the giver. What we affirm in others, we actually affirm in ourselves.

The Exceptional Life

To be realistic, one has to take into account that to choose to devote one's life to reaching enlightenment in our society is uncommon and relatively rare. The goal of society in general is to succeed in the world, whereas the goal of enlightenment is to transcend beyond it. It is important to remember that the world operates within the limited Newtonian paradigm of linear causality, which has its prevailing perceptions of what is 'real'. Spirituality, on the other hand, is based on the invisible realities and realms of nonduality and therefore may seem unreal or, at best, an oddity to the ordinary world.

To the hard-headed realist who operates out of material reductionism and measurable, concrete 'results', the values of the spiritually committed seem vague, ephemeral, and suspect. Therefore, the levels of Science and Logic, which calibrate in the 400s and dominate our society, view values and motives of those in the levels of the 500s with skepticism, and go on to deny any reality at all to the levels above 600.

Usually most people's understanding of spirituality or religion (which they confuse with each other) is that they have to do with 'right and wrong'. Society is generally pervaded by the moralistic opposites of good and bad, which results in the whole panorama of cultural institutions of law, prisons, government regulations, taxes, bookkeeping, courts, police, military, politics, and war.

By contrast, purely spiritual organizations lack authoritarian structure, own no buildings or edifices, have no officers, treasuries, goods or monies, and they avoid expressing any views and remain uninvolved with outside issues. Intrinsically, spiritual organizations make no public statements and operate solely out of voluntary adherence to spiritual principles. Neither do they proselytize, and although they have no employees, they operate out of service. They have no debts, obligations, or investments, and thus, the truly spiritual can be said to be 'in the world, but not of it'. Spirituality seeks neither credit nor does it accept blame.

The best examples of such a group in our current society are the so-called 'twelve-step' groups whose only power derives from their spiritual purity and that have evolved to the point of addressing themselves to a major number of human sufferings. These groups calibrate at 540, which is the level of Unconditional Love.

The 'exceptional life' becomes so by virtue of context and meaning whereby choice sets up a hierarchy of values that motivates all activities. The difference between the ordinary and the exceptional life is primarily one of context. To value love above gain is already such a major shift of attitude that it transforms life.

When people become spiritually inspired and dedicated, their whole life may go through a very major disruption. Many such persons abruptly leave jobs, careers, family, friends, and positions and frequently go off to seemingly remote places. This major move is often viewed with alarm by family and associates who seek plausible psychological explanations. In the ordinary world, sane people do not just suddenly bolt and leave everything in order to find God. Spiritual aspirants confound the worldly with their willingness to give up everything to follow some invisible inner calling. Because the spiritually oriented person's goals are invisible, it seems to the ordinary world that the person may have gone mad, insane, or is trying to 'escape reality'.

Families or friends may also be angry and resentful at the seeming desertion and rejection of the very goals for which the world strives. To leave privilege, money, power and position seems outrageous or even insulting. Many devotees adopt the simple nonmaterial lifestyle, which again seems to previous associates as 'deserting responsibility'.

Spiritual Groups

Joining a spiritual group or organization is a personal choice determined by many factors, both present and past. The most important factor to consider is the actual calibrated level of consciousness of the group or organization and its leaders. Classically, the 'grace of the guru' is the inner source of power of specific spiritual teachings, which is in agreement with the calibrated levels of consciousness. Thus, the actual calibrated levels of the originator of a teaching and of the teachings themselves are critical. This is a point that cannot be emphasized too strongly.

Zealous enthusiasm is no substitute for truth, nor is the belief in the faith of thousands or even millions of followers. Spiritual discernment is a rare gift and, historically speaking, it does not occur until the 'third eye' opens with spiritual vision. Until that happens, any spiritual seeker, no matter how earnest, can be easily fooled. If spiritual imposters were not impressive, charismatic, believable, and convincing, they would have no followers. It actually takes an expert or a person of very advanced consciousness to tell the difference. The reason for this spiritual error is that the error of the false guru is one of context, and the context is beyond the limited perception of the initiate.

Erudition is also not a guarantee of truth. There are teachers of great brilliance, but when one does research, one finds that the heart chakra is out of balance. In contrast, very loving teachers who are 'all heart', but in whom the third eye or crown chakra is 'out', lead followers down an errant path to possibly the most painful of all human experiences in which spiritual disillusionment leads to depression and even to suicide.

Traditional Major Religions

The admonition, *caveat emptor*, applies without exception. Many of the world's great religions originated from primitive nomadic tribes and cultures. Ignorance at the time was very major. Ignorant people tend to be easily swayed and impressed, especially through fear and superstition, and they tend to think in anthropomorphic terms. In those days, cults were rampant. Science was missing and therefore many events in nature were attributed to supernatural powers. To influence these supernatural powers, amulets, pieces of animals, bones, stones, carved figures, magical sounds, and symbols evolved. Included were earthly locations and phenomena of nature, mountains, and volcanoes, along with sacred lands or 'holy' places and ruins.

The 'gods' were responsible for major earth disasters and qualities. Famine, flood, earthquakes, eclipses of the sun, and positions of the stars were all involved with supernatural significance and magical powers. People worshipped animals and animal spirits. Animism was prevalent. Involved in all this were the 'spirits'. Therefore, manipulating spirits became prevalent. Sacred drugs, charms, spells, trances, incantations, and sacrifices were considered to have great value. The angry gods were to be assuaged by self-starvation, flagellation, animal sacrifice, mutilation, playing with dangerous beasts and cobras, lying on beds of nails, mortifications of the flesh, disease-ridden 'holy' poverty, ritual infliction of pain, and the killing of animals, fowl, and virgins.

This morass of savagery and ignorance was often the very culture out of which religions arose. Why God could be considered to be pleased by the spilling of animal blood or the death of a maiden cannot be understood unless one realizes that these cultures had created belief and deified that which was the exact opposite of God. These gross distortions of truth arose as projections from the dark side of the ego, and these negative 'gods' were really the gods of the spleen, given to revenge, jealousy, envy, spite, retaliation, condemnation, rage, destruction, punishment, casting souls into Hell, and smiting whole civilizations with pestilence, famine, flood, fire, and storm.

As a religion arose out of this morass of negativity, it tended to emphasize and focus on the negatives of sin, Hell, punishment, and righteousness and used these as an excuse for all forms of cruelty, war, mutilation, persecution, conviction, burning at the stake, banishment, imprisonment, and the cutting off of hands.

All this was believed to be holy since suffering in all its forms was deified. Therefore, the killing of infidels was lauded, and conflict was seen as justified. It could always be rationalized by invoking past cultural injustices that seemed to justify retribution for many centuries and generations on end.

In the grip of this negativity, religion became society's worst oppressor and perpetrator of rampant injustice and cruelty. A culture that lives by the venom of the spleen expects and projects a god that is menacing, cruel, and violent. To misidentify the 'gods of Hell' with the God of Heaven is such a massive and staggering spiritual error that the extent and gravity of consequences to mankind are almost incomprehensible.

The totality and extent of human suffering had at one time earlier in life revealed itself to this consciousness, and the revelation was shocking. In that instant, atheism replaced religion. Belief in a god as creator of such extensive horror and suffering was not comprehensible. Years later came the realization that the error was made by attributing the qualities of the ego to God. In retrospect, it is clear that the atheism was merely the rejection of the false gods of mankind because there was a prevailing spiritual intuition that held that a real God would be the opposite of that which was preached by religion. That intuition was later confirmed when the emergence and the radiance of Divinity within this consciousness obliterated the remnants of any such absurd beliefs.

A simple inspection of the Scale of Consciousness reveals that the historic, angry 'gods' calibrate well below 200 and are therefore not in integrity; they are in the direction of falsity rather than truth. On the Scale, 'God', as seen by the negative energy fields, is described as indifferent, vengeful, punitive, condemning, vindictive, and despising. (God despises all sinners.) These are the gods of hate with which mankind has justified its cruelty and barbarism throughout the ages.

Surely, the history of civilization for at least the last five thousand years has been that of repetitive horror, which culminated in the last century with the slaughter and mayhem of millions of people. The misidentification of demons as gods has had vast consequences of staggering gravity to mankind.

In this historic setting, there were still those of greater spiritual advancement who protested the ways of destruction, but society soon labeled them as the enemy that had to be silenced. In a blind society, a protester who can still see the light is viewed as unpatriotic, or an iconoclast, or psychotic, or a coward and certainly a threat to the status quo. To not go along with socially current delusions is to be viewed as dangerous and subversive.

In history, the rare spiritual devotees who experienced higher states of consciousness, or even enlightenment, were called mystics and were often branded as heretics and were persecuted, excommunicated, and burned at the stake. Their teachings were threats to the power structures that were based on spiritual error. The rule of guilt, sin, and fear was indeed threatened by a God of infinite mercy, compassion, and unconditional love. Until now, it has actually escaped man's discernment that truth brings peace, whereas falsehood brings fear. By that sign, it is possible to tell the difference.

In the late 1980s, the consciousness level of mankind finally leaped from 190, where it had been for many centuries, and crossed the crucial and critical level of 200, which is the level of Integrity, to its present level of 207. This higher level of consciousness is no longer hospitable to savagery and hate, and most of society, including the churches, no longer emphasizes sin and fear. They speak now of the God of Love. The current Pope speaks against killing, execution, and inquisition and about the failure to defend the innocent and downtrodden.

Like springtime, the promise of a new era in man's understanding of God is emerging. Now the level of consciousness of mankind is high enough to be able to recognize the truth of a God of Love instead of worshipping the god of guilt and hate.

Mankind now stands at the great threshold of real awakening, which may be the actual nature of the Second Coming of Christ as foretold in scripture. Civilization almost reached the point of nuclear self-extermination before it 'hit bottom' and turned again to the Light. The subversion of spiritual truth into its opposite can occur only if the consciousness level of mankind is below 200, but it begins to correct itself when the prevailing level of consciousness crosses over the line to Truth and Integrity at 200.

It is only in recent years that mankind has accepted the grace of the discernment of truth from error. The guillotine is no longer a symbol of equality, freedom, and brotherhood but can now be seen for what it is. Society now encounters new moral dilemmas with the interfacing of the residuals of the old god and the new paradigm of reality. We now have such paradoxes as atheists going to court to establish their God-given right to freedom as promised by the Constitution and the Bill of Rights, which state that such freedoms and rights stem from God's having created all men as equal.

At just over the consciousness level of 200, God is seen as the epitome of fairness, equality, and freedom. He has at last become benign and friendly. That Heaven is actually attainable now seems like a plausible reality as new hope arises out of the bleak despair of mankind's generations of hopelessness. Humanity is in the process of being reborn, and the God of Joy is replacing the God of dread and fear.

Emergence of The New Paradigm of Reality

As the level of consciousness of mankind advances, major shifts automatically occur in prevailing attitudes and social styles. The negative becomes progressively less attractive, less acceptable, and less persuasive. Hate, revenge, pridefulness, and self-righteousness find fewer and fewer enthusiasts. Punitive actions are now seen to have very unpleasant consequences; inequality and injustice become harder to rationalize. Pulling up historical negative gods is no longer fashionable or persuasive, and such extremes lose their ring of acceptable validity.

Responsibility replaces sin, ethics replace vindictive moralizing, and understanding replaces condemnation. Such terms as 'good' and 'bad' become relative, and increasingly, context is defined and appreciated as a contributing factor. Social sanity begins to replace hysteria, and the propaganda of hate is not so easily sold to the populace.

Although this progression of consciousness now

prevails in much of the Western world, it is still resisted by areas of the globe where the old gods prevail. There, the religious wars and their political adherents continue to distort spiritual truth and propagate human conflagration and war.

Most interestingly, the veil of ignorance that clouds such cultures is now being pierced by the electronic communication media that obliterates political boundaries. Who thought that evil would eventually lose its grip via the transistor chip?

The message of truth and freedom is now freely available to almost everyone. Tyranny falls beneath the onslaught of the Internet. Information is now the mightiest tool invented since Gutenberg invented the printing press.

Via free communication, all mankind is at last coalesced and united in an emerging freedom and brotherhood. The different 'tongues' that have separated mankind into conflicting divisions are now uniting in a shared language that even children readily comprehend.

The emergence of a new paradigm of reality was also reflected in the rather spontaneous, recent demise of totalitarian, atheistic communism in the former USSR and Eastern Europe. Its decline in the rest of the world is also inevitable and guaranteed by free communication as well as economic necessity. Communism in the USSR fell without a shot. It was not 'defeated' by a 'war against evil', but by the emergence of its opposite. Evolution is not via vanquishing the negative but through choosing and adhering to the positive. This was also demonstrated by the peaceful realignment of North and South Korea.

In the world of science as well, a major shift also was occurring during the latter years of the last century. The previous blindness of science was its limitation to the deterministic materialism of the Newtonian linear paradigm of reality that condemned scientific awareness, causing it to stop at the consciousness level that calibrates at 499. This is the level of Newton, Einstein, Freud, and all the other great thinkers and scientists. Information that was not explicable by integral calculus was ignored as 'chaotic' and outside the realm of scientific investigation.

Inasmuch as all life and its intrinsic processes are nonlinear, all such knowledge and reality were far outside the paradigm of what was possible in the view of classical science. All this was profoundly changed with the discovery of *chaos theory,* or *nonlinear dynamics,* which opened all life for investigation. A bridge appeared to enable understanding between science and spirituality via the clarity made possible by the calibrated Scale of Consciousness.

Science had decided that unless something was definable and measurable ('reality is measurement'), it was unreal and imaginary. Thus, science invalidated any serious study or inquiry into the human value of love, compassion, beauty, forgiveness, inspiration, faith, companionship, loyalty, gratitude, hope, and happiness—in other words, all that constitutes the actual core and reality of human existence and motivation.

Science is also unable to grasp the significance of the subtle and the intangible. It is, however, the best tool man has had thus far for evaluating and manipulating the physical world. That it has limits is not a defect but merely defines its range of usefulness. In fact, to know one's limits is a strength, not a weakness.

An important element in chaos theory is the discovery of so-called 'attractor fields'. These reveal that behind what appears to be inexplicable, chaotic, and random events is actually a hidden energy field whose pattern influences the appearance of 'stochastic', or random, data. These patterns are discernible behind what appear to be senseless or incomprehensible occurrences in nature and include explanations of global and environmental changes and weather patterns as well as the actual beating of the human heart.

The inexplicable remains unpredictable but it becomes comprehensible. The hierarchical levels of spiritual reality are now verifiable and approachable as previously invisible domains whose importance has been unsuspected. That all of human behavior and belief is dominated by levels of consciousness of increasing power with their own hidden attractor fields is an understanding that elucidates the underpinnings of the behaviors of mankind throughout history.

To know the calibrated level of consciousness of any culture, nation, group, person, or institution reveals a very predictable range of expected attitudes, thoughts, emotions, and mental content. Like flocks of birds that follow an invisible pattern, the behavioral patterns of whole segments of society are open to study and awareness. A given population can only accept the paradigm of reality that is within or not too far outside its own parameter as denoted by its innate, calibrated field of consciousness.

These invisible energy fields extend beyond time and space and are present everywhere throughout all history, at all times, and for everyone. Like a radio receiver, each person attunes to the thought field of their own level of consciousness. Those in the 300s, for example, reverberate quite differently from those in the 400s. Each level tends to discount the reality of the other levels. For instance, at 190, pride is a very powerful motivator, e.g., Hitler's Germany. Pride then becomes the justification as well as the means and the end to self-fulfillment.

By contrast, in the 400s, reason, logic, and scientific information prevail. It is not until consciousness reaches the 500s that love and compassion take on any real meaning, or reality, or basis for behaviors.

Conflict between the different levels of the energy fields influences the resulting class troubles and the clashes of society with all its political positions. The pendulum of public opinion tends to swing from one extreme to the other in which the ruling group tries to eliminate the views of those who differ from its prevailing thought forms and beliefs. At the higher levels, conflict is resolved by understanding, compassion, and comprehension, while at the lower levels, conflict is resolved by strife, persecution, and war.

The emergence of mankind out of the darkness and ignorance of the past into the hope and promise of the Light has thus far been unrecognized for what it is and for the profound shift that it really implies. This major shift from 190 to 207 *is the most profound and significant event in all of man's history.* Characteristically, its occurrence was silent, unspoken, and beyond perception. The possibility of this eventuality as man's destiny was foretold by the appearance in mankind of the great avatars.

The infinite power of Divinity radiates down

through the levels of consciousness like sunlight in the forest. It sustains all life. When deprived of the power of Light, consciousness reverts to its temporary, illusory substitute called force. Force is limited, whereas power is unlimited. Therefore, the end is certain as force cannot stand against power, and without the infusion of power, force, by its very nature, expends and extinguishes itself.

With the expansion of knowledge to include the nonlinear nonduality of reality, it will become stunningly apparent that the most profound, radically scientific statement that is possible to make is, in fact, *Gloria in Excelsis Deo."*

CHAPTER 6

The Resolution of the Ego

Revelation occurs when the obstacles standing in its way are removed. These obstacles fall of their own accord when their underpinnings are taken away. Such an underpinning is the concept of 'cause'. Why this realization is so important can be grasped when we see that the belief in cause is a major support of the illusion that one is a separate, self-existent, and independent self, or ego.

'Cause' is implicitly dualistic—there is a 'this' that causes a 'that'. There is, therefore, an imputed, logical necessity for an 'I' that is the explanation and the cause of the 'that' of actions. Thus, there is an imaginary 'thinker' behind thoughts, a 'doer' behind actions, a 'feeler' behind feelings, an 'inventor' behind inventions, etc.

Also characteristic is the confusion of identity with actions and behaviors, roles, or titles. This confusion arises from the misidentification of the self not only as a separate doer, but it also goes on to blur into a self-image that one is one's actions, behaviors, feelings, thoughts, etc. The belief that one is certain qualities, such as good or bad, or one's vocation, tends to embroider the illusion of a separate doer behind the actions, with an endless list of descriptive adjectives.

The 'I' becomes submerged beyond recognition into an endless morass of self-definitions. If they are 'good' definitions, one feels happy; if they are 'bad', one then feels depressed or guilty. In actuality, all self-definitions are fallacious and equally misleading.

It is useful to recognize that the illusion of a

separate self or entity creates a false identity whose tenacity is seemingly difficult to overcome for several reasons. One becomes enamored of this precious 'self', which then becomes an obsession and the subjective focus of languaging and thought. The self becomes glamorized as the hero or heroine of one's life story and drama. In this, the 'I' self becomes the perpetrator, the victim, the cause, the responsible recipient of all blame and praise and the principle actor in the melodrama of life. This also requires that the self be defended and that its survival becomes all important. This includes the necessity to be 'right' at any cost. Belief in the reality of the self becomes equated with survival and the continuance of existence itself.

To transcend the identification with the self therefore requires letting go of all the above mental propensities. This requires the willingness to 'sacrifice' all these traits and mental habits to God out of love and humility. Radical humility can be arrived at only by confining thoughts and opinions to their verifiable validity. This means the willingness to let go of all presumptions of thought. With persistence, the vanities disappear as truths and are now seen as the basis for errors. In one final, glorious crash, one realizes that the mind does not really 'know' anything. If anything, it only knows 'about', and it cannot really know because to really know means to be that which is known, e.g., to know all about China doesn't make one Chinese.

To limit the mind to what it provably knows is to reduce it in size and influence so it becomes one's servant and not one's master. It becomes obvious that the mind actually deals in presumptions, appearances, perceived events, nonprovable conclusions, and mentations that it misidentifies as reality. No such reality as that constructed by the mind actually exists.

The mind tends to be expansive and credits itself with 'worthy' thoughts and opinions. When carefully examined, one finds that all opinions are worthless. They are all vanities and have no importance or intrinsic merit. Everyone's mind is loaded with endless opinions, and when seen for what they are, opinions are really only mentations. What is of more importance, however, is that they stem from and reinforce positionalities, and it is these positionalities that bring on endless suffering. To let go of positionalities is to silence opinions, and to silence opinions is to let go of positionalities.

The value of memory also becomes diminished by the realization that not only does the mind misperceive in the present, but also it routinely does so in the past, and what one is remembering is really the record of past illusions. All past actions were based on the illusion of what one thought one was at the time. There is profound wisdom in the rueful saying, "Well, it seemed like a good idea at the time."

With contemplation and meditation, the belief in an imaginary 'I' as one's actual self diminishes as all phenomena are realized to be happening of their own and not as a consequence of an inner volitional 'I'.

The phenomena of life are not being caused by anything or anyone at all. It is at first sometimes disconcerting to realize that all the events of life are impersonal, autonomous interactions of all the facets of prevailing conditions of nature and the universe. These include bodily functions, mentations, and the value and meaning the mind places on thoughts and events. These automatic responses are the impersonal consequences of prior programming. In listening to one's thoughts, one realizes one is just listening to all that programming. There really is not an inner 'me' that is causing this stream of consciousness. This discovery can be made through the simple exercise of demanding that the mind stop thinking. It becomes apparent that the mind completely ignores one's wishes and goes right on doing what it does because it is not acting out of volitional choice. Frequently, in fact, it does the exact opposite of what one wishes.

Basic to the ego's continuance and capacity to dominate is its claim to authorship of all subjective experience. The 'I thought' is extremely quick in interjecting itself as the supposed cause of all aspects of one's life. This is difficult to detect except by intense focus of attention during meditation on the origination of the thought stream.

The time lapse between an internally sensed occurrence and the ego's claim to authorship is about 1/10,000th of a second. Once this gap is discovered, the ego loses its dominance. It becomes obvious that one is the witness of phenomena and not the cause or doer of them. The self, then, becomes that which is being witnessed rather than identifying with it as the witness or experiencer.

The tracking capability and function is interesting. The ego actually interposes itself between reality and the mind. Its function is like the tape monitor function of a high-fidelity set. The tape monitor plays back the program that has just been recorded a split second prior to the playback. Therefore, what the person experiences in ordinary life is an instant replay of what the ego has just recorded. In this split instant, the incoming material is instantly edited by the ego in accordance with its previous programming. Thus, distortion is built in and automatic.

This screen obscures reality and hides it from awareness. One of the first things noticed when the ego is transcended is the enormous transformation of all life into intense aliveness. One gets to experience reality before it has been distorted, muffled, and edited by presumption. The impact when one first experiences life presenting itself as it actually is, is overwhelming. Just moments before the illusion of the false self disappears, it has, in its remaining seconds, an emerging glimpse of Reality as it never could have even imagined it. The demise of the ego's perceptual apparatus reveals wondrous splendor. In that split second, actual death was also felt as the remnants of the ego's structure expired with the belief that it alone was real.

In summation, it can be said that the ego is a compilation of positionalities held together by vanity and fear. It is undone by radical humility, which undermines its propagation.

Another underpinning of the ego is our belief that it is our source of comprehension and survival, and we look to it as the font of information about ourselves and the world. We see it as our interface with the world, which, like a TV screen, brings the world and its meanings to us, and we fear we would be lost without it.

Throughout one's lifetime, the ego-self has been the focus of one's endeavors; therefore, the emotional investment in it has been enormous. The ego is both the source and the object of striving and is heavily imbued with sentiment as well as the whole gamut of human feelings, failings, gains and losses, victories and tragedies. One becomes obsessed with and enamored of this entity, its roles, and its vicissitudes. The sheer mass of investment in this self makes it seem too valuable to relinquish. We are anchored to it by all the years of intimate familiarity—the hopes, the expectations, and the dreams. One becomes attached to this 'me' that is thought to be central to the experience of life itself.

In addition to this enormous lifetime investment in what we believe to be our self, there appears on the horizon of the future the specter of death. The awful information that this 'me' is actually fated to come to an end seems incredulous. The prospect of death as an ending to the 'me' seems unfair, bizarre, unreal, and tragic. It makes one angry and frightened. The whole panoply of emotions that have been lived through as a consequence of being alive now has to be replayed, but this time, about death itself.

The relinquishment of the ego self as one's central focus involves the letting go of all these layers of attachments and vanities, and one eventually comes face-to-face with the ego's primary function of control to ensure continuance and survival. Therefore, the ego clings to all its faculties because their basic purpose, to ensure its survival, is the 'reason' behind its obsession with gain, winning, learning, alliances, and accumulation of possessions, data, and skills. The ego has endless schemes for enhancing survival—some gross, some obvious, others subtle and hidden.

To the average person, all the foregoing seems formidable and bad news indeed. For those who are involved in advanced spiritual work, however, the good news becomes apparent. In actuality, the ego-self doesn't have to die at all; life doesn't come to an end; existence does not cease; and no horrible, tragic fate is waiting to end life at all. Like the ego itself, the whole story is imaginary. One does not even have to destroy the ego or even work on it. The only simple task to be accomplished is to *let go of the identification with the ego as one's real self!*

With this relinquishment of identification, it actually goes right on walking and talking, eating and laughing, and the only difference is that, like the body, it becomes 'that' instead of 'me' or 'this'.

All that is necessary, then, is to let go of ownership, authorship, and the delusion that one invented or created this self and see that it was merely a mistake. That this is a very natural and inevitable mistake is obvious. Everyone makes it, and only a few discover the error and are willing or able to correct it.

The likelihood of correcting this error of misidentification is a transformation that actually cannot be done without God's help. To let go of one's seeming very core of existence appears to need great courage and resolve. At first, the prospect seems formidable and involves fear of loss. The fear that "I won't be me" comes up. There is fear of the loss of security and the familiar. Familiar means comfort, and there is the underlying phrase, "The 'me' is actually all I have." To let go of this familiar 'me' brings up the fear of voidness, nonexistence, or possibly the dreaded 'Nothingness'.

To ease the transition of identification from self to Self, it is helpful to know that the lesser becomes replaced by the greater, and thus, no loss is experienced. The comfort and security that were gleaned

from clinging to one's identification with the small self
is miniscule compared to the discovery of the true Self.
The Self is much closer to the feeling of 'me'. The Self
is like 'Me' instead of just 'me'. The little me had all
kinds of failings, fears, and sufferings, and the real Me is
beyond all such possibility. The little me had to carry
the burden of the fear of death, whereas the real Me is
immortal and beyond all time and space. Gratification
at the transition is complete and total. The relief that all
one's lifetimes of fears were groundless and imaginary
is so enormous that, for a period of time, it is very
difficult to even function in the world. With the
reprieve from the death sentence, the wondrous gift of
Life springs forth now in its full splendor, unclouded by
anxiety or the pressure of time.

With the cessation of time, the doors swing open to
an eternity of joy; the love of God becomes the Reality
of the Presence. The Knowingness of the Truth of all
Life and Existence stands forth with stunning Self-
revelation. The wonderment of God is so all encompassing and enormous that it surpasses all possible
imagination. To be at last truly and finally home is
profound in the totality of its completeness.

The idea that man fears God then seems so ludi-
crous that it is a tragic insanity. In reality, that which is
the very essence of love dissolves all fear forever. There
is also a divine comedy in the absurdity of mankind's
ignorance. At the same time, the blind struggles and sufferings are seen as pointless and needless. Divine Love
is infinitely compassionate; that people believe in a
God who gets upset and angry at people's limitations is
hard to believe. The blind world of the ego is an endless nightmare; even its seeming gifts are evanescent

and hollow. The true destiny of man is to realize the truth of the divinity of one's source and creator, which is ever present within that which has been created and is the Creator—the Self.

To be content with living in the confines of the ego is a pathetic price to pay for the measly crumbs that the ego repays for submission and subservience to it. Its little gains and pleasures are pitiful and only fleeting and transient.

Another reason the ego is tenacious is its fear of God. This fear is aided and abetted by the prevalent misinformation about the nature of God and on whom, in this process of personification, all kinds of anthropomorphic defects are projected, which distort man's imagination about the nature of deity itself. Like a giant Rorschach card, man's fantasies about God become, as Freud correctly said, the ultimate repository of all man's fears and delusions. Freud's limitation was that although he was correct in stating that no such false god exists, he did not suspect that, on the contrary, a true God does exist (which accounts for Freud's calibrated level of 499). Carl Jung, one of Freud's contemporary psychoanalysts, went beyond Freud and proclaimed the truth of man's spirit and the validity of spiritual values. (Jung therefore calibrates at 540.) In these observations, we clearly see the demarcation and the limits of reason, intellect, and rationality.

To understand the nature of God, it is necessary only to know the nature of love itself. To truly know love is to know and understand God; and to know God is to understand love.

The ultimate awareness and knowingness in the presence of God is Peace. That peace proclaims infinite safety and preservation with infinite protection. No suffering is even possible. There is no past to regret and no future to fear. Because all is known and ever present, all possible uncertainties or fears of the unknown are dissolved forever. The guarantee of survival is absolute; there are no clouds on the horizon nor is there such a thing as a future or a next instant that could be hiding someone awaiting misfortune. Life is a permanent 'today'.

The state of Reality precludes any causes, and there is no possible relationship between a subject and an object. Thus, there are no nouns, no pronouns, no adjectives, no verbs, no 'other', and in fact, no such thing as relationship is even possible in Reality. Neither gain nor loss is possible. The Self already is All That Is, and nothing is incomplete. There is nothing that needs to be known, and no questions remain. All goals have been totally completed and all desires satisfied. The Self is without desire and free of wants or cravings. It already has everything by virtue of the fact that it is everything. To be All That Is precludes all possible lack, and there is nothing left to do. There are no thoughts to think. There is no mind to be concerned with. The Self-God-Atman has no needs. It does not get pleased or disappointed. It has no feelings or emotions. It has no beliefs or attitudes. The existence of the Self is effortless. That which is the very source of existence is forever free and unconditional. The resplendent power of God is self-luminous in the very light of consciousness itself, which has no necessity for a body nor any materiality or form. That which is formless is the very substrate of form. The Self is noncritical, impartial, totally available, present, and accepting.

It is completely safe to surrender the self to the Self.

The unconditional love of the Self for the self is its guarantee of mercy. The emanation of Self to self is the province of the Holy Spirit, which is the link between spirit and ego. By prayer we request, permit, and choose through free will to allow the Holy Spirit to be our guide. By God's grace the transformation to enlightenment is made possible.

It is said that the resolution of the ego is made difficult by resistance. The ego doesn't want to change or be changed despite its sufferings, fears, and regretful miseries. It clings to being 'right' at any cost and frets and jealously guards its cherished beliefs. It is, in fact, not an enemy to be vanquished, but a patient that needs to be healed. The ego is actually ill and suffers from delusions that are intrinsic to its structure. The return to sanity requires only the willingness of humility. Truth becomes self-revealing; it is not something to be attained or acquired, but instead shines forth of its own accord. The peace of God is profound and absolute. Its presence is exquisitely gentle and complete. Nothing is left untouched or unhealed. Such is the nature and quality of Love. The Self is the very fulfillment in manifestation of the Creator as existence itself. Nothing exists that is outside the love of God.

The story of Truth has been told repeatedly throughout the ages, but it bears telling again. Into the void-like space created by the ego's realization that in actuality it knows nothing suddenly flows the love of God, like a dam that has been opened. It is as though Divinity had been waiting all these millennia for this final moment. In a moment of serene ecstasy, one is home at last. The Real is so overwhelmingly, obviously, and totally present that it seems incredulous that belief in any other kind of 'reality' is even possible. It is like some strange kind of forgetting, like the story of the Hindu god who willed himself to be a cow and then forgot that he had done it and had to be rescued by another of the gods.

Sometimes the ego misidentifies itself more specifically as the personality. It thinks, "I am such-and-such a person." And it says, "Well, that's who I am." From this illusion arises the fear that one will lose one's personality if the ego is relinquished. This is feared as the death of 'who I am'.

By internal observation, one can differentiate that the personality is a system of learned responses, and the persona is not the real 'I'. The real 'I' lies behind and beyond it. One is the witness of that personality, and there is no reason one has to identify with it at all. With the emergence of the real Self as the true 'I', the personality, after some delay of adjustment, goes right on interacting with the world, which does not seem to notice the difference. The personality continues to be sort of entertaining and often comical, and like the body, becomes sort of a novelty. Instead of 'me', the persona has become an 'it' that runs on its own generator, so to speak. It has its habits, styles, likes, and dislikes, but they are no longer of any real significance or importance, and they have no consequences of happiness or unhappiness. Likewise, a lingering semblance of ordinary human emotions also seems to come and go, but they have no influence or power because they no longer have any identification or ownership as 'mine'.

People in the world seem to expect certain responses and get upset if these do not occur, so out of love, they are allowed to seem to occur, although they are actually slight and of no real importance or significance. With the relinquishment of identification of Self with the ego, it is difficult and not natural to become involved in the details of the world that require linear processing. The focus now seems to be on essence rather than on details of form that require extra energy to handle. This is partially due to the fact that the brain's EEG frequencies that accompany advanced states of consciousness or enlightenment are slow Theta waves (4-7 cycles/second). They are slower than the Alpha waves (8-13 cycles/second) that occur in meditation. In contrast, the ordinary mind, which is an experience of the ego, is predominantly at 13+ cycles per second of beta waves.

The world seems to pay endless attention to the irrelevant, and it is necessary to recall that it considers such things as important, significant, or even worth dying for. Out of respect for people's feelings, some approximation with normal social responses is reassuring, or else people feel rejected or unloved. For instance, people react with happiness or sadness to what they perceive as gains or losses. In actuality, neither is really occurring, but it is obvious that it is experienced as real by the individual. Sympathy, in the meantime, has been replaced by compassion and awareness rather than by a concordant emotionality.

What the people in the world actually want is the recognition of who they really are on the highest level, to see that the same Self radiates forth within everyone, heals their feeling of separation, and brings about a feeling of peace. To bring peace and joy to others is the gift of the benevolence of the Presence.

The Pathway of Consciousness

CHAPTER 7

The Mind

Introduction

The traditional pathways to God classically have been generally described as the great yogas: Raja Yoga, Karma Yoga, and Advaita, among others. These are the pathways through the heart, surrender, love, service, worship, devotion, and lastly, *Advaita*, the pathway through mind. It has been said that the pathway of the mind is not suitable for most seekers during this Kali Yuga (an eon, or 58,000 years of one complete revolution of the Zodiac) as there are too many worldly distractions. The pathway of mind requires the capacity for concentration or one-pointedness of mind. However, it may be the best way for the person who channels their energy through thought and thinking rather than feeling.

What follows is a general orientation to approach and start on this pathway. Most seekers also do the heart pathway at the same time; it is merely a matter of emphasis on one or the other. They, of course, are not exclusive, and in the end, they become the same. This will also lead into a discussion of a concomitant style of meditation.

Observation

The mind at first observation seems to be a non-stop talking machine with a constant barrage of endless thoughts, ideas, concepts, meanings, memories, plans, apprehensions, doubts, repetitions, and nonsense verses. Then arise fragments of music, past events, stories, paragraphs, scenarios, opinions, speculations, images of objects, and people past and present. Next come imaginations, fantasies, daydreams, fears, speculations, and numerous phantasmagoria. Interspersed with all this endless babble are fragments of news, media events, scenes from movies, television shows, and Internet conversations. On top of all this are financial and business worries, bills to be paid, schemes, family, culture, politics, concerns, and so on, ad infinitum.

At first glance, there is a seeming overwhelm and a hopeless morass over which one has very little, if any, control. With focus and concentration, some logical thought sequences are possible, but then the mind quickly lapses back into its restless sea of thoughts, images, and fantasies, with no surcease.

Can any sense be made of all this? Is there any place one could start to even approach this utter madhouse?

The Buddha said that the true self is glimpsed in the space between thoughts, and yet, there seems to be no cessation in the mind's endless activities. If anything, the mind seems to engage in endless frenetic activity as though it dreads a moment of silence more than anything else. Does it fear that silence will mean its end has come? It seems to pin its hope of survival on non-stop chatter. It will, in fact, quickly fill in any possibility of silence with nonsense rhymes or senseless sound bytes; it will start chanting "cha-cha-cha" or "itty-bitty-boo" or "bee-bop-a-boo"—anything rather than silence. What in the world is going on with the mind?

Motive

By observation it can be seen that beneath the images and words themselves, there is a driving energy, a desire to think, to mentate, to keep busy with any input the mind can find to fill in the gaps. One can detect a drive to 'thinkingness', which is *impersonal.* With observation, one can detect that there is no 'I' thinking the thoughts at all. In fact, the 'I' rarely intervenes. The real 'I' has trouble even getting in a few sensible words or thoughts. When it is capable of this, we call this intervention 'concentration,' but it takes effort and energy to push aside the babble and distractions to be able to organize a sequence of logical thoughts.

The first part of such a process is to focus on the desired subject and limit the stream of content to the topic chosen for contemplation. Psychologists here surmise that the stream of thought is determined by instinctual drives, or that the content of thought is organized according to associations and conditioning. All the theorizing about the nature of thoughts surmises that there is an inner 'thinker', an invisible homunculus who sits in charge of this ongoing, multifactorial set of processes called mentation.

Computers study these phenomena and hope to come up with artificial intelligence programs. However, at best, these merely imitate certain limited logic processes. The multifaceted, complex processes of the total mind are nonlinear and unable to be encompassed within the Newtonian paradigm to be suitable for computerization. Its primary content is best described as seemingly random or chaotic, with interspersed runs of logic, reason, or intelligence that just as quickly fade back into the noise of endless chatter again.

The periods of intelligent logic sequences seem to appear chaotically. Like reveries, fantasies, or daydreams, the mind just as randomly selects short periods of reality-focused, sequential processing. Intuitive leaps occur with no warning. Just as likely are periods of thought blocking, lapses, forgettings, and various fragments lost in an endless maze.

One thing is obvious—the mind is totally unreliable. It cannot really be depended upon at all. It is not able to be consistent, and its performance is sporadic as well as erratic. It will forget to take the keys to the office, forget telephone numbers and addresses, and be the source of frustration or annoyance. The mind is contaminated by emotions, feelings, prejudices, blind spots, denials, projections, paranoias, phobias, fears, regrets, guilts, worries, anxiety, and the fearsome specters of poverty, old age, sickness, death, failure, rejection, loss, and disaster. In addition to all the foregoing, the mind has also been innocently and erroneously programmed by endless propaganda, political slogans, religious and social dogmas, and continual distortions of facts, not to mention falsifications, errors, misjudgments, and misinformation.

Even carefully orchestrated and disciplined traditional social institutions, such as the law and legal proceedings, trials and legal processes, are rife with error (as starkly revealed by DNA testing). Even eyewitnesses are dead wrong over and over again. Above all else, the primary defect of the mind is not only its content, usually irrelevant or in error, but it has no means of telling truth from falsehood. It is merely a game board.

How To Proceed

From the foregoing, it can be seen that it is futile to try to find truth via the mind. (The benefit of the way of the heart, or Unconditional Love, is that it bypasses many of the traps and quagmires of the so-called mind.) Even if the mind could be trusted to produce a logical, stable product, it easily fails to grasp the significance of context, and it interprets the results or misapplies them, e.g., the current 'politically correct' game that never seems to anticipate unexpected consequences.

The pathway through the mind is really the pathway of 'no mind' in that its techniques are designed to bypass the mind and thinkingness altogether. We could liken the mind to a goldfish bowl. The water is consciousness itself. The fish are the thoughts and concepts. Beyond the content of mind is the context or space through which the thoughts occur. The water always remains the same and is unaffected by the thoughts. We tend to cling to thoughts because the ego, in its vanity, classifies them as 'mine'. This is the vanity of possession that automatically adds value and importance to anything (possessions, country, relatives, opinions) as soon as the thought 'mine' is prefixed. Once the supposed value of a thought has been enhanced by the prefix 'mine', it now takes on a tyrannical role and tends to dominate thought patterns and automatically distorts them. Most people actually dread their own mind and live in fear of it. It can assail one's peace of mind at any time, without warning, with sudden fears, regrets, guilts, remorses, memories, etc.

To undo the dominance of mental content, it is necessary to remove the illusion that thoughts are personal, that they are valuable, or that they belong to or originate from one's own self. Like the body, the mind and its contents are really a product of the world. One is born with an organ called a brain, which is predetermined by genetics to have certain structures and capabilities as well as limitations, depending on chromosomes and gene combinations, DNA sequences, etc.

From all this genetic garble arises a fragile, complex growth pattern of brain neurons and synapses now subject to intrauterine influences and post-natal fates, such as nutrition, nurture, and emotional and intellectual climate. Together with this is the influence of an infinite number of neurotransmitters, neurohormones, environmental hazards, and accidental programmings. The IQ is already set; the convolutions are already in place, and now one has to make the best of it because society, with all its complexity and error, then proceeds to systematically program this defective organ with software of questionable accuracy, usefulness, or veracity.

Like the body, the mind is not one's real self, and like the body, it is basically impersonal. It has thoughts, but these thoughts are not a product of the self. Even if the person does not want a mind, they have one anyway. There is no choice in the matter; the mind is imposed and thrust upon one unasked. The fact that having a mind is an involuntary imposition helps with the realization that it is not a personal choice or decision.

Further Observations

After one has observed the general field of mind, it is apparent that the specific content of the thought stream itself is not likely to be rewarding. One has to stand back, move farther into the next level of consciousness, and ask what is it that is watching, observing, being aware of, and registering the flow of thoughts. Just as the eye is unaffected by what is observed or the ear by what is heard, there is the ongoing process of witnessing, which is unaffected by that which is witnessed.

Here again, there is no entity that is doing thinking; neither is there a witness behind witnessing. Witnessing is an impersonal, inborn aspect and characteristic of consciousness itself. One can retreat from involvement with the content of thought and choose to adopt the point of view of observing or witnessing. To be proficient, this does take some practice. To get a feel for it, one can practice watching out the window of a car by fixing one's gaze through a specific spot on the window; the focus is then no longer on each object specifically but on an imaginary slit through which objects seem to stream by, and as a result, one cannot with certainty identify each object because one does not focus upon them individually.

Witnessing or observing does not focus on any idea or image but allows them to flow by without involvement. One then realizes that the thought images are occurring spontaneously and the thoughts are not choices made by personal decision but that the thought stream is impersonal. The thoughts are not 'mine' as there is no 'me' involved. As the physical eye sees images, it does not claim authorship of the images nor does the ear claim authorship of sound. Therefore, with some experience with witnessing and pure observing, it also becomes apparent that the thoughts are not authored by a unique personage called 'I'. They are the result of combinations and permutations of ideational and emotional programs that are playing on the game board. The realization that the mind is not the

same as 'I' or 'me' breaks the identification of the self
with the mind.

This realization also extrapolates to the body as one
realizes that one is merely the witness, experiencer,
and observer of sensation. One does not actually experience the body but only the senses.

Proximate to witnessing or observing is experiencing. There is witnessing and observation, and then
there is the experiencing or that which is witnessed
and observed. By moving the point of observation from
what is being witnessed to that of witnessing, the next
step into the field of consciousness is awareness of
experiencing. Is experiencing done by a 'who' or by a
'what'?

One will, by observation, discover that 'something'
rather than 'someone' is functioning as the impersonal
experiencer and observer, which is unchanged and
unaffected by the content of that which is being experienced, observed, or witnessed.

The next thing to notice is that the content of mind
is form. For form to be observable, it must occur
against a background of nonform. Analogously, objects
are visible only in space because space is empty and
without form. Similarly, one can only hear sound
against a background of silence. The use of white
sound to blank out speech is an obvious example.
Because consciousness is formless and devoid of
content, it is able to recognize form. Thoughts are only
discernible if they move in a field of non-thought. The
background of the mind is therefore the silence of the
field of consciousness itself. In turn, consciousness,
which is a field of potential energy, is detectable
because it is illuminated by the light of awareness,

which is the Self.

Meditation: Observation of The Mind's Stream of Consciousness

Intentional

The stream of thought is propagated and energized by layers of motives and intentions that can be identified as follows:

1. The desire to language emotions: This takes the form of recall, rehearsing, and repetitious processing of events and ideas that are linked to emotions. This process is sometimes referred to as the mind working through its failings.
2. Anticipation: Making plans for expected or possible future events or possible conversations or encounters.
3. Rehashing the past.
4. Rewriting scenarios, real or imaginary.
5. Creating imaginary scenarios—daydreams.
6. Remembering—reruns and recalling.
7. Solving problems.

Unintentional
1. Unasked repetitions of the above.
2. Senseless ramblings, phrases, fragments of mentations, background voices, and music.
3. Commentary.
4. Dysphoric memories, painful moments, unpleasant events and feelings.

Silencing the Mind; Going Beyond It

Motives

One can observe that the mind gains satisfaction from its musings and thought processing. Pleasure results from thinking and the function of 'doing something,' e.g., "Don't bother me; I'm thinking." Part of the pleasure of doing something is the illusion that one is accomplishing some goal, creating solutions by rehearsal and planning, righting imaginary wrongs, or giving other people a piece of one's mind. There is, therefore, the motive of reworking one's life and its history into a more favorable and satisfying picture that reflects more favorably. There is an attempt to restore self-esteem and increase one's capacity to survive. The basic intentions of ordinary mental activity are (1) to feel better, and (2) to survive.

The Formation Of Thought

To accomplish the objectives, it can be observed that the mind is primarily concerned with its own moment-to-moment operation with the control of the next instant; it is endlessly poised in anticipation of being on top of the next split second, and it tries to monitor each succeeding instant of experiencing. This core intention underlies all the forms that mental processing can take, and it is ever present. It lies just beneath the surface of the content of thought itself. Its motive is the survival and perpetuation of its own functioning. The mind seems to have a fear that it will disappear if it is silent for even a moment. (Most people drown out silence with background music and conversation.)

To quiet the mind, certain motives have to be surrendered and relinquished to God:

1. The desire to think.
2. The desire for the pleasure of thinking.
3. The comfort of the guarantee of the continuation of one's existence.

It is not recommended to try to stop thought by an act of the will as that merely perpetuates the mind by forcing it to continue to will its own stoppage. A more effective technique is to let go of the wanting to think and the imaginary rewards or benefits that one's thinkingness would presumably bring about. There is actually no personal entity behind the thoughts. They are self-motivated out of habits. Thoughts actually serve mere convenience but not survival because when the mind becomes silent, life goes on joyously without them.

As one approaches surrendering the mind, one will first notice that the mind is creating stories and lengthy scenarios. Its desire to do this can be surrendered. Then the mind talks in shorter paragraphs and then in shorter sentences, phrases, and word groupings. Underneath whatever form the thoughts take, irrespective of the thought content or images, there is the same motive for the desire for self-propagation and thinkingness directed toward controlling and anticipating the experience of the next instant.

Thoughts take on increasing detail of form as they emerge from a more diffuse *anlage* that arises out of the energy field that supports and propagates thought. As one focuses on letting go of the motives behind thinkingness, it is possible to catch the thoughts as they are in the very process of formation. This thought-form matrix can be detected in the split second just preceding the formation of a specific thought. This matrix is the locale of the subtle pressure behind thought production. Surrendering this intention results in the cessation of thought. In the silence that ensues, the stillness of the Presence prevails as All That Is. The divinity of its Essence radiates forth as the formlessness behind all form in exquisite perfection beyond all time and space.

The letting go of thinkingness is facilitated by the awareness from the spiritual viewpoint that all thoughts are vanities with no intrinsic reality or value. Their attraction stems from the exaggerated value that accrues from their being considered as 'mine' and therefore special, worthy of respect, admiration, or careful preservation. To undo the grip of the mind requires a radical humility and an intense willingness to surrender its underlying motivations. This willingness receives energy and power from the willingness that arises from the love of God and the passion for surrendering love of thought for love of God.

One reluctance to letting go of thought is the illusory identification of the thoughts not only as 'mine' but also as being the 'me'. The mind tends to be proud of its thoughts as though it were preserving a great treasure. It is helpful to realize that the Self is comparable to the hardware or the main frame of a computer, and the thoughts are really just on the software as replaceable programs of external origin.

Of all the programs, opinions are often highly valued, although when looked at critically, opinions are basically worthless. Every mind has endless opinions on everything, even it if knows nothing at all about the subject. All opinions are vanities with no intrinsic value and are actually the result of ignorance. Opinions are dangerous to their owners because they are emotionally charged triggers for dissent, strife, argument, and positionality. One cannot hold to an opinion and at the same time transcend the opposites. The undoing of opinion is facilitated by humility; when the mind penetrates through its own self-infatuation, it discerns that it is not actually capable of knowing anything in the true sense of what knowing actually means. The mind has only information and imaginations about anything; it cannot actually 'know' because to know is to be that which is known. All else is only speculation and supposition. When the mind is transcended, there is nothing to know because, in reality, the Self is All That Is. There is nothing left out to ask about. That which is complete lacks nothing, and that completion is self-evident in its Allness.

The letting go of all pretensions to knowledge or of knowing about anything is a great relief and is experienced as a tremendous benefit instead of as a loss as one had feared. One had been, without knowing it, in bondage to the content, and therefore the release from mind is accompanied by a profound sense of peace and absolute security. When this occurs, one is finally profoundly at home at last, with no doubts remaining. There is nothing more to be gained, nothing that needs to be accomplished or thought. Its finality is absolute, profound, motionless, and still. The endless nuisance of desires and wants and pressure of time have come to a final end and their hollowness stands revealed.

Positionality

As positionality ceases, one becomes aware that it was the source of all prior miseries, fears, and unhappiness and that every positionality is inherently in error. All positions that were held can be forgiven. Because of programming and context, they sounded like a good idea at the time. All such ideas were based on the same erroneous notion that, in some way, they served to propagate the survival of a separate, independent ego/self identity. Actually, when it disappears, no loss is possible and no gain is necessary. It was illusion itself that was the actual cause of endless pain and suffering.

By its very nature, structure, and qualities, the false ego/self is not capable of realizing peace or true happiness. At best, it experiences pleasure, which is based on conditions whose loss brings about grief and the return of unhappiness. In the end, it will be found that the sacrifice of letting go of the mind is actually the greatest gift one can receive. The reward so greatly exceeds any expectations one could have had that it is not explicable. As the ego dissolves and the mind loses its insatiable grip on one's sense of identity, some new fears arise. Without a mind to ensure survival, how will the 'I' survive and life go on? How will dinner get made if I don't plan for it? How will the necessities of life be met? Isn't the ego/mind necessary for survival?

All these questions are based on the limitations of the ego/mind's concepts of causality. These in turn are based on the imagined duality that there is a thought-self identity which, by its thoughts and desires, causes things to happen through actions. A 'that' is said to occur as a result of a 'this' in the world.

There is, therefore, an illusory separation between cause and effect, between a separate 'I' and an event in the world caused by this 'I's' plans and ideations. Therefore, if it is believed that if there are no ego/mind's thoughts to cause anything to happen, how will survival be supported? This is the source of much fear, insecurity, and raging anger when obstructions to plans appear and threaten this imaginary survival mechanism.

In serious spiritual work, it is necessary to have a few simple basic tools that are absolutely dependable and safe to rely on in order to walk through fear and uncertainty. One basic truth that is of inestimable value and usefulness is the dictum that all fear is fallacious and not based on truth. Fear is overcome by walking directly into it until one breaks through to the joy that the fear is blocking. The joy that follows facing any spiritual fear comes from the discovery that it was merely an illusion without basis or reality.

The ego/mind is limited to the Newtonian para-digm of reality and is not capable of really understanding the nature of life itself. In reality, everything occurs of its own, with no exterior cause. Every thing and every event is a manifestation of the totality of All That Is, just as it is at any given moment. Once seen in its totality, everything is perfect at all times and nothing needs an external cause to change it in any way. From the viewpoint of the ego's positionality and limited scope, the world seems to need endless fixing and correction. This illusion collapses as a vanity.

In Reality, everything is automatically manifesting

the inherent destiny of its essence; it doesn't need any external help to do this. With humility, one can relinquish the ego's self-appointed role as savior of the world and surrender it straight to God. The world that the ego pictures is a projection of its own illusions and arbitrary positionalities. No such world exists.

Another source of hesitation when doing spiritual work occurs because there seems to be a transitory conflict between customary social attitudes and the work of spiritual evolution. Out of habit, there is claim to sets of beliefs and values that derive from customary values, expectations, and programming. These are believed to be of value to oneself and society, and there may be some reluctance to relinquish them. For example, one may feel guilt over abandoning cherished, mechanistic, or religious convictions or good-person programming held to be ideals. To move through these sources of conflict, it is useful to remember that the spiritual journey requires the relinquishing of all beliefs and attitudes in order to create space 'for Reality to shine forth'.

The emphasis on and expectations of one's efforts shift from the expected and the mundane to what appear at first to be exceptional and unusual. There is a temporary abandonment of what was fantasized to be of value to society. What were thought to be crucially important viewpoints are seen to be impertinent presumptions and hollow rhetoric. The relinquishment of pet slogans reveals them to be primarily forms of operational propaganda with hidden motives to control others and influence their minds.

With humility comes the willingness to stop trying to control or change other people or life situations or events ostensibly 'for their own good'. To be a committed spiritual seeker, it is necessary to relinquish the desire to be 'right' or of imaginary value to society. In fact, nobody's ego or belief systems is of any value to society at all. The world is neither good nor bad nor defective, nor is it in need of help or modification because its appearance is only a projection of one's own mind. No such world exists.

Another habit of the mind that creates temporary obstacles is the frequent use of the hypothetical as a source for argument and doubt. It is always possible for the intellect to construct an imaginary set of concepts in such a way to refute anything. The unconscious purpose of the hypothetical position is always the vanity of being 'right' and refuting some other point of view. The hypothetical has no validity and no existence in reality. The 'what if ' never has to be addressed in spiritual work inasmuch as it is a spurious product of imagination and languaging whose motive is self-justification of a positionality.

The consciousness level of intellectualization calibrates in the 400s, which is useful in the physical world of human endeavor but a limitation and a great barrier to enlightenment. The intellect itself is a great limitation, and the greatest geniuses of science and the intellect all calibrate at approximately 499. That is as far as the intellect can go due to the limitations set by its context of reality. To go beyond that limit requires a greater context and takes one into noncausality, nonduality, and the nonlinear and non-Newtonian dimensions of thought and understanding.

It is necessary to see that everything is what it is as a consequence of the entire universe's being what it is in its totality throughout all time. Every 'thing' we think we see is, in itself, perfect, total, and an expression of the entire universe. At most, the intellect could merely grasp this as an idea but not experience the actual truth of it. Even if the ego could comprehend totality, it would still speak of its perception of an event and not comprehend its own existence. It is helpful to realize that nothing can be described or experienced except from outside itself. All descriptions, no matter how elegant, are nothing more than perceptual measurements and definitions of imputed qualities that have no self-existence.

Nothing is as it can be described; therefore, all descriptions are of what a thing is not. The realization of absolute reality and truth is the greatest gift that one can be to the world and all humanity. Spiritual work, in its essence, is therefore a selfless service and surrender to the Will of God. As one's awareness increases, the power of that field of consciousness increases exponentially in logarithmic expansion, and that, in and of itself, accomplishes more than all effort or attempts at relieving the suffering of the world. All such efforts are futile because they are necessarily misguided by the falsifications and illusions of the perceptual function of the ego itself.

The Impersonality of The Ego

While there is a belief in a singular 'me' or 'my', it seems as though one is sacrificing by letting go of the ego/mind. It is viewed as a sacrifice because it is thought to be something unique and precious because it is personal. It is helpful to realize that the ego is impersonal; it is not unique at all. Everybody's innate ego operates about the same as that of everybody else. Unless modified by spiritual evolution, all ego/selves are self-serving, egotistical, vain, misinformed, and committed to endless gain in all its customary forms, such as moralistic superiority, possessions, fame, wealth, adulation, and control.

Because of its positionality, everybody's ego results in guilt, shame, greed, pride, anger, rage, envy, jealousy, hatred, etc. Because the ego is constructed of positionalities, it has no option to be anything else than what it is. It therefore becomes an inescapable source of endless suffering and loss. Above all else, it fears the future and the specter of death itself, which is intrinsic to the ego's structure. What the ego clings to most is its conviction of its own existence as an independent reality. For a while, the ego even resorts to seeking enlightenment as a secret means of securing its survival unto Eternity. By this slight of hand, the spiritual ego emerges in a desperate but now sophisticated form of survival. Our fantasies about our reality are dear to us, and we are reluctant to relinquish them. The process requires both courage and faith. To let go of the known for the unknown requires great commitment, willingness, and devotion to surrendering one's faith to God.

Causality

Certain realizations bring about major leaps in consciousness and are therefore worth repeating because they are often comprehended primarily through the process of familiarity rather than sequential linear logic. Progress is facilitated by letting go of certain limiting but strongly held belief systems that themselves are positionalities.

In Reality, nothing is 'causing' anything else. Everything is the expression of its own essence and is self-existent. Its appearance is dependent on everything else in the universe and the point of view from which it is observed. Everything is actually self-existence in its reality because everything is part of All That Is and has no individual parts, separateness, or independent existence.

Inasmuch as it is not separate from everything else, its existence as it is requires no external cause. That which appears as manifest arises directly out of the unmanifest by the process of creation. It does not arise as an effect of something else. There is no 'else', and only in duality does it seem to require an explanation, such as causality, to explain what appear to be separate events. Actually, there are no separate events, no separate things, and no happenings to be explained.

The Newtonian paradigm of causality, which is the main limitation of the calibrated level of the 400s, postulates a mysterious process called 'causality'. If we watch and closely examine sequences of events, we note that they are actually sequences of appearances. They are created by an arbitrary selection of a beginning and an end in time or space. Causality is an abstract concept, and like all abstractions, has no intrinsic reality. It is a linguistic concept useful in the physical world of ordinary activity. We can only see conditions. An obvious example is that one can only 'start from where you are'. We could say that the prerequisites for 'events' are not causes but certain necessary conditions. Even intellectual humility requires the relinquishment of hypothetical constructs that have only heuristic value as linguistic explanations. This is clear from the child's question, "Why does the flower turn to face the sun?" 'Heliotropism' is the explanation given, which fulfills the question but which is really a non-answer. A rhetorical question can only produce a rhetorical answer.

Because the mind that operates out of the paradigm of Newtonian causality has no means of discerning truth from falsehood, the scientific mind substitutes skepticism or even cynicism in an attempt to defend itself from being misled. All kinds of devices are utilized to overcome this limitation, including elaborate statistics that are subcategorized under the title of "Scientific Method." This results in so-called double-blind experiments or dependence on replicability of results, implying statistical and mathematical criteria that become self-reifying with causality as a purported operative mechanism. From nonlinear dynamics, however, we observe that it is out of sameness that difference arises or all of Creation would be at a standstill. It is out of a hundred million generations of black beetles that a white beetle suddenly emerges.

The blocks of skepticism in the hypothetical arguments are all delays to spiritual progress. Faith implies a voluntary suspension of disbelief, which supports the humility that underlies all spiritual progress. Conviction occurs later since truth is self-revealing, self-evident, and comes about as an effortless, self-fulfilling presentation.

If there is no causality and nothing is causing anything else, then how do we bring about desired goals or changes? In actuality, there is the setting up of necessary conditions that, by historical observation, have always been present. What is desired is the witnessing of a sequence; then causality is implied as operating through that sequence.

When observed closely, it will be realized that sequence itself, like heliotropism, is merely an intellectual construct. There is neither a sequence nor a happening but, instead, successive points of observation on an imaginary time scale. At best, one could see that they obscure what appears to be a change of appearance.

To let go of assuming an arbitrary, artificial point of observation in time, the illusion of change disappears. The assumption of a 'this' as compared to a 'that' is an artifact of duality and an arbitrary point of observation.

In Reality, there is no 'this' or 'that', no 'here' or 'there', no 'now' or 'then'. These are only mechanisms of mentation, just as locality cannot be described without a basic point of reference. In Reality, there is no 'this' to become a 'that', nor is there either time or distance other than the illusion created by the arbitrary selection of a point of reference. The arbitrarily selected point-of-reference locality is not possible or describable; therefore, Reality is spoken of as nonlocal, beyond space and time. It is not describable in those terms that are only categories of thought and abstractions of the reasoning process. These are useful, however, to the levels of consciousness that calibrate primarily in the 400s. At 500, there is a major paradigm jump so that what was real now seems unreal, and what is unreal now seems to become 'the real'. Each level of awareness has its own understanding of truth, and clarity comes from understanding this quality of levels of consciousness.

If causality has no reality and mechanistic determination is not the explanation for what we observe, what other explanation could be substituted in the interim until a greater awareness reveals itself? The mind is life's conundrum, so we can answer its questions with the temporary but obviously satisfactory explanation of Creation.

If the unmanifest becomes manifest through continuous creation, then no other intellectual devices or premises are required as attempts to explain the obvious. We could say that everything is created to be self-evolving because that is intrinsic to its existence and the nature of Creation itself. This explanation then imputes another duality, that of 'created' versus 'creator'. This can be transcended easily by seeing the obvious, that Creation and Creator are identical. In nonduality, there is no separation between a creator and that which is created. As limitations are released, the universe reveals itself to not be different from Divinity. As the Self is realized, the divinity of all Creation in all its expressions goes forth with shining power and absoluteness. It is self-effulgent, self-revealing, self-identical, and complete in total unity and oneness.

The Absolute is exactly that. The infinite Presence within all that exists is beyond all time and space, forever complete, perfect, and whole. All points of observation disappear and there is the omnipresence of that which Knows All by the fact that it Is All.

As Reality stands forth in its stunning self-evidence and infinite peace, it appears that the block to Realization was the mind itself, which is not different from the ego; they are one and the same.

The state of Awareness is the level of 'no mindedness,' which is not the same as 'void' or 'nothingness'. Those terms refer to form. The Ultimate is the realm of nonform, nonlimitation, and nonlocality, and therefore of the ever presence of the totality of the All.

There is only Existence. Existence requires no cause, and to think as much is to create a fallacy of logic. By Existence, we mean discernible through observation, and it imputes a hypothetical change of conditions from nonexistent to existent. However, that which is always was in its completeness beyond all time; looking for a primary cause is an artifact of mentation that arises along with the concepts of time and space. Beyond time and space, there are no events, no beginnings, and no endings, which are beyond the categories of human thought or reason.

CHAPTER 8

Beyond Causality

By watching the phenomenon of the mind in its operations, its mechanisms become apparent and then tend to dissolve. The presumptions of the mind are its separateness, its belief in a progression of time with its beginnings and endings, and the categories of thought that constitute and ensure its survival. To survive, the ego has to believe it is real, and that it has a separate, independent existence. The other motive for its continuance is the belief that through the ego and its betterment, happiness can be found at last and the perfect conditions for it are secured. Therefore, the ego/mind constantly seeks control and gain in all its various forms and appearances. It seeks successes by whatever yardstick it measures that illusory goal. Happiness is always around the next corner, so it strains harder to achieve its goals.

At some point, the illusion breaks down and the opening for the start of the spiritual quest commences. The quest turns from without to within, and the search for answers begins. With good fortune, one comes upon the teachings of true enlightenment and does not deviate from the core of those teachings. Over time, many of the explanations and understandings that were presented along with the original teachings have been lost and have slid instead into misunderstandings. Over the centuries, some of the greatest teachings have been distorted to arrive, amazingly, at their exact opposite meaning. These then become the basis of strife and the obstruction of truth.

It is not only useful but also critical to have some

authoritative source available to recheck one's bearings and what directions to follow. It cannot be said often enough that the calibrated level of truth of any teacher or teaching should be obtained and confirmed before becoming a student or follower, much less a devotee or initiate. One's commitment should be to God and Truth only. Teachers are to be respected, but devotion should be restricted to only the Truth. As Buddha said, "Put no head above your own," meaning that one's only true guru is the Self (the Buddha nature).

The Self of the teacher and one's own Self are one and the same. The teacher becomes a source of inspiration and information. It is the inspiration that supports the quest.

Does spiritual commitment mean one has to give up the world? No, of course not. It means merely that worldly life needs to be recontextualized, restructured, and envisioned differently. It is not the world that is a trap but one's attachment to it, along with one's observations that cloud the search for Truth. Some attractions themselves are merely time wasters, while others are serious traps with grim consequences in which the unaware become immersed. On the other hand, it is sometimes only as the result of the sheer agony of one's having gone astray that hitting bottom, letting go, and accepting better choices occurs. Therefore, one can never say it is wrong for anyone to follow any particular pathway for it may be the very means of their ultimate salvation, as painful as it may be. We can say with certainty that anything that fails to make one go strong with the muscle-test method is not a direction that a committed spiritual seeker of enlightenment wants to follow.

One source of error is often the seemingly innocuous human capacity for curiosity. The lure at the door to disaster is not obviously something negative but a more sophisticated bait that conceals the wolf in sheep's clothing. It is therefore necessary to avoid that which does not make one go strong with the muscle test because that which makes one goes strong supports life and leads to Truth.

Can one explore the domains that lead away from Truth and return unscathed? The answer, at least for the present, is that it is unlikely. Let us look at the fact that seventy-eight percent of the world's population tests as being below the level of Integrity (200). There is also the social reaction to be dealt with, which might be called the 'crab phenomenon'. In a pail of crabs, as one or more try to get over the edge to freedom, the other crabs reach up and pull it or them back; in some people, there is a contrary reaction toward those who are seeking the light. Indeed, if a member of a negatively calibrated cult begins to discern the negativity that is present behind the façade of holiness and tries to leave, they are often denounced and subjected to abuse or even violence. Most traditional pathways therefore recommend that one congregate with others who have a similar spiritual dedication. It is also significant that the consciousness level of mankind, which stood at 190 for many centuries, has now recently jumped to 207; therefore, the sea of consciousness of mankind as a whole now supports the positive instead of the negative.

The Spiritual Direction

It is helpful to remember that neither Truth nor Enlightenment is something to be found, sought, acquired, gained, or possessed. That which is the Infinite Presence is always present, and its realization occurs of itself when the obstacles to that realization are removed. It is therefore not necessary to study the truth but only to let go of that which is fallacious. Moving away the clouds does not cause the sun to shine but merely reveals that which was hidden all along. Spiritual work, therefore, is primarily a letting go of the presumably known for the unknown, with the promise of others who have done it that the effort is more than well rewarded at the end. On the earthly level, gold is not created but merely revealed by chipping away that which obscures it.

One of the main spiritual tools is intention, which sets up priorities and hierarchies of values that energize one's efforts. Spiritual work is a commitment and also an exploration. The way has been opened by those who have gone before and set the possibility in consciousness for others to follow. Just as Roger Bannister broke through the 'M-field' of the four-minute mile, so have beings of advanced consciousness left markers for others to follow. In turn, every advance that we make in our awareness benefits unseen multitudes and strengthens the next step for others to follow. Every act of kindness is noticed by the universe and is preserved forever. When seen for what it is, gratitude replaces spiritual ambition. In traditional Buddhism, one seeks enlightenment for the good of all mankind; all gifts return to their source.

In due time, one's spiritual intention and focus come to replace worldly ambitions and desires. It is as though one is progressively drawn into the Self as if there were a spiritual gravity acting by attraction. A style of knowingness replaces reason and logic, and intuitive awareness focuses on the essence of life and its activities rather than on goals or the details of form.

Perception begins to change and the beauty of creation literally shines forth from all persons and objects. A simple scene may unexpectedly suddenly become overwhelmingly beautiful as though revealing itself in three-dimensional Technicolor. There are moments when suddenly all is still, and the experience of the quality of All That Is takes place within an all-encompassing Presence. It is this Eye of the 'I' that gives the sense of reality to life. That which enables us to experience what we think of as an individual 'I' is actually the Infinite 'I'.

The radiance of God is the light of awareness that reveals the divinity of all that exists. In the stillness of the Infinite Presence, the mind is silent as there is nothing that can be said; all speaks for itself with completeness and exactitude. With this realization, one transcends the final duality of existence versus nonexistence because only existence is possible. The opposite of Truth does not exist because Reality excludes nonreality. In this realization resides the peace of God.

Evolution Versus Creation

This is a favorite source of contention for politicians, school boards, and courts. In reality, there is no conflict. Evolution and creation are one and the same. Creation is the very source and essence of evolution. Evolution is the process by which creation becomes manifest. The physical world is a world of effects and has no power of causality within it.

From paleontology, we can see that species and life

forms have changed over millions of years. Likewise, the early versions and forms of mankind that are available for study demonstrate a progression of form.

Evolution occurs as a progression within consciousness itself to form through greater adaptability to the environment. This evolution occurs on the plane of consciousness, which includes intelligence and intention as well as aesthetic awareness. Thus, evolution occurs within the invisible domain of infinite potentiality and then becomes manifest as the consequence of creation, which is intrinsic to the essence of the universe itself and is continuous and ongoing.

If Creation were a solitary act by God at some point in the distant past, then all living things would be exactly as they were millions of years ago. Inasmuch as neither God nor Reality has any beginning or end and exists outside of time, no single act of God in time and space is tenable. Continuous creation by an ongoing and ever-present God does fit with what is apparent. Basically, there is no conflict between evolution and creation as one is merely an expression of the other in the visible domain. Evolution does not negate God but reflects God's presence as ever present in everything that exists. Because of creation, all that exists takes joy from its existence because of its innate Divinity, which is the consciousness of God.

Consciousness: The Way to God

The Intellect

The risk in providing information is that the listener's ego will try to assimilate the information as data by the intellect, and there it stops. There are spiritual students who have attended literally hundreds of workshops and lectures and have rooms full of spiritual books but have not moved forward in awareness at all; they are at a standstill. Their search goes on to the next workshop and the next, the next book, the next guru, and so on.

Spiritual work is not of the intellect (which leads to a Ph.D. in Comparative Religion or Theology). True metaphysics is an abstraction to facilitate languaging and verbalization in order to communicate that which, in truth, cannot be communicated in words. The words are not the things to be realized. The truths learned have to be put into daily practice to be effective, and they exist beyond the words. If this is done, change takes place. The purpose of information is for it to be absorbed with familiarity and then mature into understanding.

Understanding

In spiritual work, understanding in itself has the capacity to bring about change. It acts as a catalyst and opens new ways of looking at things. It brings about growth and spiritual advancement. As spiritual growth continues, old styles of thinking and contextualizing are surrendered and accompanied by the joy of new discoveries. Anger at the absurdities of life is now replaced by laughter, and what a lot of the world bemoans and makes much of as melodrama is now seen as comical. Spiritual teachings need to be accepted to become integrated. Resistance comes from the ego, which lacks humility, and that, out of pride, resents being 'wrong'. It is better to realize that one is not giving up wrong views but instead is adopting better ones. That peace is better than war and that love is better than hate makes sense to the intellect, but the ego may rebel at giving up its favorite hate and justified resentments.

There is a multitude of millions of people on the planet, whole cultures and societies, whose only theme and reason for survival is hate. Their entire society is based around revenge and the duality of victim and perpetrator. Whole areas of the world are devoted to the expressions of hatred, which are constantly rejustified by reiterating the distant past. In society, there is no dearth of justifications for hatreds. One can always cite long-dead ancestors and justify hatred toward their ancient enemies. This can even be seen as heroic, patriotic, laudable, or politically correct.

Willingness

Letting go of the old is facilitated by willingness, courage, and faith. Spiritual progress literally benefits all mankind in that it raises the general level of consciousness. Even one iota makes a difference.

Another obstacle to spiritual growth is impatience. This can be overcome only by surrender.

Meditation

A general orientation and a technique have been described elsewhere. We may think that thoughts are connected together by associations or some other seemingly plausible psychological explanation. By observation, however, one will note that, on the contrary, thoughts are occurring in a senseless, random fashion. They jump from one subject to another, with no real connection to each other at all. The thought stream is usually described from the limits of the

Newtonian linear paradigm that imputes causality where none exists in reality. Thoughts appear to be random, nonlinear, and chaotic, with no calculable predictability. They seem to be haphazard. Despite laudable efforts, there is really no verifiable explanation for thoughts, images, concepts, memories, fantasies, feelings, hopes, or fears, and the content of mind refuses to be controlled. The sum stratum of mind, the matrix of thinkingness, is the constant production by thinkingness that prompts an endless succession of thoughts. These are purposely interjected to prevent all possibility of silence. The more one attempts to control it, the more it plays tricks, becomes rebellious, refuses to be controlled, and appears to be untamable.

In meditation, one can see from the viewpoint of the witness, the observer, that the field of consciousness itself is watching the mind and that it is futile to struggle with it. It is helpful to realize that the mind is not 'me'. It is an impertinence; it is seductive. It tries to convince you that you are it. The identification with the body is not overcome by destroying the body. Neither is the identification with the mind transcended by destroying the mind. If neither the body nor the mind is the real self, there is no need to destroy it, conquer it, or do battle with it. Thoughts are occurring on their own, not because they are caused by anything or anyone.

The nature of the mind is to think. One can force it into sequential, logical thought for short spurts by focus and intention. In this way, it can solve 'problems'. The mind is fast and clever. It claims credit for its thoughts (good thoughts, that is). One has to be razor sharp and focused with attention to catch that the claim of authorship of the thoughts happens a split nanosecond after the thought occurs. The illusion of 'I thought' disappears when the mind is caught red-handed.

The Buddha said the same thing; 'Buddha mind' is discovered between the thoughts. Thoughts actually don't mean anything and are not necessary for survival. The ego's claim that it authored the thought actually takes place in about 1/10,000th of a second. In reality, everything is actually happening of its own. One's life is a continuous gift, and its continuity from moment to moment is sustained by God, not by the ego. There is no point in trying to block out thoughts; they just return. People fear that if they let go of their mind or thinkingness, or do not carefully watch it or try to control it, they will either die or go insane.

The objectives of the ego/mind can never be achieved. Its efforts are noisy and upsetting. In actuality, one is much better off without it.

Once one observes that it is hopeless, one can begin to abandon it by withdrawing interest from it. One can begin to disown its hypnotic fascination and step back progressively from watcher to observer, to witness, to consciousness itself, and finally to the awareness that illuminates consciousness and enables awareness to be aware. The Self can be pictured as a space that is essentially clear of form.

The mind is under the constant pressure of anticipation to attempt to control the next split nanosecond of experience. One can focus in on the source of this will to think and let go at the level of the willfulness that underlies its obsession and drive to control the experience of the next moment.

Spiritual work is thus an endless surrendering,

letting go, turning away from, withdrawing from, and ignoring that which is irrelevant and essentially unrewarding. The direction of focus then moves from the content of thought to that which is observing and experiencing the thought, and then to the discovery that the awareness is aware as the result of an innate quality and is not really a volitional act by an imaginary, independent self.

Awareness transcends location, body, space, time, mind, thought, and feelings. Like the sky, it is the backdrop through which the clouds float. The ultimate witnessing of awareness is undisturbed by any content and does not depend on content for its own existence.

To go beyond the known requires courage, faith, and conviction. It also requires spiritual power and energy whose source is innate with the higher fields of consciousness and the great teachers and their teachings. Enlightenment itself is by the grace of God, but it also occurs only by one's own inner agreement and choice.

Forgiveness and the Innocence of Consciousness

Forgiveness is a difficult step for the average mind to take by virtue of its arbitrary positionality that creates a conflicting duality of right and wrong, deserving versus undeserving, fair versus unfair. This is the 'problem of the opposites'. The resolution of the opposites requires some understanding about the nature of consciousness.

Compassion for human frailty tempers judgmentalism. The human mind places hypothetical standards on human conduct that has a moralistic attitude. In this country, for instance, what is termed morality is actually merely an expression of Puritanism. They are not the same at all. Puritanism is judgmentalism, which is devoid of compassion, love, or forgiveness. Its attitude is harsh, pitiless, and punitive. It appeals to egotism by feeling right, virtuous, and righteous. It operates by condemnation, shame, guilt, and fear and seeks retribution and punishment.

In contrast, consciousness itself is innately innocent. It becomes progressively programmed, often merely by accidental social influences. It is born into a specific subculture. At the lowest level, it finds itself among neighborhood gangs or peculiar secular cults with allegiances, symbols, secrets, initiations, and obedience to the group and its leaders. On this level of society, consequences for violation of group codes may result in death. There are group clothing styles, symbolic gestures, utterances, and tight group control. The members are brainwashed and intimidated; the chance to escape is slim. From one view, these behaviors are anti-social. From another, they are merely adaptational and dissocial. Although these attitudes are dissonant with society as a whole, they are internally consistent.

The core of subcultures is programming. The content is spelled out in the lyrics of the music of the subculture. The norms of society are ridiculed and have no significance.

On progressively higher social levels, the same type of programming takes place but is less obvious or blatant. Again, group loyalties to social programs are expected. Variance is punished by subtle means or rejection.

The consciousness of people on every level of society is entrained by a calibratable level of consciousness that prevails as a hidden 'attractor field'. Attractor field is a term derived from nonlinear dynamics and signifies that within what appears to be random or unconnected occurrences, there is actually an invisible, organizing pattern field of influence that affects the occurrence of phenomena within each level of consciousness. It also establishes parameters that limit understanding and awareness. If a concept is beyond the reach of understanding of a certain level of consciousness, people say, "I don't get it."

When we look at the nature of consciousness, we could say that the mind is innately innocent as it has no means to prevent its becoming programmed. It is an instrument that can be involuntarily imbued with any 'software'. Unaided, human consciousness cannot discern truth from falsehood. The mind lacks a protective mechanism and is easily damaged. Emotions further decrease capacity for mature or balanced perception. In addition, the mind has an inherent defect in that it operates via perception itself, which automatically dissociates reality into duality and creates the spurious pseudoreality of the seeming polarity of the opposites.

Consciousness is like the hardware of the computer, and social programming is like the software. No matter what the content of the software, the hardware remains uncontaminated and innately innocent.

In the past, spiritual progress was limited by the dominance of religious authority, and dogma and was surrounded by fear and threats of persecution. Anyone who transcended the commonly held belief system, such as mystics, was suspected of heresy and was treated as though they were threats to the ecclesiastical establishment and its authority. (This still prevails in some countries.)

In the Western world, this has changed and is continuing to change in a favorable direction. Cruelty is no longer acceptable or condoned. The Holy See of the Catholic Church now speaks against capital punishment and has renewed its spiritual authority and power by the demonstration of humility and spiritual integrity. The fault was not within religion itself but in the misinterpretations of it by those who did not truly understand its essence.

Because ordinary human consciousness is blinded by the very nature of perception, it is completely unable to tell truth from falsehood. Because of its innate innocence, it can be misled, and all error is ignorance. The consciousness level that prevailed in mankind for the past centuries was actually inhospitable to spiritual truth, but now that the consciousness level is at 207, truth has found a fertile ground in which it is welcome and can grow.

The Will: Understanding and Comprehension

Will is determined by understanding and comprehension that, in turn, is influenced by meaning, which is then determined by context. Out of meaning and context arises value and, therefore, choice. The will energizes the efforts to achieve that which is valued by virtue of its meaning. To the worldly, motivation is based on wants and desires and the seduction of attraction. These wants and desires lose motivational force when they become overruled by will and decision. Will is thus the basis for spiritual growth and the evolution of consciousness. One becomes attracted by truth rather than repelled by falsehood. Spiritual evolution is almost like a space ship taking off from Earth's gravity; it is difficult at first, but it finally leaves the gravitational field. Energy-consuming intentionality eventually dissolves into effortless surrender, and one becomes the recipient of unfolding awareness. Revelation replaces discovery. Understanding presents itself and becomes self-revealing by grace, without effort.

The inner pressure to achieve spiritual awareness is replaced by being the witness of Truth rather than its seeker. Effort is replaced by the effortlessness of spontaneous discovery. Essence progressively shines forth through form, which loses its delineation. Then, even essence fades into the domain of the awareness of existence itself with its self-revealing Divinity.

On The Nature of Peace

The Profound Peace prevails in the Silence, which marks the ending of the experience of time. The illusion of time precludes Peace in that it occasions an expectation of a feeling of loss or anticipation. At ordinary levels of consciousness, this time pressure and its accompanying anxiety are outside awareness and go unnoticed, just as people who live next to elevated trains eventually become oblivious to the noise. But, if the trains stop, they are overwhelmed by the sudden, strong silence. Some people who have become used to tumult and noise feel upset by silence and peace and seek to return to the familiarity of noise and disruption of people. Many people cannot tolerate the quiet of the country or an empty room. The silence of Divinity, by contrast, is profoundly comforting and fulfilling.

CHAPTER 9

Advanced Awareness

Nature of The Pathway

The direct avenue to advanced awareness via consciousness bypasses form, duality, and perception. Conflict and error arise from form, which is also the home of force. Power resides within the 'domain' of the formless. Formlessness might be said to emerge noticeably at the consciousness level that calibrates at 500 and progresses to 600, at which level form disappears into formlessness. Eventually, it is recognized that form is constituted by the formless, and that they are one and the same, but until that realization occurs, form itself is a distraction and a delay that is best avoided.

Avoid The Distraction of Form

Many 'spiritual' teachings that are expressed in form frequently lead to what is best termed as 'astral' realms of consciousness, which in themselves can be seductive, unending, and pleasurable, but they do not lead to enlightenment.

Form reinforces the illusion that there is a seeker on some sort of pathway with rungs and signposts and even 'spirit guides' positioned along the way. On the spiritual climb to the peak of Enlightenment, there actually are no entities to meet you along the way.

Astral 'planes', like teachings, can be calibrated. There are low planes (hells), intermediate planes (purgatory or limbo), and the higher astral planes (celestial). These are all possible destinations of the soul or spiritual body, or focus of consciousness. Each of these levels has its own hierarchies, 'gods', and folklore that are 'real' to the inhabitants of these planes. These may be gratifying, even joyful and thrilling, but they are not enlightenment.

That which is Reality is beyond all form and yet intrinsic to it. Let form reveal its own nature. There is no need to seek it. Also, one needs to be wary to not be caught in the supposed opposites or alternatives of form versus formlessness, or Allness versus void, or fullness versus emptiness. These are merely descriptive linguistics, with no intrinsic reality. One does not have to choose between the real and the unreal since the unreal does not exist.

The Direction of The Exploration

The search is progressively 'within' to discover the source of the knowingness of the sense of 'I'. People say, "I know myself." But what does that mean? In ordinary parlance, it means to be aware of the nature of the ego and therefore implies awareness of one's own psychology, the ego, and its forms.

The awareness of the Self is an actuality that replaces the ego as the seat of the sense of 'me' or 'I'. In the process of spiritual discovery, one looks instead to discover what it is that is aware of and has the authority to sense the existence of 'I-ness' or the quality of 'I-ness', rather than a specific or circumscribed 'me' as the 'I'.

Note that both God and all references to the Divine are capitalized, and that of all the possible pronouns, only 'I' is capitalized. The individual 'I' can only be aware of itself or its existence as a consequence of the greater Awareness. This is the innate quality of the Divine 'I' that is its source and the focus of the spiritual search. As such, it is thus nonverbal and the source of experiencing, witnessing, and observing. By analogy, one comes to realize that one is the water and not the fish.

The Basic Process

To look within is an attitude rather than a technique or spiritual practice. This means to relinquish the fascination with the content of mind and the world that it reflects. This detachment may be felt initially as a possible loss, as if one is facing experiencing the death of the world and all its promises. Such a death may be passively experienced as such, but it is merely the passing of an illusion. The source of pleasure never was without but was always within. It was never the world that granted pleasure at all but one's own enjoyment of it.

It is not really the loss of the world itself that is feared, but boredom. Boredom passes when it is recognized as merely the consequence of clinging to a yearning for the past or the future, and it is only the ego that can be bored. The ego thrives on novelty and is completely dependent on what is happening 'next'. The ego therefore thrives and lives on anticipation of future satisfaction instead of experiencing the absolute completion that is available only in the Now.

Akin to the fear of boredom is its underlying illusion that boredom is constituted by nothingness. The illusion of a possible void presents itself and seems a threat. The path, then, is from letting go of the illusion of the realm of the everythingness of the mind/world, through the illusion of void/nothingness, to the goal of the awareness of Allness that replaces both prior illusory states. It is reassuring to remember that all states are illusions and capable of being traversed by the spiritual will and progressive awareness.

Who Is Doing The Seeking?

The illusion of the ego dissolves as the prefix 'I' is removed from all action. What ego claims as its actions are merely self-existent characteristics whose functions are automatic, determined by local conditions, and without an imaginary 'I' to activate them. One does not think, feel, or even exist because of an action or decision by some inner, invisible 'I'. Thinking and feeling occur unasked. What is searching for higher truth is not a personal 'I' but an aspect of consciousness itself that expresses as inspiration, devotion, dedication, and perseverance, all of which are aspects of the spiritual will. Therefore, the source of the search for the Self is the Self itself actualizing the necessary processes by virtue of its own qualities, which are facilitated by Grace.

As another example, curiosity is a quality that exists without a personal self or decision to activate it. Curiosity, one might say, is an independent, impersonal quality of consciousness and is universal throughout the animal kingdom. It does not need an 'I' to be curious. There is no inner, independent personal 'I' that makes decisions; to prefix all thinking, action, and feeling with the pronoun 'I' is just a convenience of speech. The inner personal self could be referred to just as well as an 'it'. There are stages during spiritual evolution when both the mind and body do seem, for periods of time, to be 'its'. The body goes about its business as though it had rehearsed, and the mind speaks to others in conversation without an inner personal self to direct it. There is no inner 'thinker' behind thoughts, no 'doer' behind actions, no 'seeker' of enlightenment. Seeking occurs on its own when the time for it is right, and it emerges as a focus of attention. All aspects and qualities of consciousness are self-actuating and energize each other under the general direction of the Will.

The Will As A Tool

The capricious and carnival-like nature of the mind's activities precludes it as a fruitful focus for spiritual evolution. One can order the mind to do one thing or another, but it will refuse. To try to control the mind is like a cat chasing its tail. To try to control the mind already results in the duality of the 'controller' and the 'controlled', as well as the contents of what is to be controlled and the 'how' of controlling.

The only space from which to address mind is from that quality called Will. One can locate this area without too much difficulty. Whereas thoughts, feelings, and images pass through the mind continuously, the will is relatively motionless and fixed. It tends to persist in a more stable and therefore approachable manner. The will can indeed be quite fixed, committed, one-pointed, and immovable, unlike the mind that flits about like a nervous butterfly. Therefore, the most profitable point of view from which to approach the mind is afforded by focusing the sense of Self as emanating from the will. The will is malleable, but only slowly and deliberately so by reflection. It is a workable 'place' from which to proceed and explore. The will is closer to the true Self than is ordinary mind with its thoughts, beliefs, concepts, ideas, and fluctuating emotions.

Contemplation

This is the most fruitful and meaningful activity of spiritual work. With very little practice, one can acquire the capacity to function in the world with only minor interruption of reflection and contemplation. Meditation as it is usually practiced, however, is limited in time and place and often involves seclusion and cessation of activity. Although contemplation and reflection seem less intense, actually, by their constant influence, they wear away the obstacles. Contemplation is therefore a mode of meditation that is not less than or inferior to sit-down, cross-legged meditation.

Empowerment of The Spiritual Will

The will is activated and empowered by devotion, and it responds with inspiration, which leads to illumination by Grace. The personal will dissolves into Divine Will, and the spark that leads to the spiritual search and inquiry is a divine gift.

The readiness to initiate the journey cannot be forced nor can people be faulted if it has not occurred in them as yet. The level of consciousness has to have advanced to the stage where such an intention would be meaningful and attractive. Once inspired, a seeker will often forego all customary conveniences and life styles and sacrifice anything that stands in the way.

The illusions of the ego are tenacious but relatively fragile when subordinated to the spiritual Will. The ego/mind is fortified by habit that crumbles when its underpinnings are removed. The ego is not an enemy to be subdued but merely a compilation of unexamined habits of perception.

The Self that activates the spiritual Will is the home of infinite power against which the ego's house of cards cannot stand. The Self is like an infinitely powerful magnet that has the capacity to dissolve the structure of the ego if and when the spiritual Will gives assent. There is no one to take credit for the progression of spiritual awareness, nor is there anyone to blame if it does not seem to occur.

With spiritual work, the terms 'is' or 'are' become progressively replaced by the term 'seems to', which is due to the increasing realization of the degree to which perception is the mask that hinders truth. Until the Absolute Reality reveals itself, it is closer to reality to hold all seeming knowledge as merely hypothetical. Even now in society, this understanding is surfacing as evidenced by the frequent use of the term 'perceived', e.g., the person reacted to a 'perceived' threat.

The emergence of this discernment is a very important and significant development. It is the first real indication of an emerging awareness of the limitations of the ego and the fallibility of perception. This increase in social awareness of the limitation of the ego is reinforced by the recent discoveries of false judicial verdicts as revealed by DNA testing, and by the research which shows that witnesses are actually very unreliable and prone to serious error to a great degree. Psychologists have also discovered retrograde falsifications of memory, with displacements of events in time and place. Society thus struggles to differentiate truth from falsehood but thus far is not aware of how it can actually be accomplished dependably.

The spiritual Will is enforced and activated by love and devotion and its willingness to surrender. Love is without form and is that capacity through which one becomes willing, out of that love, to surrender one's positionalities to God. The classical way of the great religious saints was the adoration, love, and worship of God, either unmanifest or manifest as the great, divine teachers. Profound dedication and devotion can overcome all resistance, and thus the way of the heart and the way of the mind or consciousness eventually merge.

Meditation

It is rewarding to initiate the meditative process from the viewpoint that the 'I' or 'me' is located within the spiritual Will. Because the will is relatively steady and unchanging, it becomes the seat from which to progress through consciousness to the transcendent awareness of the self, which is the expression of God as the Absolute 'I', the Eye of Reality.

It is actually the spiritual Will that determines destiny or karma. The Will is the seat of power of the Self as it extends to mind and, as such, is the region of direct contact with the Holy Spirit. At the level of Will, form and formlessness 'meet'. Here the formless qualities of love, devotion, gratitude, humility, inspiration, and faith meet with the particulars of the mind with its forms of ideas, thoughts, memories, conflicts, and images. In the spiritual Will, the goals that are valued or desired are now exposed to the formless spiritual qualities of love, forgiveness, and devotion. Through humility and the choice of peace out of love, one can relinquish even the most cherished of negativities, such as revenge, spite, or hatred.

The small self is dissolved by the Self. The healing attitude of the Self to the self is compassion; it is through forgiveness that one is forgiven. This willingness to surrender, arising out of the grace of God, permits the power of God expressed as the Holy Spirit to recontextualize understanding and, by this device, to undo the reign of perception and its attendant duality that is the source of all suffering. The dissolution of duality is the ultimate gift of God, for it dissolves the very source and capacity for suffering. In nonduality, suffering is not possible.

Dogma

The way to God via the nonduality of consciousness involves no dogma or belief systems. Sufficient, useful information is available, the truth of which can be verified by one's own inner quest that is crucial to progress, especially if one is dedicated to Enlightenment in this lifetime. The value of any piece of information can be easily calibrated. It will also be discovered that each time this exercise is done, something more is learned that was not part of the original question verbatim.

Diets, Rituals, Exercises, Breathing Techniques, Mantras, and Symbols

Although none of these is actually necessary, they can be helpful to some spiritual devotees. It is useful to recognize that religions have their own agendas and limitations. The spiritual pathway to enlightenment is unique. It is not the same as 'practicing a religion'. Religions tend to emphasize historical events, their geographical locations, and past cultures with political alliances.

Enlightenment happens in the present moment and is outside time, history, or geography, which are therefore irrelevant. Theology is concerned with the consciousness level of the 400s; Enlightenment is concerned with the levels of 600 and above.

What of Music, Incense, and Architectural Beauty?

These are inspirational and supportive of a spiritual and reverential mood and attitude and help to remove the focus of attention from thought content. Beauty is uplifting and calibrates in the high 500s, which is akin to perfection.

What Is The Essence of Spiritual Practice?

To activate by inspiration, dedication, and decision of will those aspects of consciousness that become progressively self-actualizing. They are empowered by compassion, devotion, humility, and the willingness to surrender to unconditional love. Perception then transforms into spiritual vision. This evolution evokes a supportive response from the highest levels of consciousness for it takes great power to overcome the 'gravity' of the earthly life and its habits of perception. The act of worship is an entreaty and invitation to these higher energies for assistance in one's spiritual endeavor.

What of Daily Life?

There is a shift of values from worldly accomplishment to spiritual realization, which colors all activity. It places it in a different context. The overreaching goal of life becomes altered, and life's events take on a different significance and meaning as though placed in a new dimension. Eventually, the focus is on the inner, silent, motionless, still presence of Awareness itself rather than on its passing content. Suddenly, the sense of 'I' shifts from the content to the context, which is the universal 'I' of the Self.

Why Is 'Work' Even Necessary in Spiritual Endeavor?

The ego can be thought of as a set of entrenched habits of thought that are the result of entrainment by invisible energy fields which dominate human consciousness. They become reinforced by repetition and by the consensus of society. Further reinforcement comes from language itself. To think in language is a form of self-programming. The use of the prefix 'I' as the subject, and therefore the implied cause of all actions, is the most serious error and automatically creates a duality of subject and object.

To overcome the gravity of worldly thoughts and beliefs requires the work of implementing the decision of the spiritual Will to deprogram consciousness. This includes the refusal to accept the ego/mind's presumptions and statements as though they were reality. Instead, there is an insistence on a higher understanding.

Familiarity with more compassionate viewpoints of life tends to potentiate them; thus, the traditional spiritual advice to 'mingle with holy company' and avoid negative companions. This potentiates progressive discernment of more appropriate attitudes and habits of thought.

Of What Use Is Prayer?

Supplication is an act of humility. To lower levels of consciousness, prayer is an attempt to 'get' something for self or others, such as a new car, a job, recovery from an illness, or special favors. With progress, this intention to control God is given up, and the act of supplication becomes a dedication instead of a request. In war, both sides pray to win. With progression of consciousness from selfishness to selflessness, the quality of prayer shifts to the willingness to be a servant of the Lord and a channel of His Will without trying to specify the what or the how it is to be done.

Prayer becomes surrender rather than supplication. Many children lose their faith in God by using prayer in the form of pleading and then become disappointed when the requested benefit fails to appear.

What Is The Healing Power of Prayer?

All love arises from God. On the scale of consciousness, Love calibrates at 500, and as it is perfected, it reaches Unconditional Love at 540, which is the level of healing. Healing prayer services thus seek to replace negativity with an energy field of 540 or over. Some spiritual organizations calibrate at 540 or above and therefore provide a field of healing energy that is capable of accomplishing 'miracles'.

What Is A Miracle?

If an event occurs outside the domain of explanation or expected linear causality and the Newtonian paradigm, it is termed a miracle. It is an eventuality that is brought into actuality by removal of the impediments of negativity. This may involve relinquishment of limiting belief systems, such as, "It's impossible," or "It is not deserved," or other ego viewpoints. For those who have reached higher levels of consciousness, the miraculous is not only commonplace, it is the natural course of events and becomes continuous. The miraculous comes out of creation and not causality.

Spiritual Principles

Attitude

The 'way' of spiritual advancement through consciousness is actually uncomplicated and simple. The primary quality is really one of attitude in that one looks at life not as a place to acquire gain but as an opportunity for learning, which abounds even in the smallest of life's details. A spiritual attitude leads one to be friendly, kind, and well meaning to all life. We find ourselves walking over an ant carefully rather than squashing it, not as a compulsive 'must' or a religious rule, but out of a greater awareness of the value of all life. All animals will be discovered to actually be individuals that respond to respect and attention. Even plants are aware of it when you love and admire them.

Humility

This again is an attitude, an awareness of the limitations of the mind and appearance. There is an increasing awareness that life is filtered through perception, and that what is going on is primarily attitudes and perceptions rather than self-existent, external realities.

Willingness to Overlook and Forgive; Kindness

As a serious spiritual student, one has to resign from the self-appointed duties of being the one to judge, correct, control, direct, change the world, and express opinions about everything. As a serious spiritual student, one is no longer obligated to continue these chores and, instead, they are turned over to Divine justice. Inasmuch as the mind has no idea of what Reality even is, relinquishing these former duties will be a relief and also bring an end to a lot of guilt. It is therefore quite helpful to give up 'causes' and rallies for the oppressed, downtrodden, other victims, and sentimentalities. Each person is merely fulfilling their own destiny; allow them to do so. With detachment, it will be observed that most people derive satisfaction from the melodrama of their lives.

Observation of People

Physical appearance is a great deceiver. Most people look like adults but are not really adults at all. Emotionally, most people are still children. The emotions and attitudes that prevail in kindergarten and on the playground continue on into adult life but are hidden in more dignified-sounding terminology. Within most people is a child who is merely imitating being an adult. The 'inner child' we hear so much about is actually not inner at all; it is actually quite 'outer'.

As people grow up, they take on various identifications and copy what they conceive of as adult behaviors and styles; however, it is not the adult who is doing this but the child. Therefore, what we see in daily life are people acting out the programs and scenarios that they identify with as a child. The young child, as well as most animals, already exhibits curiosity, self-pity, jealousy, envy, competitiveness, temper tantrums, emotional outbursts, resentments, hatreds, rivalries, competition, seeking the limelight and admiration, willfulness, petulance, blaming others, disclaiming responsibility, making others wrong, looking for favor, collecting 'things', showing off, and more. These are all attributes of the child.

As we watch the daily activities of most adults, we realize that nothing has really changed. This realization is helpful for compassionate understanding rather than condemnation. Stubbornness and opposition, which are characteristic of the two-year-old, continue to dominate personalities well into old age. Occasionally, people also manage to go from childhood to adolescence in their personality and become endless thrill seekers and challengers of fate; they are preoccupied with the body, muscles, flirtation, popularity, and romantic and sexual conquests. There is a tendency to become cute, coy, seductive, glamorous, heroic, tragic, theatrical, dramatic, and histrionic. Again, this is the child's impression of adolescence being acted out. The inner child is naïve and impressionable, easily programmed, and easily seduced and manipulated.

Curiosity About The Nature of Consciousness

It is easier to stop reacting to people internally as well as externally by becoming familiar with the nature of consciousness. Human life is very difficult, even in the best of circumstances. Frustrations, delays, lapses of memory, impulses, and stresses of all shapes and forms beset any individual. Demands often exceed capabilities, and life is pressured by time requirements. It will be noticed that everyone's ego is about the same as that of everyone else.

The mind is inherited and has a brain run by genes, chromosomes, and a genetically determined personality 'set'. Research shows that many of the personality's major characteristics are already present at birth. Few people can actually be different from what they are. It is only the minority of people that seeks self-improvement or spiritual growth. This is because whatever one's self-criticisms, one secretly really believes that one's way of being is okay and probably the only correct way. They are all right as they are, and all problems are caused by other people's selfishness, unfairness, and by the external world.

Seek to Give Love Rather Than to Receive It

Most humans believe that love is something that you get, that it is an emotion, that it has to be deserved, and that the more they give away, the less they will have. The opposite is the truth. Lovingness is an attitude that transforms one's experience of the world. We become grateful for what we have instead of prideful. We express our lovingness when we acknowledge others and their contributions to life and to our convenience. Love is not an emotion but a way of being and relating to the world.

Avoid Creating 'Enemies'

People fall into the trap of getting even or making constant remarks. They create enemies and animosities. These preclude a peaceful life. Nobody needs enemies. They can retaliate in ways unseen and so bring on unfortunate consequences. There is no such thing as winning a conflict; that results in hatred by the loser.

The majority of domestic violence is a physical response to verbal provocation. However, in our society, victims seldom take responsibility for the provocation, temptation, or hurled insult.

It serves spiritual progress to always accept responsibility for all that befalls one and avoid the trap of being a victim. From a higher view, there are no victims. Nothing in the world of appearances has the power to cause anything.

Choose A Benign Role and View of Life

Harsh viewpoints are not conducive to spiritual growth. Even if they are 'right' or 'justified', a spiritual seeker cannot afford them. One has to give up the luxury of revenge or enjoying that 'justice has to be done' when a supposed murderer is executed. One cannot violate basic spiritual principles without paying a price. The spiritual seeker sees through the illusion and therefore gives up the role of judge and jury. Nobody goes 'scot-free', as people indignantly protest.

With muscle testing, one can quickly affirm that not one iota is missed by the universe; literally, every hair is counted, every fallen sparrow noted. No kind word goes unnoticed. All is recorded forever in the field of consciousness.

Give Up Guilt

Guilt is an attempt to purchase salvation, manipulate God, and purchase forgiveness by suffering. These attitudes stem from the misinterpretation of God as a great punisher. We think we will assuage His righteous wrath by our pain, suffering, and penance. There is actually only one appropriate 'penance' for wrongdoing, and that is change. Instead of condemning the negative, we choose the positive.

To make progress and to change takes more effort than feeling guilty, but it is a more appropriate response. We note from the Scale of Consciousness that Guilt is way down at the bottom, whereas God is way up at the top. Consequently, wallowing around in guilt at the bottom of the field of consciousness does not get us to the top.

Humility means that we see our own life as the evolution of spiritual consciousness. We learn from mistakes. Maybe the most useful of all quotes to revise whatever the past behavior is, 'It seemed like a good idea at the time'. Later, of course, in retrospect, it becomes recontextualized and seems to be in error. However, if other people are intrinsically innocent because that is the nature of consciousness, then so is the self of the spiritual seeker.

Along with giving up guilt, it is also very helpful to give up sin as a reality. Error is correctible; sin is a mistake and is forgivable. Most of what people call sin is an attachment, an emotionality stemming from the child within. It is actually the child who lies, steals, cheats, calls other people names, and hits other people; therefore, sin is really immaturity and ignorance of the true nature of Reality and the nature of consciousness. As spiritual values replace worldly ones, temptation diminishes and error is less likely to occur.

Willingness
This is the keystone to all spiritual progress as well as success in the world. It means letting go of

resistance and finding the joy of going one hundred and one percent. Unpleasantness is due to resistance, and when resistance is let go, it is replaced by feelings of strength, confidence, and joy.

In any endeavor, there is a point of resistance that becomes a block. When this is overcome, the endeavor becomes effortless. Athletes often go through this discovery, and so do physical laborers. There is suddenly the release of enormous energy, an emergence into an almost enlightened state in which all is happening of its own. There are a peace, a serenity, and a stillness. The exhausted ballerina or laborer is closer to the discovery of God than they think. The awareness of the presence of God is preceded by surrender.

In Zen, it is said that heaven and hell are only a tenth of an inch apart. It is often in the pit of despair that the ego lets go so that all crises can be turned into the opportunity of spiritual discovery.

Realize That 'Truth' Is Dependent on Context

Truth is only relative and not absolute. All truth is only so within a certain level of consciousness. For instance, to forgive is commendable, but at a later stage, one sees that there is actually nothing to forgive. There is no 'other' to be forgiven. Everyone's ego is equally unreal, including one's own. Perception is not reality.

Nonattachment

This is an attitude of withdrawal of emotional entanglement in worldly affairs. It leads to serenity and peace of mind. It is supported by refusing the emotional seduction of other people's upsets and problems. It also involves a willingness to allow the world and its affairs to work out its own problems and destiny. Reactive involvement and intervention in the world can be better left to people who have a different calling.

A 'good person' is one thing; enlightenment is another. One is responsible for the effort and not the result, which is up to God and the universe.

Nonattachment is not the same as indifference, withdrawal, or detachment. Misunderstanding that the development of detachment is required often ends up as flatness or apathy. In contrast, nonattachment allows full participation in life without trying to control outcomes.

Acceptance

Acceptance is the great healer of strife, conflict, and upset. It also corrects major imbalances of perception and precludes the dominance of negative feelings. Everything serves a purpose. Humility means that we will not understand all events or occurrences. Acceptance is not passivity but non-positionality. The development of a spiritual ego can be avoided by the realization that spiritual progress is the result of God's grace and not the result of one's personal endeavors.

Avoid False Gurus

This cannot be overemphasized. The naïve spiritual initiate is easily swayed by trappings and reputations of spiritual figures and the charisma of those who have many followers. Without the spiritual awareness of advanced states of consciousness, the spiritual seeker has no means of guidance, and popularity clouds judgment.

At this time in human history, there is actually not a single guidepost that can be relied upon other than the muscle test of the actual calibration of the level of consciousness of a teacher, organization, or teaching. The naïve are impressed with claims of supernatural powers, paranormal feats, and fanciful titles and dress.

Earmarks of true teachers are humility, simplicity, lovingness, compassion, and peacefulness. There is no financial charge for conveying truth, as there is no interest in money, personal power, or gain.

It is irrelevant to a true teacher whether others become followers or join a spiritual group or organization. All are totally free to leave the spiritual group. There is the avoidance of the development of a personality cult. There is no desire by a true teacher to control others, and, therefore, a true teacher has no interest in coercion or persuasion. Neither does the teacher attempt to appropriate knowledge or force it on others inasmuch as it was freely received. Therefore, the true teacher is gracious in manner and spirit. The student of a true teacher is the totality of all mankind.

Avoid False Teachings

It is often recommended that one use muscle testing to sort out the content of one's spiritual library. Put the books that allow one to go weak on one side and the ones that make one go strong on the other. It is highly educative.

It is very important to remember that it is an impersonal fact that the consciousness of the seeker is naïve and has no means of discovering truth from falsehood. Avoid the attractive but irrelevant. There are astral realms and universes without number, each with its own teachers, masters, spiritual hierarchy, and belief systems. Many are quite intriguing. The unwary can be easily entrapped by these fascinating and esoteric doctrines; however, the seeker of enlightenment will remember that the ultimate state is not reachable via the levels of form.

Many people think they ought to be involved in spiritual endeavor but are intimidated by what appears to be complexity, rituals, requirements, sacrifices, commitments, complicated readings, dogma, and money. Some spiritual groups even insist that the applicant become 'initiated' and go through strange ceremonies, pledges, and agreements. Proprietary groups have mandatory attendance, training courses, and the payment of many fees. In reality, there is nothing one has to join, do, or study. There are no rules, regulations, or requirements; there are no rituals or strange garb, and no odd breathing exercises or postures are necessary.

Many new-age groups sound less demanding but rely on misleading sources of information. There is emphasis on strange garb, odd diets, weird headdresses, and all manner of necklaces, symbols, card readings, psychics, channelings, mediums, chantings, and mantras. It is best to beware of and avoid all manipulation of energies, light fields, mystical visualizations, colors, mystical numbers, signs, and 'ancient secret teachings'. Some misleading figures claim special private instructions from God and become self-proclaimed prophets and visionaries. It is simple to see through all this with a simple muscle test.

These distractions all rely on form and specialness. The whole field takes on a carnival-like atmosphere, with reference to spaceships, UFOs, extraterrestrials, and doomsday prophecies. All these aspects are mistakenly labeled as spiritual and tend to be accepted at face value. One is easily misled into the astral circus thinking that it is 'spiritual'. The whole new-age community becomes enamored of an endless array of 'babas', 'masters', and legendary figures, most of whom cause one to go weak with muscle testing. Research reveals that many famous gurus have sold out spiritual integrity for power over others and delusions of grandeur.

CHAPTER 10

The Nature of God

Introduction

Although it may seem like putting the cart before the horse, it serves the spiritual aspirant to know something of the destination in order to avoid being led off track by the fallacious. Error is rampant and often pervasive by the sheer masses of people who follow erroneous and misleading concepts and proselytize error.

To know God via direct experience is extremely rare. Enlightenment occurs to less than one person in more than ten million people. True teachers are few and pretenders abound. If the masses were headed in the right direction, sainthood and enlightenment would be common. They are not. The Buddha said, "Put no head above your own. Follow the true teachings only." The true way is simple and direct.

The Qualities of Divinity

This knowledge is important to comprehend so that one can quickly discern what God is *not*. Many religions teach what God is *not* in the form of misunderstanding and distortions of truth that occur because of the ego's misinterpretations and projection of anthropomorphic perceptions. To know what God is and to have a tool available that can calibrate levels of truth is to be very well prepared indeed for what can be at times a difficult journey or process.

God is everywhere present, including the here and now. God is not elsewhere, such as only in a distant heaven or in the future so as to be available only when one gets to heaven. The presence of God is thus available to everyone all the time. To realize this is just a matter of awareness. It is said that without the help of a guru, savior, or avatar, this awareness is unlikely to occur in the lifetime of most people, which may be true.

God is beyond perception, duality, positionality, or having parts. God is beyond all opposites, such as good and bad, right and wrong, win and lose. Like the sun, God shines equally on all. God's love is not reserved for the favored few. It is, however, experienced directly only by the few, but it does shine through the clouds via the love we experience with others, including even pets and nature. The degree to which one experiences the presence of God's love varies markedly from one person to another, depending on one's level of consciousness.

The presence of God is the quintessence of profound peace, stillness, and love. It is overwhelming in its profundity. It is totally enveloping, and the love is so powerful that it dissolves any remaining 'non-love' held by the residual ego.

Like empty space that is unsullied by its content, or water that is unaffected by the fish that swim through it, the Reality of God is beyond, yet within, all form. Like space, it is equally present in the objects therein.

That which is omnipotent, omniscient, and omnipresent is not vulnerable to threat or emotional upset; thus, God is not prone to revenge, jealously, hatred, violence, vanity, egotism, or the need for adulation or compliments. The beneficiary of worshipping is the worshipper. God is totally and absolutely complete and has no needs or desires. God is not unhappy or upset if you have never heard of him or do not believe in him.

Many of the old-world descriptions of God are actually reprehensible and figments of man's guilty projections of fear. Primitives thought that every storm meant that God was angry and needed sacrifices to calm down. Volcanoes also indicated that God was angry. The ego demands explanations and looks for 'causes'. God was therefore rationalized to be the 'cause' of earthly events that created fear, such as earthquakes, famine, floods, pestilence, storms, drought, barrenness, or ill health. God was considered the great punitive enforcer as well as the great rewarder. Thus arose the numerous gods with many different descriptions in the traditions of the cultures within which these myths originated. (Note that natural disasters occurred before mankind was even on the planet.)

The god of old is the projection of the ego energies associated traditionally with the chakra of the spleen. The gods of the spleen are really serious misconceptions and account for the fact that many old religions and scriptures make one go weak with muscle testing. They represent the demonic gods of fear, hatred, envy, jealousy, and retribution. The fear of God's 'righteous anger' is still prevalent today.

One can see at a glance that righteousness is merely an arbitrary vanity of positionality, and anger would hardly be an emotional limitation to an ever-present, all-powerful God.

God is not injured by anybody's wrongdoing and therefore has no trauma to avenge. The image of God as a retaliatory, cruel punisher is hard to eradicate from one's thinking. God is blamed for all that is actually the product of the ego itself. It is the ego that is the source of guilt, sin, suffering, condemnation, and creation of all the hells. It seeks salvation by blaming it all on God. It does so by turning God into His opposite. The gods of the lower regions are really demons. In actuality, God cannot be manipulated, cajoled, bargained with, or maneuvered into a position of being either a perpetrator or a victim. God is not codependent or neurotic and does not suffer from a paranoid psychosis with grandiosity.

That which is all knowing and all present registers everything. Consciousness detects and instantly registers every event, thought, feeling, and occurrence and thus knows everything completely forever. One can verify by simple muscle testing that every hair on every head is indeed counted, noticed, and filed away in the knowingness of Infinite Consciousness itself. This occurrence is impersonal and automatic and happens because of the innate qualities of consciousness. God has no personal stake in all this nor does he react. God does not get upset or offended or get his nose out of joint at any impertinence or lack of good taste.

The infinite mercy and forgiveness of God is beyond any and all conception and is totally unconcerned with the trivialities of world events. God is not half of a duality. In Infinity, there is no 'this' (bad) to react to, nor 'that'. God is neither sadistic nor cruel. He cannot be injured and therefore has no desire for revenge.

The experience of God is not possible to the ego, which is limited to perception and deals in concepts, feelings, and form. God is nonmaterial and is not detectable by x-rays, spectrometers, photo film, Geiger counters, metal detectors, or ultraviolet or infrared detectors, which are the favorite tools of paranormal investigators looking for 'spirits'.

The love of God is unconditional. It is not arbitrary or evanescent, nor is it parceled out to the deserving. To understand that God is love precludes all such notions. God does not make decisions, does not need any news, and does not need favorable reports in order to function. That which is completely and fully the totality of love has no capacity to stop being what it is.

By analogy, one can say that space cannot decide that it will suddenly become non-space. Everything is totally identical with the essence of its own existence. Love cannot turn into non-love, nor can God turn into non-God any more than a giraffe can turn into a non-giraffe.

God is not a disturbed child or a parent. He does not read the news or punish the wicked. No arbitrary judgment is required in a universe that is innately just and self-balancing. Each entity experiences the consequences of its own doing, its own choices, its own wishes and belief systems. That which is all still, silent, peace, and love repels back onto itself all that is unloving, non-silent, and unpeaceful. This is experienced by the ego as hell, which is thereby self-created.

All actions, events, thoughts, ideas, concepts, and decisions are accompanied by an energy field that can be calibrated. Thus, by its own acts, the ego brings itself to its own level in the sea of consciousness. Like buoyancy, the impersonal quality of the sea of consciousness automatically determines the level to which one rises or sinks. This is merely the nature of the universe's being what it is. The explanation that the ego and perception use to describe the automatic outcome of actions is called 'judgment', which is an illusion, just as an explanation of events in the material world is ascribed to 'causality'.

God is not limited by concepts, ideas, thoughts, or languages. Because of the quality of the omnipresence, the presence of God includes All That Is, including man's thinking, but of itself does not partake of it. God does not talk to anybody. A voice booming out of the heavens is at best an interpretation of an inner experience that has been projected onto the physical world. Sound is a physical vibration. God is all present within the physical. That which is formless does not manipulate sound waves.

Enlightened beings do not relate any experiences of being spoken to or verbally addressed by God. This would surmise a duality of God versus a person to whom God is speaking. In reality, the Self, God, and Allness are one. There is no separation between a speaker and that which is spoken to. Mystics attune to God by an unspoken knowingness. Messages from God are from the spiritual ego, which has become dissociated and projected as some 'other' reality. 'Voices from God' are usually hallucinations. Occasionally, they are due to astral entities, some of which claim 'Godship'.

The Infinite Presence has no intentions because, here again, there would have to be the duality of an intender, that which is intended, and that to whom the intention is directed. All such constructs are conceptualizations based on perceptual duality.

God is nondualistic, total, complete Allness and Oneness. Misinterpretations of God arise because the ego deals in perception and form. It also misidentifies force as power.

Power is analogous to a gravitational or magnetic field in that everything that occurs within in it is impeccably and automatically the consequence of the nature of the field itself. The field does not 'choose' to attract anything, nor does it have different rules for different objects. The field represents total equality. Likewise, in a spiritual field of power, everyone and everything is attracted and influenced by virtue of its own constitution or spiritual 'weight', vibration, or attractor field.

Some entities or personal egos are repelled by a positive field. Many people are sincerely 'turned off' by anything loving, spiritual, or benevolent. Lots of people really hate both silence and peace; it drives them crazy. Are not solitary confinement and silence the ultimate punishment?

It seems that at consciousness level 200, a polarity shift occurs. It is as though from 200 up, the entity is positively charged, and below 200, negatively charged. It is obvious in society that those who tend toward criminality are attracted to criminality and to others of the same ilk, whereas those who choose peace and love are attracted to others with the same propensities.

Principles that are obvious and attractive above the level of 200 can become repulsive absurdities and are often ridiculed below the level of 200. Societies whose power derives from keeping the consciousness level of the people extremely low, such as the recent society in Cambodia, even take official political positions against love or its expressions.

In contrast, peace and love would be seen as the greatest of opportunities for a person who is spiritually motivated. Although it may seem absurdly simple and obvious, unfortunately, to most of mankind, it is an unfamiliar fact that God is at the top of the Scale of Consciousness and not at the bottom. It is also obvious to the spiritually advanced, but not to the masses, that creation and power radiate from the top down and not vice versa. The power of creation belongs to God alone. The physical world does not possess the power of creation or causality; thus, it is impossible for creation to proceed from form and materiality into life and eventually nonform. People are not 'co-creators' with God. God doesn't need help. What would a human being be capable of co-creating, anyway? God is beyond all form.

Ordinary people think in terms of form. Why would that which is omnipotent, omnipresent, and formless be interested in worldly games? There is nothing that 'needs' to be created.

The effects of the presence of God emanate from the Divine Essence itself and are not selective acts by God. In Reality, there are neither happenings nor events, and, therefore, there is no need for correction or intervention.

Between God and man there is a hierarchy of spiritual energy levels and fields of graduated power. These are intuited and referred to as the Holy Spirit, the Higher Self, the Grace of God, angels, archangels, and heavens. Consciousness levels beyond 1,000 and up through the spiritual hierarchy represent power beyond the capacity of human imagination.

The touch of an archangel is so powerful and devastating that the ego is as if paralyzed or stunned and goes silent. The power is absolute and total. (An archangel's power calibrates from 50,000 and above.) If life continues in the form of a physical body, it may take years to be able to function again in worldly terms.

Each existence is then the consequence of the Presence and is given the capacity to fulfill its destiny. The strength to sustain and survive the enlightenment experience itself is provided by the Holy Spirit as a powerful energy that sustains the remainder of destined life. It is by means of the Holy Spirit that there is a return to function of the faculties necessary, but they have been transformed forever. Even the 'experience' itself cannot be spoken of for many years. There is no one to tell and nothing to report. There is no speaker and no one to decide to speak. Life is directed and propelled by the Presence. The illusion of an independent, personal will or decision maker is gone forever. Perhaps subsequent actions are the momentum of a prior covenant or commitment. Everything happens of its own. Ongoing life is self-actualizing and fulfilling. There is no personal self to do anything; there is no thinker to think, no actor to act, no doer to do, no decider to decide. All verbs, adjectives, and pronouns become meaningless.

The Reality of God

God does not direct floods, conflagrations, earthquakes, volcanoes, storms, lightning, or rainfalls. These are impersonal effects of conditions within the physical world and its universe. God does not get mad and 'trash out' cities, civilizations, towns, or ethnic groups. All these things occurred on the planet before there were any living societies. God does not get involved in human conflicts, political and religious struggles, or strife. God has no interest in war's battlefields. He has no enemies that need to be slain. There are no 'Holy Wars'—the term itself is self-negating and absurd.

Infidels, believers, or the like are all positionalities of the human ego. Even sensible humans are beyond such smallness of mind and its judgmentalism. God does not 'care' whether one believes in 'Him' or not; however, the consequences will be quite different.

Love gravitates towards heaven, and hate sinks into the other direction. Goodness rejects no one. Like goes to like; love is attracted to love. God takes no actions against anything or anyone. Some souls are attracted by light and others by darkness. The selection is from within the ego and not imposed from without.

God Is Beyond Form

It is important to recognize that that which is beyond form is not reached through form or by the manipulation of form. Therefore, involvement in esoteric or occult practices is a snare and a delay. These practices are byways that lead to astral planes, enthusiasts, and proselytizers, all of which are endless in number. There is no power in geometric figures, mandalas, icons, paintings, statues, or recitations. Any value that ensues is by the intention, dedication, commitment, and faith of the believer. The world is full of well-intentioned but naïve reciters of mantras; lightworkers; worshippers of sacred objects, amulets, charts, holy places, Druid remains, mystical charms; and sites for pilgrimage, such as Machu Picchu, Stonehenge, the pyramids, the Ganges, ancient temples, energy vortices, and all the rest. This could be called 'making the circuit', but eventually, one has to go within. "Heaven is within you," said the Lord Jesus Christ.

God is self-revealing and beyond all form, yet present and innate within all form. God is silence, still, serene, peaceful, unmoving, all-inclusive, everywhere present, all-knowing by virtue of being All That Is. God is total, complete, quiescent, loving, beyond time and space, without parts or partitions, nondualistic, and equally present in All That Is, not different from the Self. Only existence is possible. Despite translation errors and misunderstanding, God is not nothingness or void. Nonexistence, as one can see by its own self-definition, is not a possibility.

The Presence is beyond all thought, mentation, or even observation. The awareness is Self-awareness that stems from the knowingness of actually being All That Is; therefore, there is nothing to know 'about'. There is no knower or known; they are one and the same. In the state of Oneness, the objective and subjective disappear into each other.

The Presence is incredibly soft, gentle, loving, melting, and paradoxically, simultaneously rock-like, immutable, all-powerful, and an infinite cohesion that holds together 'all reality' as a universe that is perpetual Creation. In the presence of God, the illusions of cause and effect disappear. The Presence does not cause anything to happen; instead, it is all that appears to be happening.

In the Presence, all sense of time disappears, which is a crucial aspect of peace. Once the pressure of time ceases, it is recognized to have been perhaps one of the primary sources of distress that accompanies the human condition. The sense of time creates stress, pressure, anxiety, fear, and endless disgruntlement in a myriad of ways. The 'time stress' accompanies all activities and pursuits, creating the illusion of sequence and cause. Every human action is couched in an unspoken pressure cooker of time and the mind constantly calculates how much 'time' can be 'spent' at every activity. This results in panic, fear, or worry, as well as guilt, shame and anger. "Too much time spent on this. Not enough time spent on that. There are many things we would like to do but we do not have enough time. Time will run out." Until the sensation of time stops, one does not have any possibility of knowing what real freedom or peace feels like.

God Is Freedom, Joy, Home, and Source

In the presence of God, all suffering ceases. One has returned to one's Source, which is not different from one's own Self. It is as though one had forgotten and now awakened from a dream. All fears are revealed to be groundless; all worries are foolish imaginings. There is no future to fear or past to regret. There is no errant ego/self to admonish or correct. There is nothing that needs changing or bettering. There is nothing about which to feel ashamed or guilty. There is no 'other' from which one can be separated. No loss is possible. Nothing needs to be done, no effort is required, and one is free from the endless tug of desire and want.

God Is All-Merciful

That which itself is absolute perfection sees nothing to forgive. All 'happenings' were the ego's perception and had no real existence. There are no 'events' to explain, account for, or that require retribution. Mercy is the quality of unconditional love. Perfection does not see imperfection or lack.

God May Be Revealed as a Sudden or Unexpected Presence

The difference between the ordinary state of consciousness and sudden awakening is very extreme, and there is really no way to prepare for it. It quickly reveals itself with no advance warning. The remaining shell of the outworn ego is felt to 'die'. One is now in a new and splendorous realm, and there is a different dimension, the presence of a different state or condition. No spirit guides, saintly figures, or angelic forms appear. There are no higher beings to meet or greet one. All considerations, expectations, and mental or emotional activity cease and are replaced by a silent knowingness that is without form or content. To be All That Is leaves nothing unanswered or unknown. That which formerly thought itself to be an 'I' or a 'me' has vanished. One is now invisible.

It is like one has been trudging along to reach a mountain and suddenly finds oneself alone at the top of Mt. Kilimanjaro, with only the infinite sweep of snowy mountains to be seen. On the peak, one notes that in some mysterious way, one is also the mountain as well as the sky and far-reaching fields of snow. No one is there; even the body stands there as though it were something unimportant, like a sled. It appears to be a curiosity of the landscape and nonessential. One looks down at the sled and marvels at the insanity that one once thought that one was a sled.

The Self is self-aware beyond the senses. Divinity shines forth as a massive revelation. Its obviousness is stark and forceful as a radiance. Its essence is certainty and finality, totality and completeness. All searches have ended.

An aspect of awareness is the quality of being everything that is, in contrast to ordinary consciousness, which seems to live and perceive the surface of things. The vision of the Presence is the inner knowing of everything. The Self is equally the sled, the snow, the mountain, the sky, the clouds, and the wind. It is All simultaneously, and yet none of them. The world seems to have turned from the equivalent of a black-and-white movie to one in three-dimensional Technicolor. Everything now has great depth and texture.

All things are equally aware and conscious of the Presence and share in the joy and realization of timelessness. If it is so destined, the ongoingness of life is autonomous and continues on its own. The physical body moves itself and goes about its remaining business. It even, if prompted, takes care of itself; however, without prompting, it would be unlikely to do so. One no longer needs a sled or is a sled, so it just does whatever it does, which can sometimes be amusing. The body is like a pet that has been discovered—it is a lovable animal.

Discussions and Lectures

Transcripts of talks and meetings in numerous countries with groups of spiritual students having a variety of spiritual backgrounds.

CHAPTER 11

Along the Pathway

Visitors have questions that are not specifically about the Self or Reality but are concerns that arise earlier in the course of spiritual exploration.

Q: I saw a program on television about out-of-body and near-death experiences. They seemed to equate the two. Aren't they really quite different?

A: They are decidedly and altogether different. One might say that one is transcendent, and the other is considered paranormal. An out-of-body experience can arise at any time, even in sleep or dreams. It is often triggered by physical calamity or illness, such as an accident or surgery. In the out-of-body experience, there is location, position, and duration. An almost invisible energy body leaves the physical body and travels to a different location in the room or perhaps even at some distance. Sensory awareness accompanies the energy body and stops being associated with the physical body, which is then experienced as being separate. The sense of 'I' is also associated with the energy body and not the physical body. Eventually, there is a returning of the energy body to the physical body and life resumes as before. This adventure is recallable and often related to other people. The calibrated level of consciousness of the individual does not change significantly. The personality does not change; however, there may be a dawning that the 'I' is not just a physical body.

    In contrast, the near-death experience is not

local in setting. One enters a much grander and more splendid domain. An infinite, radiant love is always present. There is a distinct awareness that a state of revelation is occurring, and calibrated levels of consciousness show a sharp increase. One sign of the experience is that the personality changes and results in transformation. These changes are often quite noticeable. Often, there is a major shift of attitudes and diminished interest in worldliness. The fear of death disappears. There may even be a shift of vocation. Generally, there is an attraction to spiritual subjects as well as a marked lessening in the level of overall fear. This is reflected in greater peacefulness, grace, and the replacement of negative attitudes by positive ones. The transformation of personality may be quite profound in some cases. In others, it could only be aptly described as saintliness. Some people who have these experiences become healers and are drawn to the healing professions or ministries.

Q: **What spiritual practices are practical to pursue in a busy world? Most people have jobs, families, and many distractions.**

A: The conscious pursuit of spiritual goals is the result of a choice and a decision. It actually requires only willingness and the capacity to follow through. Even a simple spiritual concept is a deceptively powerful tool. The simple decision to be kind, forgiving, and compassionate to all life in all its expressions, including one's own self, is a scalpel that is capable of removing the major impediments to spiritual progress.

With humility, one can see that the mind is limited and incapable of seeing all the circumstances surrounding any event. Out of this arises the willingness to let go of condemnation and judgment. This process results in a willingness to surrender one's experience of the world to God. It becomes apparent that the world does not really need one's personal opinions about anything at all. If one decides to take a charitable view of life's events, then alternate ways of interpreting circumstances, appearances, and other options open up.

Q: The Buddha said that desire is the source of the ego. How does one overcome this attachment?

A: There is a meditation we might call "What for?" When we note a desire, we can ask, "What for?" The answer is always, "…and then I'll be happier." Thus, the locus of happiness is always something that is outside oneself and in the future. This results in viewing oneself as the victim of outer circumstances. This is also a projection of one's power. The possible source of happiness is actually coming from within. There is neither time nor locus of happiness other than at this very instant.

The true source of joy and happiness is the realization of one's existence in this very moment. The source of pleasure always comes from within, even though it is occasioned by some external event or acquisition. In any one instant of time, no such thing as a problem can exist. Unhappiness arises from going beyond the reality of the Now and creating a story out of the past or the future that, because neither exists, has no reality.

Q: What are some other useful tools?

A: There is another meditation we could call "What if, and then what?" This exercise is based on the willingness to surrender the ego's illusions to the reality of God. We start with, "What if we let go of something we desire or value?" and ask, "And then what?" That brings up the next obstacle. We ask if we are willing to surrender it to God, which brings up the next obstacle. Eventually, the willingness to surrender every illusion that happiness is 'out there' brings an awareness that one's existence from moment to moment is solely by the grace of God. One's life is sustained as a function of the presence of God, and the materiality that we thought sustained it is in itself an expression of God's will for us. One's own efforts to sustain life is a 'given' and not a personal invention. The ego thinks we survive in spite of God's will rather than because of it.

Q: Is spiritual progress sudden or gradual?

A: There is actually no contradiction in this question, which implies the either/or state of duality. Both conditions prevail simultaneously. Seemingly small steps in spiritual evolution often occur almost unnoticed, but it is the small shifts which occur out of sight below a mountain of snow that result in an avalanche. Sudden leaps in consciousness can occur with no warning. Therefore, it is best to be prepared for such a possible eventuality.

Q: What about getting past the great block of

the intellect?

A: This leap is also made as a result of willingness and inspiration. Only four percent of the world's population is able to transcend the consciousness level of 500, the level of Love. Love approaches Unconditional Love at level 540, which is the level of Healing. In the calibrated level of the 500s, progress becomes clear and obvious. The goal is best described as lovingness towards all life and dedication to its support. Thus, in the 500s, one becomes forgiving, charitable, benign, peaceful, and easygoing. One's happiness is independent of external circumstances or events. Judgmentalism disappears and is replaced by desire for understanding and compassion. The innate beauty and perfection of all things begin to be revealed. It is common to break into tears at the extent of the beauty that is apparent in all that exists. The recurrence of any thoughts or feelings that are less than loving is experienced as painful or unwelcome.

Q: What about justified resentments?

A: The willingness to let go of resentments reveals that all so-called justifications are rationalizations and excuses.

They are the projections of blame and represent a narcissistic positionality. Resentments are really childish and based on kindergarten notions of fairness. Nothing in the universe has anything to do with fairness. Instead, everything represents universal justice outside present time and locality.

All resentments represent the justification of blame, the projection of responsibility, and seeing oneself as victim. For the spiritual student, even if the other person was 'wrong', they still have to be forgiven. All resentments calibrate below the level of 200 and are not in integrity. There is no gain in harboring them.

The modern trend toward 'political correctness' is a great source of conflict, strife, and suffering (calibrates at 190). It is based on imaginary 'rights'. In reality, there are no such things as 'rights'. These are all social imaginings. Nothing in the universe has any 'rights'. The whole area of 'rights' leads to a 'chip on the shoulder' paranoid attitude, confrontiveness, conflict, concepts of perpetrator and victim, illusions of causality, and revenge. All this displaces taking personal responsibility for one's own experience of life, which is the level one has to reach for integrity.

Q: How does humility undo the hold of the intellect?

A: By fearlessly exploring logic and reason, science itself comes to realize its limits and its proper domain. Eventually, reason and logic become circuitous so that one ends up defining definitions, categories of thought, and modes of description from preselected points of observation. Logic has practical and useful applications in the everyday material world that are salutary and beneficial, but they do not lead to enlightenment, which is an entirely different endeavor.

Q: But what about morality? Doesn't letting go

of right and wrong and judgment of others lead to immorality?

A: Denotations of right and wrong are practical guides to behavior for people who are not yet spiritually evolved. They are a temporary substitute for a greater awareness. Thus, we teach a child that it is 'bad' to cross the street alone because they lack the awareness of danger. By adulthood, such a contextualization as right or wrong about crossing the street is no longer meaningful or significant. We look both ways before crossing the street to avoid being run over, not because it is wrong or bad. With spiritual progress, ethical values replace moralistic dictums, just as awareness of spiritual truth replaces dogma and coercive belief systems. Behaviors that have to be outlawed to suppress their occurrence in the general population have lost any meaning to people who are far more advanced.

Q: **If there is no 'objective' right or wrong, then what guides behavior?**

A: One's awareness of Reality recontextualizes all meaning and significance as well as any appearances. There are no gains to be desired, no wrongs to avenge, no winners or losers, no causes to sacrifice for. The guide to all action becomes an unconditional lovingness, kindness, and compassion. All choices have consequences, and there is actually no injustice anywhere to be seen when one's vision is unlimited by time, space, and perception.

Q: What about karma?

A: We can avoid controversy and contention by not using that term, which, in the Western world, is associated with Eastern religions and spiritual traditions. Instead, we can observe the association between actions and choices, both mental and physical, with consequences. In reality, these are not sequential but are actually concordant and seemingly separated by perception. From outside the duality of perception, an 'event' and its 'effects' are one and the same thing. Nothing actually moves except the point of perception itself. All religions, without exception, teach that decisions, choices, and actions are connected with consequences that appear and occur later in 'time'. If life is seen as a continuum from one realm to the next, then all religions are the same in that they teach that actions have consequences in another realm or condition of sequential life frame.

All the religions teach that there will be a nonphysical life that supersedes the physical one. The confusion here arises from the misidentification of this life as physical and other lives as nonphysical, or recurrently physical. To begin with, this life is an inner, subjective experiencing that includes, but is independent of, the physical body. Thus, this current existence is not actually physical, either.

This life is the subjective adventure of that mysterious entity called 'I'. This current experience of the 'I' may consider itself physical, but that in itself is an illusion. Whether successive life experiences include the illusion of physicality or not is really irrelevant to the inference and significance of the sequential progress of conditions. All 'lifetimes' are subjective, nonphysical, interrelated, and actually continuous. Each is conditioned and determined by choices, positionalities, and their consequences. All possibilities are included in the evolution of consciousness. Once consciousness stops identifying with form, it is then beyond karma.

It is of considerable interest that newborns already have a calibratable level of consciousness at the time of their birth, and that this level in most people tends to persist throughout their lifetime. The progression of consciousness in the average human being during one lifetime is an advance of about five points. Paradoxically, however, the level of consciousness of mankind as a whole remained at 190 for many centuries, and only recently crossed the critical line of 200 to the current level of 207. The rate of increase of the general level of consciousness is held back by the immense number of people who continue to make negative decisions and choices.

Q: Is karma therefore related to form?

A: Preexisting conditions of consciousness consist of patterns expressed as prevailing energy fields of relative power. Each level contains within it the unresolved issues and limitations that characterize that level and thereby confront the individual. Let us say that at birth, one's energy field calibrates at 150. This person's main confrontation will certainly be anger. They may spend a lifetime, or many lifetimes, with anger as the central theme. Persons who are in the energy field that calibrates in the 50s will face a life of poverty and deprivation and may be born in a starving population, ravaged by disease and war.

Q: Aren't conditions at birth pure chance, depending on genes, chromosomes, and the accident of geography and time?

A: Nothing in the universe happens by chance or accident. The universe is a coherent concurrence and interaction of innumerable conditions attendant on the infinite number of energy patterns. In the state of Awareness, all this is obvious and can be clearly seen and known. Outside that level of awareness, it could be likened to innumerable, invisible magnetic fields that automatically coalesce or repel one's position and interact according to the positions and relative strengths and polarities. Everything influences everything else and is in perfect balance.

In Awareness, the subtle inner workings of the universe reveal themselves as a magnificent dance of incredibly complex design and execution. It becomes clear that what the world calls miraculous occurs as the consequence of a shift of energy, such as that created by love or prayer. It is also possible to arbitrarily select any aspect of human activities and interactions and calibrate the power of the energies involved. The intrinsic energies associated with all that exists determine their fate, depending on all prevailing conditions in an entire universe. In the entire universe, these are expressed locally as prevailing conditions. No accident or unfairness is possible. Every action, decision, thought, or choice alters the interacting balances and has consequences.

Q: Is karma then a general condition?

A: The entire unfolding and interaction in evolution of everything in the universe is totally karmic. Human life is no exception. Likewise, all possibilities are determined by the entire set of the universe and everything in it. A cat does not suddenly turn into a dog. It is 'karma' that results in the selection of the genes and chromosomes of one's birth, as well as the place, location, and conditions of it. A potential cat's energy field does not get attracted to enter the body of a dog. One can, with muscle testing, track the 'karma' of any entity. Within each entity, karma is a field of possible choices as well as consequences of past choices. Commonly, these prevailing sets of conditions are referred to as destiny, fate, or luck.

Q: What is the interaction between the visible and invisible domains?

A: Any separation between the two is arbitrary and one of perception only. Both the manifest and the unmanifest are an integrated whole. The physical world of perception is a world of effects. That which is the ordinary world has no power to cause anything. The power of causality exists only in the invisible domain. The Empire State Building came into existence first as a thought and design within the mind of its creator, which was then empowered by volition to appear as a consequence in the visible world. As a physical building, it has no power of

causality to cause anything to happen. Its presence
represents a local condition that has consequences,
such as wind currents or shadows, but the power of
causality is not intrinsic to the structure or its parts.

Q: What accounts for the existence of anything?
A: Divine Grace determines all Creation in all its
expressions and aspects. We say that the unmanifest
comes into expression as manifestation by ordi-
nance of Divine will. This is made possible and activated by the Presence whose quality is to potentiate the evolution of possibility into actuality. We
could say, for instance, that a seed is dormant and
inactive, but in the Divine Presence, it begins to
grow. The potential patterns for the emergence of
materiality reside within the invisible domain as
energy patterns. The quality of 'realness' is only the
radiance of the Self that imbues the quality we call
realness. The ordinary mind attributes this quality of
realness to any material and imagines that the realness emanates from the material itself. The only
thing that is real is the Self that, by the nature of its
divinity, radiates forth the qualities of life, reality,
and existence. Life is either present or not.

There is no self-existent reality such as death,
just as there is no such thing as 'off-ness' in an
electrical wire that is without current. Divinity
expresses itself as form and/or life, depending on
local conditions and potentialities. Without the
prior potentiality ('karma') for life, no one could
be born. The entire universe and everything in
it is actually a synchronous karmic display and
single event.

Q: **It sounds as though all life is pretty much pre-determined. Isn't that predestination?**

A: No. Predestination is something quite different. As a term, predestination implies limitation and outcomes, whereas karma sets up opportunities and areas of freedom for choice. The range of choices available is limited by prevailing conditions that are attracted or set by one's karmically patterned energy field. Choice supersedes karma and can overrule it or change it by an act of the will.

Q: **What of free will?**

A: As part of one's energy-pattern inheritance at birth, there is an innate capacity for choice and decision. These are available in quality and quantity, depending on one's calibrated energy field. Within an individual's inheritance and evolution into the world, we experience that one has the opportunity to forgive or to hate and condemn. It might be said that one's spiritual buoyancy goes up with the choice of forgiveness and down with hatred. Each choice then moves one into a different 'locale' in an overall energy field of human life. We say, "Birds of a feather flock together"; "Like seeks like"; "Birds go home to roost"; "What goes around comes around", and, "We reap what we sow." The Buddha said there is no need to attack or punish one's enemies for they will bring themselves down as a result of their own natures. All religions teach that this life influences the next one; whether the next is actually physical or not is therefore irrelevant. Life cannot become nonlife; it can only change form and expression.

Q: Is not an energy field of a higher calibration 'better' than a lower one?

A: It is not 'better', only different. Each entity has its work to do in its contribution to the whole. One brick is not better than another because it is bigger or higher up in the building. 'Greater' or 'lesser' or 'better' are judgmental terms arising from positionality. Each entity that lives takes equal joy from the awareness of existence. The Divine Presence in All That Is imbues that quality as a consequence of Creation. The animal, the plant, or the human are equal in their joy of existence. The human mind can think and ponder. A plant, if it had a mind, would probably consider thinking as superfluous and stupid. Every entity that lives loves its existence, not because it has emotionality, but because the joy of awareness is intrinsic to life and all existence. Knowingness does not require either thought or feeling because existence contains the quality of Divine awareness. Life itself knows that it exists, but it gets caught up in its identification with its current form. From the level of awareness of Truth and Reality, death is an impossibility because it has no reality, just as absence is not a state of being but a mental description. For death to occur, it would have to be part of the karmic potentiality of the universe. It is not a possible potentiality, and there is nothing to occur. Nothingness is not a thing that can happen.

Life, like existence, has no opposite, just as truth has no opposite, self-existent pseudoreality such as falsehood. Truth is either present or not. Divinity,

God, Allness, Oneness, and the Absolute are All That Is; no opposite to God can exist. Only the true is true; nothing else exists. All fear, then, arises from attachment to form due to the illusion that form is a necessary requirement for existence.

CHAPTER 12

The Search for Truth

Q: Where does one begin the search for spiritual truth self-realization called enlightenment?

A: It is simple. Begin with who and what you are. All truth is found within. Use verified teachings as a guide

Q: Where is that reality of eternal truth to be found?

A: Begin by accepting the very important statement that *all truth is subjective.* Do not waste lifetimes looking for an objective truth because no such thing exists. Even if it did, it could not be found except by the purely subjective experience of it. All knowledge and wisdom are subjective. Nothing can be said to exist unless it is subjectively experienced. Even a supposedly purely objective material world, if it existed, could be said to exist only because of one's subjective sensory experience of it. Even the most rabid materialist is stuck with the fact that in the end, it is only their own subjective awareness that gives it the authority of believability.

Q: Is there not a difference between an objective and a subjective reality?

A: All reality is subjective. Every other position is an illusion based on duality. The subjective and objective are one and the same, just different descriptions from different points of perception. Reality is not based on perception, duration, description, form, or measurement. All such attributes are those

THE EYE OF THE I

of perception itself, which is, by its very nature, transitory, arbitrary, limited, illusory, and dualistic.

Q: What is the value of the great teachers and teachings?

A: The gift is not limited to information, facts, or wisdom but the level or power of consciousness from which they emanate. Great power is sustained by purity of context. The usefulness of many teachings has been destroyed by error in the context in which they were taught, and thus their meaning has been obscured or distorted. How else could mankind be led into its historic, repetitious pattern of horrific and ghastly acts committed in the name of some religion, theological dogma, or positionality? Every human crime can be excused and rationalized by some distorted statement that claims to be truth because it was 'taken out of Scripture' by those who seek power, fame, wealth, and control over others. Dogma masquerades as truth and provides the slogans that lead whole civilizations sanctimoniously, piously, and arrogantly to grim and horrific death. All such empires expire.

Q: What is the difference in meaning among God, Is-ness, Buddhahood, Christ, Avatar, Truth, Enlightenment, Self, Krishna, Reality, Awareness, Oneness, Absoluteness, Allness, Totality, and Divinity?

A: None. Different linguistic forms reflect the culture of origin of the teachings.

Q: But are there not differences between the

truths of the different teachings?

A: In actuality, no difference is possible. All supposed differences are merely due to misunderstandings and are reflections of limitations of context. Differences may exist among religions but not among truly spiritual teachings. Spirituality unites; religiosity divides.

Q: How can that be possible?

A: All truth is self-existent, total, complete, and all encompassing without location, duration, or parts. Because truth is self-existent as itself in its totality, that which is a self-evident, subjective state of 'I' encompasses All That Is. Allness allows for no division.

Q: What is the 'I'?

A: The 'Infinite I' is that subjective reality which underlies the individual 'I' and allows for the experience of 'I-ness' as one's existence. It is the absolute 'I' that enables the statement, "I." It might be said that Descartes had it backwards. The truth is not "I think, therefore I am," but its corollary, "I am, therefore I think."

Consciousness, or the capacity for awareness, is formless and is the backdrop from which form can be identified. It is because of the formlessness of the apparent emptiness of space that form can be perceived. 'Somethingness' can be identified only because it stands out against no other things. It is due to the clarity of the sky that we can see the clouds.

Q: Is there a shortcut to enlightenment?

A: Yes, indeed. One can spend endless lifetimes studying all the spiritual and philosophical teachings of
the world and merely end up confused and discour-
aged. Seek to 'know', not to 'know about'. 'Know'
implies subjective experience; 'know about' means
to accumulate facts. In the end, all facts disappear,
and there are none to be known. If one realizes that
one's own Self is the All of Everything that is, has
been, or ever could be, what is left that one needs
to know? Completeness is, by its very nature, total
and complete.

Q: How can this be?

A: Because once you become something, there is
nothing more to know about it. To know implies
incompleteness. That which I am is Allness. To
realize that one already is and always has been All
That Is leaves nothing to be added.

Q: This sounds confusing.

A: That is only because the false self/ego identifies
itself with limitation and form.

Q: What about 'learning'?

A: With awareness of Reality, all learning stops. The
mind becomes silent. In peace and stillness, all that
exists radiates forth its own meaning and truth and
reveals that the nature of existence is stunningly
divine. Everything radiates forth its Divine essence
as Existence itself. That which Is and that which is
Divine are one and the same. Out of the Unmanifest

radiates the Manifest, which is also, in its essence, the Unmanifest as well. There is no duality of manifest versus unmanifest. All seeming differences disappear when one transcends perception, which is an arbitrary and limited point of view. It is perception that creates duality. This is an experiential fact, not a philosophical conclusion. Philosophy can be useful but it is only an intellectual parallel to reality in which no philosophy is possible.

Q: **Then what are we discussing?**

A: Descriptions, but behind them stands the subjective, experiential reality.

Q: **Of what value are teachings or discoveries?**

A: Each piece of information contributes to intuitive understanding and recognition. Truth is recognized. It presents itself to a field of awareness that has been prepared in order to allow the presentation to reveal itself. Truth and enlightenment are not acquired or achieved. It is a state or condition that presents itself when the conditions are appropriate.

Q: **What favors this occurrence?**

A: Humility is of greater value than all factual accumulation. Unless one has completely and totally experienced the presence of God in Its stunning, absolute Allness, it is safe to assume that one really knows nothing and that all accumulated so-called knowledge is but ignorance and pride. Anything within that claims, "I know," by that very statement proves that it is false or else it would not make such a claim.

Q: Why is knowledge such a block to enlightenment?

A: The thought, "I know" precludes the ultimate awareness of the real 'I Am'. The word 'know' is dualistic and assumes a dichotomy between a separate subject, the 'knower', and something external to be known.

Q: Thus, is there no division between 'knower' and 'known', no difference between subject and object?

A: That is the basic error of duality, which assumes the perceptual point of observation. Actually, the subjective and the objective are one and the same. To say otherwise is merely to be arbitrary.

Q: We hear that the ego is the block to realization. Can you explain that?

A: There is no such thing in reality as an ego; it is merely illusory. It is made up of a compilation of arbitrary points of view supplied by mentation and powered by feelings and emotions. These desires represent the attachments that the Buddha spoke of as the bondage of suffering. With absolute humility, the ego dissolves. It is a collection of arbitrary mentations that gain force only because of vanity and habit. If one lets go of the vanity of thought, it dissolves. All thought is vanity. All opinions are vanities. The pleasure of vanity is therefore the basis of the ego—unplug it and it collapses. In the higher state of consciousness, it becomes silent in the Presence. To even have a single thought in the presence of the Presence would not be within the realm of the doable nor would there be the likelihood of bringing up such an outlandish pomposity.

Q: There must be some tools to assist in lessening the hold of the ego.

A: Ideation persists because it is valued. Notice that everyone has an opinion on everything. Notice that all thoughts are merely pontifications. Everyone is enamored of their own thoughts and ideas, even though they are worthless.

Q: But what about the value of education?

A: Education gives reliability to thought processes and therefore of action. This is useful in the world but does not lead to enlightenment. To become educated is one objective; to become enlightened is another. Many are the educated, and few are the enlightened.

Q: But is there not reality to experiencing that which is myself?

A: All seeming separation is an artifact of thought. It is essential to see that the mind is at all times experiencing a point of view.

Q: What, then, is illusion that we hear about so much?

A: The entire perceptual illusion that the ego claims to be reality is completely and totally the product of positionality. This is very important to unravel and understand in one's own experiential awareness. If you observe carefully, you will note that at the time the mind is taking a position, that position stems from choice, training, desire, emotion, or political or religious viewpoint. From the arbitrary positionalities of moralizing, all actions and events can be categorized as right or wrong. From that positionality stem all the pointless sacrifice and sufferings of the world.

Q: What is the cause of this error?

A: Judgmentalism. This is the great vanity of all egos. Scripture says, "Judge not, lest ye be judged." Also, "'Judgment is mine,' sayeth the Lord." Christ said to forgive. The Buddha said there is nothing to judge because perception can only see illusion. Perception is always partial and limited by an arbitrary context. In truth, no judgment is possible.

Q: Is judgment ever justifiable?

A: It can always be rationalized. From Ethics, one learns the basic axiom that the end does not justify the means. To fail to understand this basic dictum is to be totalitarian and subject to serious spiritual error. A 'good' result can be conjured up to excuse any barbaric behavior, and it is thus used extensively in our society to justify socially sanctioned behaviors that violate spiritual premises. These violations undermine the very fabric of society and backfire as the prevalence of misconduct, crime, and human suffering in all its forms.

Q: How can mankind climb out of this pit of misery?

A: The swiftest way out of problems and ignorance is

by acquiring an understanding of the nature of consciousness itself. Awareness of the nature of consciousness catapults one through all problems, limitations, and human endeavors. It is the most important subject of all subjects to be learned because it underlies all human experience and enterprise. Science itself has progressed only to the point where it can advance no further without understanding the nature of consciousness. Thus, there are so many international conferences on science and consciousness that are the focus of much interest and are very well attended. Thus far, such endeavors have been hampered by the lack of adequate tools to explore the leading edge of human intelligence.

Q: We hear that the block to Awareness is duality itself. How can this be solved?

A: Duality is the artificial and arbitrary basis for the illusion of separation. It originates from a positionality that stems from the sum of thinkingness, with all its myriad judgments, values, selectivity, prejudices, and opinions.

These in turn stem from symbolism, limited paradigms, and limitations of context. It is only by an arbitrary limitation of context that any judgments or value statements can be made about anything at all. The fact that many opinions are held by great masses of people is hypnotic. Few minds can escape the appeal of the authority of mass agreement. People look without instead of within for guidance. As Freud said, the individual conscience is dissolved in the unconsciousness of the herd and mass action. Morality is silenced by mass hysteria.

Few can resist the propaganda of the news media. Truth eventually surfaces, but it is usually belated. How often human error underlies tragedy is revealed by the DNA-based reversal of the convictions of so many prisoners who have even been previously executed. Judicial testimony is perception, and inasmuch as perception is the source of error, the so-called justice system is understandably prone to error. Truth cannot be arrived at through voting. Jury conclusions are merely opinions, not facts. Emotions blind perception and guarantee error. Duality is thus a separation of truth and error that is sourced by the vanity of perception and the ego.

Q: How does perception result in duality?

A: Arbitrary selectivity results in a positionality that is a point of view which artificially polarizes the oneness of Reality into seemingly separate parts. These parts are apparent only and not actually separate in Reality. The separation into parts occurs only in the mind and not in Reality. Thus, we end up speaking of 'here' and 'there', or 'now' versus 'then', or we arbitrarily select out portions from the flow of life that we refer to as 'events' or 'happenings'. One serious consequence of this mental process is the production of a false understanding of causality. This misunderstanding leads to endless human problems and tragedies.

Q: I understand that you place great emphasis on clarifying the nature of causality.

A: In an attempt to reconnect that which has now been conceptually separated in the processes of the mind's thoughts, causality is invented to explain what is now viewed as 'relationship'. In Reality, there is only identity; there is no cause of anything nor is it required. In the Newtonian paradigm of linear causality, a 'this' seems to be causing a 'that'. In Reality, everything is already complete, and the total oneness is beyond time, space, and separation or definition. It is obvious that nothing is the cause of anything else as that would require a dualistic separation in time and space, which is impossible.

The manifest becomes manifest by creation. All things are because of their essence in its expression as existence. All we can observe are conditions.

It is relatively easy to see that the 'cause' of anything is the totality of the entire universe throughout all time, being what it is in all its expressions as existence. All things exist as an expression of identity, and the essence of all things shines forth by its presence. All things are self-created by divine expression as existence. Therefore, each 'thing' can only be what it is because of the totality of the entire universe. A speck of dust cannot be where it is positioned without air currents, which require a room, which requires a building, a lot, a continent, a planet, a solar system, a galaxy, a universe, and so on.

All statements made by the mind are subjective. There is no linear progression of events, sequences, or causations. All shines forth as it is in its expression of existence. All is self-existence and therefore not dependent on anything outside itself.

Q: Is the ego 'wrong'?

A: The problem with the ego is not that it is wrong; it is just that it is limited and distorted. To conceive of the ego as an enemy is to become polarized, bringing forth conflict, guilt, anger, and shame. Positionalities support the ego. By enlarging context, opposites are transcended and problems are dissolved. Humility removes the ego's underpinnings of judgmentalism, positionality, and moralizing. In Reality, there can no longer be opposites anymore than there can be winners or losers.

Within the illusion, statistics, for instance, depend on how limits are set and defined. By changing classification, statistics shift. Thus, the supposed crime rate in the United States can be made to appear to go up or down, depending on political pressures, or by including or excluding certain things in the compilation. By raising or lowering criteria, any social phenomenon can be made to appear to increase or decrease. The world as described by perception is therefore arbitrary, and social 'reality' becomes whatever one decides to call it. Definition defines perception, and the corollary is equally true.

Q: What effect does thought have on perception?

A: Thought usually takes the form of languaging. Language is based on labeling, which is therefore the result of prior separations and fragmentations of the whole. Thinking and mentation are dialogs and expressions of duality. One can ask who or what is doing the thinking or for whose benefit. Who is the speaker and who is the listener?

Q: What is the difference between ego and mind?

A: They are actually one and the same. The term 'ego' is generally used, however, to describe certain aspects of the mind, but the ego could be more generally defined as the source and the process of thinking.

Q: What is the relationship between mind and meditation?

A: The purpose of meditation is to transcend the mind and its mentations and limited perceptions, thereby transcending duality and becoming increasingly aware of Oneness.

Thinking proceeds from lack; its purpose is gain. In wholeness, nothing is lacking. All is complete, total, and whole. There is nothing to think about nor any motive to think. No questions arise and no answers are sought or needed. Totality is complete, totally fulfilling, with no incompleteness to process.

Q: If thoughts are fragmentations and artifacts of duality, how can spiritual teachings be conveyed in language without being misleading?

A: Concepts have levels of power that can be calibrated. The higher the level of truth, the greater its power. The energy of the concept results from the truth of the statement plus the level of consciousness of the speaker. Unaided by a higher energy (as from a great teacher), the ego/mind cannot transcend itself.

Q: **Many teachings seem ambiguous and confusing.**

A: Ambiguity itself is illusory. All seeming ambiguities dissolve in the presence of understanding. Within truth, no arguments are possible.

Q: **How can this be?**

A: Because only that which actually exists has Reality. There is no 'true versus false'. That which is called 'false' has neither existence nor reality, and only that which is true has existence; anything thought to be otherwise is illusion and falls away.

Q: **Can you give another example or further explanation?**

A: Opposites do not exist in Reality. They are only concepts of speech and mentation. Let us take the seeming opposites of light and dark. Actually, there is no such thing as darkness; there is only light. The conditions then can be accurately described as light is either present or not, or light is present at various degrees; therefore, all light or the lack of it of can be defined only in terms of light by its presence or degree, or not. Thus, there is only *one variable*: the presence or absence of light.

You cannot shine darkness into an area. One can, by languaging, call the absence of light darkness, but it will have no existence in Reality.

Let's use another example—the possession or nonpossession of money. In this, the only variable is the presence of money. The term 'poverty' then implies the absence of having money, but it is not a thing in itself. One cannot have poverty.

There is no up or down in Reality. These are denotations arising from an arbitrary positionality. Neither 'up-ness' nor 'down-ness' exists as a reality. This is how the whole illusory world of the ego is formed as positionality, with an accompanying naïveté that presumes that opposites have an independent existence. Therefore, the world as seen exists only in the mind of the observer. It has no independent existence. In Reality, one does not have to distinguish between 'what is' and 'what is not' but only to affirm that that which is, is. Therefore, the false need not be denied but only the true affirmed.

Q: It would seem that going beyond perception and duality to Reality is difficult and would require reprogramming of the whole mind to accomplish it. Is this possible?

A: A major move in the evolution of consciousness is classically referred to as 'transcending the opposites', and it brings about a rapid leap in awareness. Let us look at more examples that are easy to see. The supposed opposites of heat and cold dissolve in the easy recognition that heat is either present or not. We do not say that more 'coldness' takes over, but only that heat disappears. If it is present, we call the condition warm or hot. Coldness merely means the absence of heat; it does not exist on its own. We cannot say that 'non-heat' exists in the room. We cannot say that 'absence' is present or that 'nothingness' exists.

Let us use another obvious example: the seeming opposites of visible versus invisible. It is obvious that invisibility is not a thing that exists independently, so the question arises, visible by what means?

Another example would be the seeming opposites of present versus absent. Present is a reality that can be confirmed; absent is not a condition or a state in and of itself. We cannot say that absence exists.

Q: These still seem abstract. Can you give a more concrete example?

A: Electricity is either on or not on. There is no such thing as 'off-ness'. Off-ness cannot be sent down a wire. It is merely a linguistic convenience. The telegraph can only send 'on' signals; it cannot transmit off-ness. Likewise, life is either present or not; dead or deadness has no independent existence.

Q: Can you give a nonverbal experiential example?

A: There is a very simple and interesting demonstration of this principle. Most people are familiar to some degree with basic muscle testing. A simple demonstration shows that that which is positive or true makes the body's muscles go strong, and that which is not true, negative, false, or injurious allows them to go weak. To the naïve mind, it would seem that the muscle response is either positive or negative, or true or false. In reality, like the electricity, that which exists or is true has strength, and the muscle response is positive. That which has no existence or is false has no energy or power, and the arm merely goes weak because there is no power or electricity on to make it go strong. In other words, there is no such thing as falsehood that makes it go weak; those are only styles of expression.

Similarly, electricity makes a motor run; when it is disconnected, the motor stops. There is no such thing as 'non-electricity' that makes the motor stop. That which has no existence in Reality is an illusory product of mentation. It has no actual independent existence. It is therefore useless to seek an objective, independent universe because none is possible. All that exists does so only as a subjective experience. An independent, objective reality can neither be confirmed nor denied. Either statement is merely a positionality. No one can escape from the pure subjectivity of their own experience.

Q: What is the purpose of the ego?

A: We cannot say what its purpose is; that would be teleological reasoning. However, its main function is organized toward self-perpetuation to maintain the illusion of a separate 'I', with independent survival of its uniqueness and existence. As a consequence, it is subject to pain, suffering, and fear of death. Thus, the ego channels its survival strategies in all its multiple expressions, such as gain, fear of loss, and anxiety about its ultimate fate.

Q: What is the central, most important consequence of the function of the ego?

A: The belief that there is a 'doer' behind actions, a 'thinker' behind thoughts, a 'feeler' behind feelings. These are illusions that reinforce the belief that one is a separate, distinct entity subject to birth, death, and karma. Belief that one is a separate entity engenders fear that, in turn, reinforces all the drives for survival and the basic ego mechanisms of greed, desire, envy, pride, hatred, and guilt. To see oneself as a separate, finite entity automatically creates a duality based on 'me' versus 'not me', 'here' versus 'there', 'now' versus 'then', and so on.

Q: What then is the basic mainspring of the ego's self-propagation?

A: Believing it is a separate entity, the ego resists this illusion based on its fear of nonexistence. It fears coming to an end and not surviving in time. Its notion of reality is very limited, and it does not know what lies beyond itself. The ego cannot experience the Infinite or know of the exquisite Presence that will replace it. The ego clings to the small, personal 'I' because it has no knowledge or conscious experience of the infinite peace or joy of the great 'I' that comes into awareness and replaces it.

   The ego cannot be blamed for its own ignorance. It has no notion that anything exists beyond its own limited parameters. To go beyond its own self-imposed limitations and boundaries is not a goal that can originate from the ego itself. Unaided, the ego cannot transcend itself or dissolve its own hindrances and limits. It is like an isolated tribe that is unaware that there is a whole world beyond itself. Commonly, the members of primitive societies refer to themselves as 'the people' of the Earth. The ego is neither bad nor an enemy, but merely an illusion to release so that something far better can replace it.

Q: If the ego is as described, then how can enlightenment come about?

A: That is the function of spirituality, which informs, educates, inspires, leads, and supports the exploration of consciousness beyond the restrictions of the ego experience. Those who have gone farther along the road to greater awareness report their findings to the world and invite those who are interested to follow.

Although Enlightenment is statistically infrequent, it happens sufficiently often so that there is collectively a great body of teachings which have a profound influence on all humanity. Each enlightened being, by its own energy radiation, silently recontextualizes and expands the paradigm of human consciousness. That higher levels of consciousness are possible pervades and inspires all knowledge and creates the overall context for the human experience. The urge to progress is innate in all societies and cultures, both individually and collectively. Human striving creates the history of civilization in its efforts to better itself. Even though it is often mistaken in its efforts, the striving itself is still present.

Q: It is said that the world we see and experience is a projection of the mind and has no independent existence. It exists only as a perception. How can this be explained?

A: We can start with a simple example. We hear there

is a 'problem' in the world, or the observer has a 'problem'. It is relatively easy to see that all 'problems' exist only in the mind of the observer as a result of taking an arbitrary point of view. All 'problems' are products of mentation only and do not exist in the world.

Desires and other worldly passions and belief systems result in selectivity of perception. Examine the so-called 'signs of the Zodiac' and 'constellations' that supposedly exist in the sky. If you photograph the starry sky at night and look at it with no preconceived notions, it is obvious that arbitrary lines could be drawn between any group of bright spots so as to produce the outline of any familiar figure or geometric shape. One can draw on a map of the stars a dog, a cat, quadruplets, or whatever. These do not exist in reality in space; in fact, there is no such thing as a constellation except to the imagination of the observer. From a different viewpoint in space, not a single one of the famous constellations with fanciful names can be seen by anyone.

Q: Why then is there such a plethora of erroneous observations and belief systems?

A: Languaging creates and defines thought patterns and forms that are then projected onto the world. It is an anthropomorphic habit. We see a big tree next to a small tree and say the big tree is 'smothering' the little tree and 'taking away its sunshine'. Or we say that that was a savage or angry storm, or that this is a beautiful tree but the one next to it is deformed and ugly.

Naïve anthropomorphic statements are routine. When we say something is good, we mean we want it. When we say something is bad, we really mean we do not like it.

In and of itself, the world contains no objects, adverbs, or prepositions; neither is there sequence, events, or happenings. Even all verbs are inappropriate. Nothing is 'doing' anything. Even nouns are sources of perceptual illusion as a noun stands for an arbitrary selection of boundaries and qualities that have prior existence only in the observer's mind. What is difficult to see is that all is complete and total in itself and exists as its own self-identity. No 'thing' exists, and even if it could, it is not the name given to it. To say, "This is a chair," is to deny the completeness, wholeness, and absolute self-identity of all that exists. To say, "That is a chair," is to say that A is actually B. The name, the image, the idea of a chair is again something other than a chair, and the mind is easily deceived by nominalization and linguistic convenience. Abstractions are linguistic conveniences; they have no separate existence. Language is metaphor.

We are all familiar with cleverly constructed pictures that hide images. Children love to 'find the cat' in the picture. The mind does this constantly over and over out of habit. The perceptual world is formed out of familiar forms and images held together by belief systems and energized by emotions. Whether the object or situation is loved or hated, feared or admired, seen as ugly or beautiful, depends on the observer. Such qualities do not exist in the world. Adjectives have no actual existence or reality.

As consciousness evolves to higher levels, the world changes in appearance and behavior. As consciousness reaches the levels that calibrate in the high 500s, the beauty and perfection of the world shine forth with divine Radiance as the core of its existence. All apparent form and separateness begin to disappear, and everything is seen to be connected and continuous with everything else. One is then witness to the endless miracle of time-less creation. Everything is viewed as whole, perfect, and complete. With the realization of self-identity, everything is seen to be absolutely perfect in its expression of its divine essence. Imperfection exists only in the mind's thoughts. No imperfection exists in the world as it is.

As the level of consciousness proceeds upward past 600 into the levels calibrated at 700 and beyond, even the world itself disappears as such. There are only the unmanifest and the manifest that exist only as perception. The Absolute Reality is itself formless and therefore present in all form.

Q: Can one be trained to reach these levels of awareness?

A: These understandings are self-revealing; they are not acquired. Spiritual learning does not occur in a linear progression like logic. It is more that famil-iarity with spiritual principles and disciplines opens awareness and self-realization. Nothing 'new' is learned; instead, what already exists presents itself as completely obvious.

CHAPTER 13

Explanations

Q: What is the best attitude for spiritual work?
A: A 'Yin' type of position that is persistent and unwavering. The work consists of understandings, realizations, and a general attitude of allowing rather than getting. Know that what is being sought is all present, innate in All That Is, invisible, and silent. It is the requisite condition for existence itself. It is the one quality that is of prime significance and is the absolute, irreducible matrix for anything to 'be'.

This is so taken for granted that its significance is ordinarily overlooked. For the condition of existence itself to be apprehended, Awareness is the necessary prerequisite. The intrinsic, innate quality and essence of that prerequisite, awareness/existence, is Divinity. When discovered, it is unmistakable. The knowingness is silent, without words, and shines forth as a revelation. It presents itself in total completeness and finality. It is neither vague nor obscure but powerful and overwhelming.

The Presence dissolves all separateness. It feels as though one has stepped outside time. All sequence stops as if all time and creation were totally present equally in the Now. All that ever was or could be is already totally present and complete. All that is possible to know is already known. The potentiality already is. All thought stops and therefore all categories of thought, such as time, space, distance, and duration, cease and are not applicable.

The world literally looks different. Everything is
seen at much greater depth. Everything is alive and
radiant with consciousness. Everything is aware
that it is, and it is aware that everything else is
aware. Nothing is innately inert.

**Q: What is the best spiritual approach that is
appropriate for self-inquiry?**

A: It is an attitude, almost like a 'mudra', in that it is a
position of awareness or observation. It is actively
passive in that the Yin/allowing attitude is consistent and unwavering. One should not 'try' to see the
obvious but merely remove all obstacles, such as
opinions, beliefs, mental categories, commentaries,
impatience, or attempts by the mind to anticipate
or control the next split second.

As children, we have all tried to 'see the hidden
picture' in some pictorial art form, and when we
stopped trying, it revealed itself; the bush suddenly
became obviously a smiling lion, for example. To
'try' results in reinforcement of perception and
narrowing of vision, and, therefore, greater limitation.

It is a paradox to look for the invisible. It is more
like an identification that takes place with All That
Is and the very substrate of existence. By observation, it becomes clear that all emotional/
mental/conceptual phenomena are spontaneously
happening on their own and that there is no person
as such causing them.

The Self is the total field and all its contents as
well. Consciousness is the quality by which the Self
is known, knowable, and expressed. God is All That
Is, without any exclusion—sight, sound, space,

objects, form, formless, visible, invisible, solid, liquid, without dimension or location, and everywhere equal. There is no opposite to God. God is both Allness and voidness, equally form and nonform.

Q: How does one transcend the opposites?

A: This is a frequently asked question. Realize that all opposites are only descriptions of convenience and have no self-existent reality. They are an illusion created by adopting or choosing an arbitrary starting point or observational position. Their only value is an operational one to a reference point of intention or purpose of action or denotation. That they may and do have operational convenience leads to the false assumption that they are a self-existent reality rather than merely a descriptive viewpoint.

All positionalities depend on definition and all definitions are conventionalities reached by historic agreement. All conflict arises from positionalities. From a higher viewpoint, all alternative pairs of positionalities are irrelevant. All are based on a presumption of an intended or theoretically possible future action. An obvious one is the possibility of choice. If no potential value, action, qualification, or choice is desired or appropriate, the opposites disappear into meaninglessness.

Discrimination is definition for the purpose of the communication of information between separated points or entities. In Reality, where nothing is separate from anything else, there is no information necessary nor are there any spaces or gaps across which such information would be sent. There is neither a sender nor a receiver, nor any discrete or limited parcels of information that could be conveyed.

Communication is of value only in the world of perception where everything appears to be separated from everything else. In Reality, all is already known by all that has existence. No messages are necessary, just as the ocean does not need the concept of 'wetness' to be itself.

Q: Are verbalizations misleading?

A: If accurate, they can be very useful as a starting point to delineate the nature and direction of a quest. A verbalization helps to set a context that then progressively becomes nonverbal and more inclusive. Accurate information saves time and speeds fruitful inquiry by indicating which routes would be fruitlessly time-consuming and diversionary. To know which closet the shoes are in saves searching all the closets in the house. A good compass saves many miles of being lost, just as an accurate map saves a lot of fruitless and frustrating guesswork.

Q: How can one see past the opposites of duality?

A: The omnipresence and totality of God are all that is possible, which excludes all alternatives. God as 'void' is the unmanifest Godhead of infinite potentiality unexpressed, formless, invisible, and intangible. It is the infinite Brahman, the transcendental Krishna, beyond existence or beingness. It is the unborn, unexpressed source. Out of the unmanifest arises the totality that is God expressed as Creation or Allness.

God is All Presence simultaneously as manifest and unmanifest, as void and Allness, as visible and invisible, as the potential and the actual, as the expressed and the unexpressed.

The Dance of Shiva is the apparent appearance or disappearance of these seeming opposites that are really only alternatives of viewpoint. These occur just as the appearance of a hologram is determined by the position of the observer and not by any movement or change of the hologram itself. Let us use the example of the concept of temperature, which includes all possibilities within which there would be neither hot nor cold except by definition and an arbitrary point of delineation.

From this understanding, we can see that all seeming alternatives are merely options of viewpoint or definition. All definition is purely subjective; therefore, there is no self-existent 'out there' to be blamed for anything. One cannot be the victim of a storm or an avalanche; one is merely a participant observer of an actual phenomenon. One cannot, therefore, be a victim of life, but only take a stance that some condition is favorable or not favorable, desired or not desired. Therefore, all hatred, revenge, spite, resentment, and anger are without any basis in reality, and it is all imaginary.

Everyone is exposed to life in its expression as nature and also human interaction, called society. This interaction is impersonal, and the vicissitudes of life are inevitable and unavoidable. This can be either challenging or depressing, depending solely on one's point of view. Without positionalities, life is experienced as serene and interesting. It potentiates growth and, hopefully, wisdom rather than self-pity or bitterness. Everyone is free to make a choice. The rain does not determine whether one will be happy or disappointed. The surrender of willfulness/positionality brings peace in all circumstances.

Q: But aren't there rational opinions and positionalities based on being realistic?

A: These are primarily conveniences; actually, they are self-indulgences. All resentments are petulant self-indulgences of sentimentality, emotionality, and melodrama. One gets to be the martyr or the pitiful victim, or gets to cast oneself as tragic or heroic. Endless plausible explanations or excuses are available to rationalize, explain, or justify absolutely any human behavior or response. Reactivity is conditioned, but it is also selective. These temptations to be childish have to be bypassed by the serious spiritual seeker who sees them for what they are and refuses the attraction of the games of emotionalism.

On a certain level, they can all be seen to be false. They are actually one's 'act', even if one is unaware that they are only that.

Peace is literally a choice and a decision, although not a popular one in our society despite all the rhetoric about the term. The decision to overlook the seeming inequities of life instead of reacting to them is a choice.

Q: What of social problems?

A: Being a social reformer is an entirely different

career from that of seeking enlightenment. It is well to remember that spiritual advancement influences everyone else from within, whereas force tries to change the external only. Surrendering a personal grievance or grudge is more rewarding for all society than marching up and down with provocative signs and slogans. To the spiritually advanced persons, whether other people agree with them or not is immaterial as they no longer need to look outside themselves for validation or agreement.

Q: What does it mean to go into a bliss state? What does one do? What happens?

A: To be dissolved into intense, infinite love is overwhelming and incapacitating. There is neither the desire nor the capability to emerge from that state unaided. All bodily functions cease. Even breathing itself may cease and resume only in response to an entreaty from another person who is intensely loving. However, it is not necessary to do so. One has permission by knowingness to leave the body as an option.

In this case, in order to acknowledge love, breathing resumed. Perhaps it was decided by karma. However, the choice was also made with the concurrent awareness that any return to physicality was only temporary and the final dissolution back into Infinite Love was inevitable and certain. Compared to the eternity of that infinite state, a short return to the realm of physicality seemed trivial.

Q: What if there was nobody around to entreat

one to return to worldly life?

A: Whether or not those conditions prevail probably depends on karma, circumstances, conditions, Divine Will, and the interaction of the universe as a totality. If there were no entreaties, then the body would expire, which at the time would be quite agreeable. When Ramana Maharshi went into that bliss state spontaneously, he was not discovered for some lengthy period by which time he had been severely bitten by many insects and had been without sustenance for an unknown number of days. He was entreated to drink and eat. He responded slowly and eventually resumed movement and function; however, he did not speak in language for another two years.

Q: **Are there different degrees of realized states?**

A: There are different levels of *Samadhi*, classically described with Sanskrit designations. There is a state that is transcendental but which persists only so long as one's eyes are closed in meditation. There is a more intense Samadhi that persists in the meditative state even after the eyes are opened. There is a more advanced state yet that persists even if the devotee gets up and is able to walk around and function simply. These states are reflected in an electroencephalogram (EEG) as 'alpha' waves which are much slower than the beta waves that denote ordinary consciousness. The more advanced state is a permanent awareness that persists continuously so that returned functioning in the world is possible, as determined by karma or prior decision, choice, or agreement. The returnee to the world is then termed a 'sage' and may function in the role of healer, teacher, and source of information. The EEG of the enlightened sage is dominated by slow Theta waves (4–7 cycles per sec.), which make functioning in the ordinary world quite difficult.

In that state, the option to leave the world at any time persists and is a permanent, open option as though it was part of a silent agreement or knowingness. There is no obligation to persist or continue.

Q: How then does earthly life resume?

A: After a period of years, adjustment is made with the relearning of communication styles and a reacquaintance with human affairs sufficient to function. Recent history had to be caught up on. This can be accomplished by getting a television, watching the news reports, and reading newspaper headlines. There is an ongoing dialog within the overall field of human consciousness that is as though transparent by its essence; and by recognition, it offers aspects with which one has an option to respond.

Q: What persists?

A: The Presence and the awareness of the Self are ever present. The residual personality interacts with the expectations of the world in order to remain appropriate and not elicit comment or notice of anything other than the ordinary. Although this ordinariness is learned and voluntary, it requires the expenditure of energy and attention to form. Interaction with the form of human life can only be done for periods of time and can seem quite exhausting as it is not one's natural state. Not all the world's requests or wishes can be complied with, so there is a tendency to conserve energy in order to meet 'needs' rather than wants.

The sage persists only as a vehicle whose purpose is delineated by Divine Will as expressed through the Self. One is merely a witness to the action, which is spontaneous. The body continues to perform like a live puppet and behave in human fashion. Its needs are fulfilled automatically by its interaction with the universe.

Q: Is there any 'regret'?

A: Not regret, but there is an awareness that the expectations and wishes of the world often cannot be met.

Q: What would you specify as 'your' function?

A: To be that which I am to the world and explain it as clearly as possible in order to facilitate spiritual awareness and thus contribute to the relief of the suffering of mankind. The energy field with which that function is accompanied does by itself silently contribute to the well-being of human life and diminish human suffering, which itself is a satisfaction and a completion.

Q: What prayers are useful?

A: Ask to be the servant of the Lord, a vehicle of Divine Love, a channel of God's Will. Ask for direction and divine assistance and surrender all personal will through devotion. Dedicate one's life to the service of God. Choose love and peace above all other options. Commit to the goal of unconditional love and compassion for all life in all its expressions and surrender all judgment to God.

Q: How can we forgive those who do not seem to deserve it? It seems like an impossibility.

A: By understanding others' frames of reference, human limitations and conditioning, and genetic and social programming, much rancor as well as harm can be avoided by acknowledging and accepting the human limitation. Unrealistic expectations of human nature prevail and are propagated by denial and the use of hypothetical arguments. Political/sociological hypotheses are usually proven over time to be incorrect and based on false assumptions about human desires, conditions, and limitations. They are also naïve in that such formulas almost always ignore context altogether and naïvely make false presumptions about human behaviors without attention to circumstance.

For instance, honesty is possible, but only if certain conditions are present. If needs, desires, or hunger reach a certain intensity, then the 'luxury' of honesty has to be sacrificed. Poverty has its own rules of survival. Unsatisfied biological drives may overrule hypothetical ideals of behavior, e.g., the rationality of the prefrontal cortex may be overwhelmed by the arousal of the old, deep-seated animal brain. It is an artificial situation that defies millions of years of biology and the rules of racial survival, including the effects of pheromones.

Another factor overlooked in human expectation is individual variability and aberrant individual defects of control as well as deviant training, conditions, and defects in brain chemistry. These individuals are often pushed beyond their limits by circumstances or even by intoxication. All these realizations tend to temper our expectations of perfection in a world of limitation.

People in our society are not educated as to human limitation and variability. Our puritanical society tends to pontificate and put considerable emphasis on such imaginary, nonexistent faculties as 'will power', which is used as an excuse by moralists primarily to justify vindictiveness. That there is no such faculty as will power which can be relied upon becomes obvious to any student of human activity who would observe that it is entirely lacking in most people most of the time and only marginally operative in a few under favorable circumstances. The fallacy of will power underlies many of mankind's unsolvable social problems.

If we view average people as flawed, limited, and unable to be other than what they are at any given moment or in any given circumstance, then most negative feelings and judgments can be avoided. People are then seen more as being limited rather than as 'bad', 'selfish', or 'wrong'. Life is then considerably easier and more peaceful.

Individual experiences of life are tempered, tailored, and considerably determined by one's personal level of consciousness as well as that of prevailing society. As science advances, it is discovering that more and more of human behavior, especially deviant or abnormal behavior, as well as character traits, is inherited. Many predominant characteristics are already set and in operation during early infancy. There is, for instance, a depressive disorder called "dysthymia," which begins in childhood and persists for a lifetime. It is accompanied by the deficiency of an essential brain neurotransmitter. Many mood and behavioral improvements cannot be made by the individual unaided, and often the situation cannot be resolved even with expert help.

Q: Resolution of most conflict, then, is possible by education?

A: That is true. Compassion and wisdom go hand in hand. To complain about the limitations and defects of others is futile and unrealistic.

Q: What about ideals?

A: They can be hoped for but not expected. Goals are hypothetical intellectual constructs and can be sources of inspiration, but idealizations often refer to prideful conceits. Conventionally, ideals are expected of others but not necessarily of oneself for whom plausible excuses prevail.

It is very immature to expect others to live up to one's own standards or ideals. Let us not overlook that the majority of people have no reason other than to 'take what they can get'. Seventy-eight percent of the people on the planet calibrate below the level of Integrity at 200. They are not committed to spiritual truth, which to them is fiction or idealistic nonsense. Fairness, consideration, honesty, and ethics do not prevail at consciousness levels below 200. When they do, it is the exception rather than the rule.

In addition, realize that rationality and intelligence do not prevail as dominant bases for behavior and decision making until consciousness reaches the level of the 400s. The majority of people are not bound by logic but by wants, emotionalism, desire, ignorance, pridefulness, and the desire to be 'right'. Below the consciousness level of 200, society relies on force rather than power.

Q: So what can the spiritual seeker do to be of help to society?

A: To endeavor to evolve spiritually is the greatest gift one can give. It actually uplifts all mankind from within because of the nature of power itself. Power radiates and is shared, whereas force is limited, self-defeating, and evanescent. All society is subliminally and subtly influenced by every kind and loving thought, word, or deed. Every forgiveness is a benefit to everyone. The universe notes and records every action and returns it in kind. Karma is actually the very nature of the universe because of the innate structure and function of the universe itself. In the universe time is measured in eons. Beyond that, it does not even exist at all. Every kindness is therefore forever.

CHAPTER 14

The Body and Society

Q: If identification with the mind and body ceases, how can one survive?

A: There are moments when it is 'permitted' and possible to relinquish the body altogether. Destiny, karma, intention, commitment, or whatever one might choose to call it, is also operative. If destined by prior choice, continuance of life in association with this body may continue. It does so on its own. The body does not require mentation to survive. The universe provides for it.

Even now, everyone's body is accomplishing thousands of physiological processes that perpetuate its life without any conscious thought at all. It is not necessary to decide on each heartbeat or digestive enzyme. Each of these functions does what it is supposed to do because it is an integrated part of a larger whole. The body is also not separate from the whole but is part and parcel of the universe, and its survival is a function of the whole.

Necessary information is provided to the body when needed, and it does not have to originate from the mind. The nervous system and senses have automatic, learned responses.

Although the ordinary body/mind is propelled by endless wants, desires, and anxieties, when these lose their underlying motivation, it is found that the body has very few actual needs. The body itself is no longer sought or needed as a source of pleasure because the source of pleasure is in the ever-present awareness and joy of existence in each moment.

Thus, continuance of the body is dependent on local conditions, such as the presence of others who see to its maintenance and survival. If local conditions such as the interest of other people in the body's survival are not present, then it may cease to survive. Whether it survives or not is actually relatively unimportant.

Q: Are not some functions of the body 'necessary'?

A: They occur because that is the body's nature, but they are not actually 'necessary'. They do have a function; for instance, repetitive sensory experiences help to maintain a sense of locality and direction. The Self is invisible, weightless, and everywhere present so that even sound is no longer a precise indicator of position. The body is witnessed but not special. If its repetitive sensory experiences are discontinued, then time, location, and physicality drift away and there is even a loss of the sense of direction. Staying 'in the world' or functioning as 'a part of it' are the result of intentional focus and require energy.

Q: It sounds confusing to say that the mind is the main block to Realization.

A: To clarify for the sake of understanding, the mind could be 'partitioned' into 'thinking mind' and 'aware mind'. 'Aware mind' knows, recognizes, and is conscious of many things and has capacities that do not depend on thought, language, or concepts. It recognizes wholes and essential elements and patterns. If the mind stops languaging and sequencing thoughts, it is still capable of rapid comprehension on a nonverbal level. Even a dog knows or recognizes a great deal, with no language necessary.

This 'aware mind' is always present but overlooked if the mind is focused on reason/logic/thought/words. The aware mind is analogous to peripheral vision as compared to central vision. For instance, although the eyes may focus on a specific object such as a clock, they are also simultaneously taking in, registering, and recognizing the entire room.

In spiritual work, it is necessary to withdraw attention from a central focus to a more diffused and all-encompassing gaze. *Central focus is always directed to an ego interest.* It is therefore the focus of desire and limitation. One might say one has to focus in order to function. However, focusing is accomplished by excluding the whole. Peripheral unfocused vision, like 'aware mind', is inclusive rather than exclusive. It is concerned with essence and not detail and operates effortlessly at all times; it is always present.

One survives by means of 'aware mind' and achieves by using 'focused thinking' mind. One could use a mnemonic. Focus is to function and peripheral is for peace. In the enlightened state, the energy of restless 'focused thinking' mind is absorbed back into effortless, non-thinking 'aware mind', and when allowed to, it becomes only awareness itself that lies behind and illuminates 'aware mind'.

Likewise, intention results in the bodily gaze being focused on the near side of an object, whereas love results in the dilation of the pupils, and the eyes focus on the far side of an object or person so as to include them. It is a standing joke that most men cannot tell you quickly at all what color their wife's eyes are.

Focused, linear, verbal mind can learn 'about' God, but because Truth is total and all-inclusive, it is not equipped to know or capable of knowing God directly or experientially. One might say that macular, or central vision, is 'Yang' as compared to peripheral vision, which is 'Yin'. The intellect is Yang; the Self is more comparable to Yin. (Although it includes the Yang, it does so in a Yin manner!)

The moment of enlightenment or realization is like the very ultimate Yin-and-Yang 'experience'. It is a given that is received. The ultimate surrender opens the door for Revelation, which stands forth to be received. This is the ultimate power of Yin. The Presence stands forth with such enormous power that it seems like the ultimate Yang presence. Enlightenment is the product of that union; thus, it is absolutely complete and final. The occurrence is like the birth of a new nebula, the birth of a star. This may sound exaggerated unless it is realized that it is not the local, limited 'you' that becomes enlightened. On the contrary, the Self is the All of the Entire Universe; therefore, others who have arrived at that state have described it as 'cosmic consciousness' because of the enormity of the 'event'. It should not be forgotten that this occurrence impacts the total consciousness of all mankind and does so for many thousands of years, and on into time without end.

Without the consciousness of the avatar appearing on this planet, mankind would have self-destructed millennia ago. Thus, when the Buddha extols the virtues and magnificence of his 'teachings', he is merely being humble and factual. It has nothing to do with being self-laudatory. The realization of that which sustains all life is hardly a small discovery. Every sage knows the same thing but expresses it differently or perhaps in other styles of language.

Q: Why is the intellect, which is so useful in dealing with material problems, so useless and, in fact, a hindrance when it comes to reaching enlightenment?

A: The ego/mind is limited to perceptually created, linear sequential logic, abstractions, and the use of words, concepts, and symbols. The matrix of the comprehension afforded by intellection is actually an epistemological position that relies primarily on definitions. Thus, it is definition itself that is the very crux of the impediment. Definition is an artifice, an agreed-upon symbolism displayed as verbal or auditory syntax so that it will have a communicable, specific, and limited meaning. Language is as useful as it is precise.

To define, we have to deal in abstract categories of thought. We specify class, genus, and species. Thus, verbalization and languaging result in careful, progressive limitation from class to genus to species to particular individual.

The perfection of this level of consciousness calibrates in the 400s, at which 499 is the level of intellectual genius. This level is very powerful. It creates and sustains all modern science, industry, and the economy as well as space exploration and biological research. The 400s are certainly a long, long way beyond the mentality of Neanderthal Man. Modern society lives in the 400s—the age of the university, the Internet, the newspaper, and electronic communication—but self-realization is a state of a different dimension. It is unlimited, beyond form, and all inclusive.

Language and concepts consist of very limited, distinct forms. Although this generality is easy to see, it is more far-reaching and subtle in its effect than can be easily described. At the very basis of the limitation of thinking/mind/logic is the fact, as pointed out by Korzypski, that a symbol or a word is not the same thing as that which it denotes (e.g., the map is not the territory).

In Reality, everything is totally and completely self-identical and self-existent. It is exactly and only what it is in a very radical self-identity that excludes all adjectives, adverbs, verbs, pronouns, or actually even nouns. From the viewpoint of radical truth, a thing can be said only to be itself. All language is thus based on perceptual bias and limitation. For instance, if it is said that it is a great day outside, the radical fact is quite to the contrary. A day is, after all, a specified duration of time. It cannot have any color. There is no such thing, actually, as 'a great day'. With examination, it will be found that all definitions and statements are false, without exception, and thus are restricted severely and radically to self-identity only.

An individual is *not* a class, or even a genus or a species. These are all categories of thought. In Reality, each thing is perfect as a definition and expression of itself by the authority and self-effulgence of its own existence. All labels are therefore fallacious. A thing is not a word or a concept. At a deep level of understanding, all language and symbols are fallacious. For instance, people are not caused to be frozen to death by a thermometer that is reading twenty degrees below zero Fahrenheit. They freeze to death because of the absence of heat, which we (fallaciously) term 'coldness'. Even if we say someone 'froze to death', that is also fallacious. The person actually died because their heart stopped beating. Even that is not true. The person died because if the heart stopped, the brain lacked oxygen and stopped breathing. Even that is fallacious because with no oxygen, the energy production from chemical reactions of the body has stopped (cyclic amp, etc.). Even that is fallacious because when the enzymes stop, the chemical processes they catalyze stop. Even that is fallacious, and so on. Eventually we find that the person's body died because the etheric/life/energy/spirit body that had inhabited the body had left.

No thing or person can actually be an adjective. It cannot actually even be a noun. As a matter of fact, it cannot even do anything. The limitation of radical reality is that it can only 'be'. Not only that, it can only specifically be precisely that which it is, with no descriptive terms applied at all.

Abstractions have no existence or reality. They do not have the capacity to 'be'. All qualifiers are a perceptual artifice; none actually exist. Reality becomes self-evident when the obstruction of perception and mentation are removed, including all belief systems.

Q: Are beliefs also obstacles?

A: Yes and no. A belief is an operational substitute for the knowledge that can be gained only by experience. For instance, a traveler believes that a country called China exists, based on faith and information. The belief gives sufficient basis for action. The traveler first hears about China, and then reads information. At that point, the person 'knows about' China. After the traveler actually lands in China, lives there, and meets the people, then the traveler actually 'knows' China rather than 'knowing about' China. Once this occurs, the traveler needs no further beliefs or faith that China actually exists. Thus, successful action starts with plausible belief. The belief, however, cannot be substituted for the actual experience.

Most people have many religious beliefs that serve as guides and in which they have faith. However, unless these are carefully calibrated as to their actual levels of truth, the beliefs may indeed be fallacious or half-truths. Most spiritual error contains a grain of the truth that then gets lost in misunderstanding or manipulated distortions. "Kill a Commie for Christ," or, "Kill an infidel for Allah" is very far from spiritual truth, but, generically, this type of statement is accepted over and over by millions of people through endless generations.

Sentimentality and emotionalism are superimposed on fallacious beliefs, which give them added attraction and dominance in people's thinking. Religious absurdities gain momentum merely because they are 'religious'. As an example, in the year 1212, a European boy had a vision of being called to lead a children's crusade to free the Holy Land from the Islamic infidels. (Why God would be interested in who governs what real estate on the planet has never been answered.) The popular appeal of the admixture of an 'innocent child' with a 'religious vision' plus the heroics of 'saving the Holy Land' resulted in a wave of enthusiasm. The children's crusade was horrific. They died by the thousands from exposure, exhaustion, disease, malnutrition, and other disasters. Of the few thousand remaining, none actually reached the Holy Land, and all were finally captured and sold into slavery. The entire disaster was based on belief, faith, and religiosity. However, as a disaster, it was miniscule in the history of humanity in which whole continents, populations, civilizations, and major portions of human life were wiped out by fallacious religious fervor.

Thus, faith and belief are necessary to start a journey, but verifiable knowledge is necessary to complete it. Without a compass or sextant, the average sailor on the seas ends up at the bottom.

As the Buddha said, "Few are they who endeavor to make the journey, and fewer and rarer still are those who succeed." (Krishna said the same thing in the *Bhagavad-Gita*.) The concern expressed here is for the success and welfare of all mankind whose history, until very recently, has been quite tragic.

Q: You speak often of mankind as though it was your concern or identity. Why is that?

A: To own oneself completely is to own all humanity. The Self is the same Self in all, and society represents the collective ego. To look at all mankind in its totality throughout history takes us through the Scale of Consciousness. When we look at man, it brings on grief, sadness, hopelessness, depression, guilt, remorse, or regret. We see man as being miserable, evil, hopeless, tragic, and frightening. We feel anger at what has transpired in the past.

In Courage, we see that change for the better is feasible. We stop blaming, hating, and fearing and lift ourselves out of victimhood, weakness, and apathy and strive to make the world better. We give up self-blame and self-pity and affirm the power within us. To reach Truth, we have to accept that mankind has been much in error and that the reason was ignorance. Through understanding, we can learn to become compassionate and seek to recontextualize our relationship to the whole.

We can look back and see that humanity was enslaved and brutalized by the ignorance that prevailed at a consciousness level that calibrated at only 190 for so many centuries. However, at its present 207, the future of mankind promises to be very unlike the past. Each of us can progress in our own level of consciousness to that which supports life and love. That is really all that was asked of us by all the great spiritual leaders and saints of the past. Even Freud said that man's destiny was to be able to work and to love. Carl Jung then added, "and to own the spiritual truth of one's reality."

Because of the limitations of perception, mankind does not see that the Dark Ages did not even end until 1986, when the consciousness level of mankind, for the first time in history, crossed over from negativity and nonintegrity to go above the critical level denoted by the calibration level of 200 into Integrity, Honesty, and Truth.

Q: Religion and spirituality, then, did not have a major impact on society?

A: Man's problem isn't that he has not heard of spiritual truth, but that he does not understand it. That is the purpose of clarification and explanation. It takes a whole volume of words to explain that which is wordless.

The value of a numerically calibrated map of consciousness with associated descriptive terms is that it makes what might have sounded like philosophical or sociological generalities verifiably concrete. Anybody can understand simple numbers, but few people, despite ostensible piety, understand even the simplest things, such as the difference between positive and negative, 'right' and 'wrong', or constructive versus destructive.

Nonintegrity is so interwoven in almost every aspect of society that it has become invisible to the average person. The wolf is hidden under the sheep's clothing of patriotism, righteousness, and beliefs that "It's just business"; "The end justifies the means"; "Society deserves revenge"; "People are best controlled by threat and fear"; "The war against drugs"; "Greed is okay in business"; "Lying is okay by government or business"; "Pride is good";

"Materialism and gain justify all behaviors"; "It's okay to distort or hide the truth if you can get a conviction"; "Any deceit is okay to get elected"; "Anything is okay to print as long as it sells newspapers"; "Being right is more important than being truthful," or, "Profit justifies any human behavior." Even the spirit of the law is undermined by using the letter of the law to defeat it.

Q: Why is all this negativity so pervasive?

A: The purpose of enumeration was to overcome denial. In our current society, the mass media, including certain types of merchandising, tend to enhance and support negativity and target primarily young people who are thereby directed to the use of drugs, irresponsible and violent behaviors, suicide, contempt for authority, playing victim, projecting blame, and embracing moral depravity. The media are dishonest in that they claim they have no responsibility. They also disclaim any negative influence. If the media had no influence, then why would advertisers spend billions of dollars annually on media programs and broadcast them to the populace? The same conditions ensue from playing grotesque killer video games that entrain the mind into a hypnotic state where it is unconsciously programmed. This produces teenage killer robots that 'act with no reason'. In some states, there is actually a special open season for juveniles to hunt with guns and telescopic sites to kill prairie dogs, doves, or squirrels 'for fun'.

It is difficult for anyone to be human, and most do so by wearing blinders to avoid being confronted by the obvious. The reconstitution of integrity is the first step across the threshold from Negativity to Truth. In order to succeed, it is necessary to remove the sheep's clothing from the wolf and realize that we are not talking about 'sport', 'just business', or 'it's what people want'. In all this, society is both the perpetrator and the victim.

Q: You have given much attention to these matters.

A: It is because of an important point covered in *Power versus Force* called 'critical factor analysis'. In a system of considerable complexity, there is a very precise point where even a small amount of energy applied brings about a major change. A giant clockworks has a vulnerable point at which even a slight pressure stops the whole works. A giant locomotive can be halted if you know exactly where to place your finger. The great clockwork of human society likewise has points where major changes can occur as a result of a slight amount of pressure.

Do you realize the impact of the press? Imagine what would happen if they had focused on Franklin Delano Roosevelt's crippled legs or the infirmities of Harry Truman or Winston Churchill at the height of World War II? At that point, the stature of these world leaders was the critical rallying point that saved the free world. On several occasions, Hitler was only a few months away from winning the war.

Q: Why such focus on social issues?

A: Integrity is power. To refuse negativity, it first has to be exposed. If the press, for instance, once had integrity, it can make a turnaround and regain it. The current Pope (John Paul II) has been a stunning example and an inspiration to the world that one reestablishes spiritual integrity by owning error and carrying it into an inspiration to reach higher spiritual levels and regain true power. Thus did the Pope not only symbolically but literally reflect the truth back to mankind that the Dark Ages were finally over.

Q: Why do people find it so difficult to change?

A: They identify with their personality, which can be like an addiction. Styles are modish, popularized, and glamorized. Each style has its advantages to impress or control others. There is a secret payoff and satisfaction in being the victim, martyr, or loser. Each persona is a way of manipulating a specific social response. The social image is a way of influencing opinion, and it reflects a person's positionalities. These self-images also have a strong karmic component that is simultaneously a self-casting and a dramatization.

These personality styles are influenced by the media, and each has its gain as well as a price. They are cultured stereotypes embedded on a given culture. These styles change with time. The 'tough guy', the sophisticate, the charmer, and the 'no-nonsense, down-to-earth' types are all social castings. The Dudley-Do-Right, the rebel, the outlaw, the mobster, etc., also reflect group identifications. People become addicted to a style even to the point of death. The danger-prone 'macho' image often results in a violent final ending. The extreme-sports fanatic keeps going faster and faster until he hits the wall. Innate to those images is the desire to be a hero. People cherish their image and get lost in their identification with it. These influences are unconscious and often rigid self-definitions that resist change.

CHAPTER 15

Clarifications

Q: **What is the relationship between spirituality and consciousness?**
A: The domain of spirituality is that of the realm of consciousness. Spiritual development and revolution are therefore facilitated by an understanding of the nature of consciousness itself.

Spiritual progress is accomplished by aspects of consciousness that become more powerful when it is recognized that they are not personal attributes but specific qualities having to do with the nature of consciousness and not aspects of 'me', or 'mine', or the common 'I-self'. Spiritual inspiration, understanding, and the awarenesses that arise from compassion are not personal qualities but operate as catalysts by virtue of the innate quality of their essences. They are activated by spiritual motivation and intention. They are actually aspects of God's grace that become operational by consent of the seeker's will. They are facilitated by humility and surrender of the vanity and domination of the ego/mind and its belief that it 'knows'.

In actuality, the ego/mind can only 'know about'; it cannot actually know anything in the full sense of the term. To truly 'know', it is necessary to 'be' that which is ostensibly known.

Q: **What is meant by the term 'mystical'?**
A: All states of spiritual awareness are actually mystical in that they are subjectively profound and transforming but cannot be conveyed to others in an

285

objective, rational, or (to the skeptic) convincing manner. All profound, subtle, or significant awareness occurs within the nonlinear levels of consciousness, which are not describable within the ordinary Newtonian linear causality-limited paradigm of reality (which ends at calibrated consciousness level 499).The conventional world is confined to the limited level of form reflected in language and mechanistic determination. The worlds of spiritual experience are outside the limited paradigm of logic; thus, they lack the capacity to denote meaningfulness or validity to the ordinary ego.

Actually, all the most profound and significant experiences in life occur in the realm of the nonlinear. Force is linear; power is nonlinear. It is meaning that empowers and transforms people's lives, and the only importance of facts is what they actually mean to them. Happiness has nothing to do with facts but instead stems from attitudes.

Q: What is the essence of the spiritual quest?

A: The spiritual quest could be simplified as the task of transcending the limitations of linear, sequential duality created by perception so as to reveal Reality, which is unlimited and nonlinear and therefore nondual.

On a calibrated scale of consciousness, we can see that the weakest levels below 200 have to rely on force as a substitute for power. As one gets closer to Reality, the power increases exponentially at a rapid logarithmic rate. The 400s denote the realm of the highest development of the

Newtonian paradigm and indicate mastery of the
physical domain. The world of science is unsur-
passed in its capacity to comprehend and manipulate the world of materiality. Science gets us to the
moon, but only man's consciousness gives the feat
meaning or significance. Likewise, joy does not
come from figures or statistics but from what they
mean.

Q: Where is Reality to be sought?

A: Life is lived solely on the level of experience and
none other. All experience is subjective and nonlinear, and, therefore, even the linear, perceptual,
sequential delineation of 'reality' cannot be experienced except subjectively. All 'truth' is a subjective
conclusion.

Once having understood that the only significance or importance of the linear, perceptual world
is how it is subjectively experienced, the quest for
truth shifts from 'out there' to within. To the worldly,
success is something 'out there' to 'have' and to be
acquired.

To the more experienced and sophisticated, it
becomes apparent through wisdom that the source
of happiness is within the subjective inner world of
experiencing, which is the result of inner qualities,
meaning, and context.

Q: How does one arrive at meaning?

A: It is meaning that gives life its value, and when life
loses meaning, suicide results. Meaning arises from
value. The realization that it is not the facts or
events of life but their meaning that determines

happiness leads to an interest in the subject of philosophy. This is the highest realm to which the intellect can aspire; it is the realm of examination of meaning and its subtle implications. Philosophy tries to define its components and how man comes to understand meaning. This investigation leads to epistemology, or the science of how man knows anything, that then brings forth cosmology, which tries to define what it is that is potentially knowable. Beyond epistemology and cosmology arises theology, which stretches the linear intellect to try to comprehend the nonlinear Reality of Divinity itself.

The next higher step in abstraction is to move on to metaphysics, which addresses the Reality of nonduality and reemphasizes the subjective as the domain of spiritual truth. The word 'metaphysics' simply means 'beyond the physical'. Beyond the realities addressed by metaphysics are the levels of experience traditionally described as mystical. Beyond mystical states is the condition of Awareness, traditionally called Enlightenment. Enlightened states reach from the awareness of the presence of God to the final completion of spiritual evolution with the relinquishment of all duality of a self that is apart from God. The final realization is that there is only total Oneness, and that the Self and source of Self are one and the same.

The Infinite, Ultimate Potentiality is the Actuality of Existence. 'All That Is' is therefore innately Divine or it could not exist at all. The absolute expression of divinity is Subjectivity. If I exist, then God Is.

Enlightenment is the verification that all existence is not only the result of Creation, but also that
existence itself is not different from the Creator.
The created and the Creator are one and the same.
Once the false dichotomy produced by perception
is removed, the exact nature of Reality is clear and
obvious. There is no fallacious subject-object artifact of mentation left to separate Reality into the
Creator versus the created. In the nondualistic reality of pure subjectivity, all illusion disappears.

The substrate of all existence and creation is
the state of subjectivity. God is the very essence
of subjectivity. What is aware of existence is the
awareness of the presence of God within us. With
this realization, we resolve the spiritual conundrum of that which is seeking is that which is
sought; in essence, it is the subjective searching for
the subjective. The illusion that there is a dualistic
set of opposites called subjective versus objective
dissolves. It is the ultimate human paradox that
man's dependence on perception precludes his
being able to know his own identity.

As the state of enlightenment presents itself,
there is a glad moment as though experiencing a
reentry into the profoundly familiar. There is a fleeting, transitory thought that one had forgotten who
they were. This forgetting was a consequence of the
operation of perception itself. This is allegorically
alluded to in Genesis as the eating of the apple of
the perceptual domain of the opposites of good
and evil. The innocence of subjectivity was now
contaminated by a positionality that condemned
mankind to endless suffering in error. Without

divine intervention, the return to Reality is not possible, and thus, mankind's solution is only by means of the grace of God.

Q: Is the realization of God 'personal' or 'impersonal'?

A: Although the pathway to the realization of the presence of God and enlightenment has been described thus far in terms of an evolution of awareness through the levels of consciousness, that is merely due to the languaging that has been chosen in order to make the transition comprehensible. The levels of consciousness describe the terrain to be traversed, but they leave out the essential factors of love and devotion that activate the journey and give strength to the endeavor. These are the sources of the requisite energy to make and sustain the effort and commitment to persevere. By analogy, one can have a car and a map, but without gasoline, the source of energy and power, the vehicle does not move. The destination is sought because one is impelled towards it and attracted by it. The way is lighted by God's grace as the Holy Spirit, which is the Guide and Sustainer.

In the end, the God of Transcendence and the God of Divine Love merge in the Supreme. The Unification of that which is loved is the fulfillment of divine destiny and the core of salvation. Love is therefore the means and the end.

If the essential dynamic of one's spiritual seeking is not spiritual ambition (to get somewhere) but the progressive surrender of the obstacles to Love, then that which is called 'spiritual ego' does not later arise as an obstacle. A given calibrated level of consciousness is not better than another but merely represents the level that is being worked on. It is the basic building blocks that enable a structure to ascend, and it is the dedication that ensures the completion of a cathedral.

Q: How does one eliminate the obstacles?
A: The spiritual work that presents itself most obviously to the pathway of devotion is the removal of the obstacles to Love. All these obstacles stem from the errors of perception that arise from positionality. Positionality is the originator and perpetrator of 'the illusion of the opposites'. These arise from opinionating, which in turn arises from the vanities of the ego. These vanities are sustained and fed by the ego's propensity to overvalue and cherish what it conceives of as 'mine'. Once a thing is labeled 'mine', it becomes a valued viewpoint from which, like a prism intercepting light, reality now becomes split into differences, divisions, and opposing views. Thus, the one becomes the illusion of the many. The sense of 'I' now proceeds to identify with these views and defends them as the reality of 'me'. Once caught in the duality of the polarity of the opposites, the ego/mind is trapped and projects its views and holds them to be an objective reality.

Having denied its authorship, the ego-self now becomes the victim of its own projections. The sense of reality that accompanies the awareness of existence is now ascribed to these projections as arising from 'out there', and imagination produces an 'objective reality' whose original source has now been forgotten. This forgetfulness is reinforced by the well-known psychological mechanisms of denial, isolation, repression, and projection.

With the disowning of authorship, there is the relinquishment of power to a perceptually created false conception of a reality where 'causes' now explain the phenomena that have been disowned. Because the perceived dualistic images of reality are the very filter through which experiences are interpreted, the senses then reinforce the images and qualities that have been projected to be external. The physical world is said to exist separately from that which experiences it. Sensation replicates belief and is sorted and interpreted in accordance with the construction and forms of perception that have accorded the objects of sensation with separate identities and discreet and unique nominalization. Language then enforces the perceived world and subtly reinforces its appearance. An 'objective' universe then arises out of arbitrarily selected points, the imaginary distances between these points, the imaginary planes and dimensions, and the illusions of time and space.

In order to project the world of illusion, the ego-self experiences itself as separate from its own creation. The greater the feeling of separation from God, the greater the anguish. As a consequence, the self now fears annihilation, death, and even worse—perhaps endless suffering at the hands of an angry, retaliatory God who has been made angry by sin. The lower levels of perception become preoccupied with energies of negativity that are the ego's conceptions of itself at the lowest levels.

It now fears its own worst projections and struggles with the opposites of heaven and hell.

Man is therefore not the victim of an 'out there' to be feared, but is instead its originator. These imaginations are not even personal but merely consequences of the interaction of the fields of consciousness with their hidden inner attractor fields that determine the content of each level of consciousness. The ego's final victory is the belief that its own illusory reality created by its own projections was 'created by God'. Thus, religious truth becomes obscured by religious superstitions, misinterpretations, and false beliefs. It is important to realize that that which is of God brings peace, and that which is not of God brings fear.

Q: How can one avoid such error?

A: In today's world, the level of truth of any statement or teaching can be quickly calibrated. The ego has created many impressive spokesmen. It is also helpful to remember that Reality is beyond form and not definable.

Q: You mentioned earlier the path of simplicity. What do you mean by that?

A: For the average person who is involved in a busy world, the intense requirement and commitment of a spiritual seeker of enlightenment is usually impractical. This does not mean that a different goal should be sought, but that the means should be attenuated to daily life.

It is really unnecessary to comprehend the content of the discussions and dialogs that have been described primarily to convey understanding to areas of human consciousness that are not well understood. For significant spiritual growth, only one simple tool is required. It is merely necessary to select any simple spiritual principle that is appealing and then proceed with its application, without exception, to every area of life, both within and without. For example, one could therefore choose kindness, compassion, forgiveness, understanding, or noncritical acceptance. One could choose to be unconditionally loving or committed to seeing the innocence of life. Whatever principle is chosen then has to be applied to everyone, including oneself, without exception, and with absolute persistence. This process will bring about spiritual purification as the obstacles to these spiritual principles are brought up for examination.

The accomplishment of the spiritual goal will require changes of perception that will, in turn, require growth of understanding and reconceptualization.

Q: **What is a realistic spiritual goal for the average person?**

A: Any advance along the levels of consciousness is significant and very worthwhile. The practical goal that is reachable by any person who is seriously spiritually committed is that of Unconditional Love. That is a transformative level, and from there, one can relax as the prime objective has been reached. Innate within the level of Unconditional Love is the desire to perfect that condition. As that level is reached, even the slightest imperfection of Love is unacceptable and calls for correction.

Q: What is the most effective means of spiritual purification?

A: Focus on Love itself. That is the royal road to God and one that is everywhere present and available to everyone. In the beginning, love is seen as dualistic, i.e., the one who loves and that or who which is loved. Love starts out as conditional and a feeling state, but it progresses. It becomes apparent that love is a way of seeing, experiencing, and interpreting life. Later, it becomes apparent that it is a state of being.

Life itself becomes the expression of love, and that love is the way to realizing that one's life is love. In the final realization, the divinity of love transforms perception into spiritual vision, and the presence of God as All That Is becomes self-revealing. All existence radiates forth the Divinity of its essence as Creation, which is the manifestation of the love of God.

Q: Love is the pathway of devotion. Is it not therefore the most effective?

A: Love is transformative; its power sweeps away all obstacles. It is both the means and the end. It brings forth willingness and the capacity to surrender. It brings forth compassion and the desire to understand. With understanding, forgiveness ensues. With the relinquishment of positionality, one then realizes there is nothing to forgive. Judgment dissolves and condemnation and hatred are no longer possible. Ignorance born of innocence is seen to be the only 'defect' that needs to be transcended. It is seen that the nature of Creation is as it is and not in need of correction.

Q: Is love not merely a commonplace emotion? It is talked about endlessly.

A: Love is definitely not the prevailing level of consciousness of mankind. Seventy-eight percent of the world's population calibrates below 200 (basic Integrity) and is therefore focused on negativity. Only 0.4 percent of the population ever reaches the level of Unconditional Love that can be called 'lovingness'.

Love is an awareness, an attitude, a context for understanding life. Love is the leading edge of Reality and the oneness and essence of the Spirit. To deny love is to deny God. Love is obscured by positionality and judgment. Most of society invalidates love as a rational basis for decision and action. There are whole segments of the population that view love for one's fellowman as a weakness. Mankind really wants gain, pride, possession, power, and the right to revenge and retaliate with punishment.

The United States, or the land of 'freedom', has more people and a greater percentage of its population in prison than any other country except China. Society declares 'war' on its problems that, of course, then multiply. Force is ineffective and a weak substitute for power. In contrast, people will do almost anything out of respect and love and very little out of fear. Without the loyalty born of respect, even a general cannot command his troops to obey, and without that aspect of love called respect, insurrection and mutiny arise. Force can only act as a temporary stopgap. All the empires that were ruled by fear have collapsed. Religions that are based on the fear of sin rather than on the love of God are inherently weak.

Lovingness is a way of relating to the world. It is a generosity of attitude that expresses itself in seemingly small but powerful ways. It is a wish to bring happiness to others, to brighten their day and lighten their load. To merely be friendly and complimentary to everyone one meets in the course of a day is revealing. That this is not a commonplace attitude is revealed by people's responses when they encounter it. Often, they respond with surprise or even a pleased state of shock. "Nobody ever compliments what I do; they only complain," is a remark that will be heard. Most people, because they are focused on their own wants and critical attitudes, apparently do not even see the positive aspects of life and cannot respond to them. They take others' service for granted with the explanation, "Well, they're getting paid for it, aren't they?" (Which is really beside the point.)

Major segments of society operate on the level of lovelessness. Giant corporations and government agencies can only be described as dourly functioning. Gratitude does not appear nor is it even considered to be socially appropriate. Love is belittled as 'touchy-feely'. Love is therefore socially restricted to romance, mothers and their children, or one's dog. Expressed elsewhere, it becomes an embarrassment. There are a few masculine areas where love is okay, such as for family, sports, one's country, or a car.

The large area of life that is socially acceptable and open to everyone is that which is called 'caring'. To 'care for' is a wide-open avenue for the expression and expansion of love. People say they cannot find love as though it were something to be gotten. Once one becomes willing to give love, the discovery quickly follows that one is surrounded by love and merely did not know how to access it. Love is actually present everywhere, and its presence only needs to be realized.

The universe responds to love by revealing its prevalence. It is hidden to ordinary perception, but the awareness is finessed by lovingness itself. Awareness is a capacity that is beyond the senses or emotions. If one ceases anthropomorphic projections and limitations, it is revealed that all that exists is innately conscious and emanates love as a consequence of the divinity of Creation.

Every plant is aware of its surroundings and the admiration and respect for it. It returns to us by reviewing its own intrinsic perfection and beauty. Each plant stands forth as a unique, creative sculpture and is a perfect expression of its essence. Divinity shines forth from all Creation to those who can see. Nature becomes not unlike a children's cartoon where the trees smile, the animals talk, and the flowers move gaily. When perception ceases, the world of wonder reveals itself. Consciousness is in all that exists. It recognizes itself manifesting as the Allness of Creation.

Q: How can such a wondrous revelation come about?

A: By the mere intention of kindness, respect, and consideration for All That Is, without exception, and in every detail, including oneself. We see what we believe and accept that we ourselves are. The qualities of gratitude, thankfulness, gentleness, and appreciation are themselves powerfully transforming. Our experience of the world and life is totally the result of inner beliefs and positionalities. Out of love and respect for God arises the willingness to surrender all these prejudgments, and the humility that ensues opens the doors to the splendor of reality, which is the revelation of the Self. Love is the magic catalyst that brings about the awareness. In the end, faith is replaced by certainty, and, therefore, it is said that God is found by those who seek Him.

Q: You seldom mention the physical body. What is its importance in spiritual work?

A: The body is a product of nature and part of the animal world. One might say it is owned by nature but rented to us provisionally. It has only a temporary existence and thus does not justify undue attention or importance. Its value is its capacity for communication, a means of conveying information and sharing awareness. If adequately tended, it is hopefully a source of pleasure and a means of accomplishing work and expressing affection. Essentially, it is a temporality, an experience of perception or position in space and time. Perception claims it as 'me', or at least as 'mine'. This is a major restriction and limitation of identification of the self with physicality and form. Like any other living thing in nature, the body responds to kindness, respect, and consideration. It can be cared for and loved like a cherished pet without necessarily identifying with it or becoming unduly attached to it.

One of the most difficult areas for clarification of the differentiation between self and body is the functioning of the senses. These are experienced and believed to be functions of the physical body itself. As strange as it may seem, the actual locus of sensory experience is within the invisible domain of the inner energy body that activates the physical body. The physical body, in and of itself, has no capacity to experience anything at all!

The experiencing of the senses (as well as of everything else) is a quality of consciousness associated with one's presence as an energy body within the physical body image. Anyone who has ever had an out-of-body experience remembers that all modalities of sense were the function of the etheric body that was associated with their consciousness and sense of self. Sight and hearing continue even if the physical body is in a dormant or unconscious state. The 'self' experience migrates out of the body along with the sense of positionality or movement. In that state, the 'I' sense is located within the energy body, and the physical body becomes an 'it'. It is seen as 'a body', not 'my body'.

High numbers of people report identical experiences, so there is common agreement as to the nature of the phenomenon. Likewise, near-death experiences often involve the 'self' traveling down tunnels of light, meeting people, and encountering various colors, and then having a reluctant return to re-inhabit the physical body. Thus, we can say that we inhabit a physical body, but we are not a physical body. It is clear that the spirit, soul, or energy self is a resident of the body and tends to blend in and diffuse with it, and so loses its unique identity. Some people are prone to leaving their body accidentally or at will; astral projection as a technique can in fact be taught as a skill so that one can leave one's body at will and even choose locations to visit (e.g., at the Monroe Institute).

Distant viewing and clairvoyance are the partial projections of the sensory faculty of the energy body. The 'experiencer' is the inner presence within what has been variously called the astral, etheric, soul, or spirit body. The spirit body is not controlled by the usual forces called physical but instead exists on another dimension or plane.

Mind also travels with the spirit body and realizes that it is separate from the brain. Consciousness does not depend on physicality but exists independently of it. When localized, however, it tends to identify itself with form and location.

Q: What about purification and mortification of the body?

A: There is nothing to purify except illusion. Desires

are for specific experiences and sensations that can be sought through the body, but the problem is not that of the body but of the mind. It is the mind that is trying to anticipate and control experience.

Q: **Does the experience of the body change with advanced spiritual awareness?**

A: There are changes that occur in the nature of the bodily experience. The sense of location is more general and less specific. There are periods during spiritual work when the body seems to almost disappear as though forgotten. There are also times when very intense energies seemingly flow through the nervous system, and various burning sensations are experienced as though the nervous system were on fire. There was also a period when the kundalini energy flowed with intense pleasure up the back and spine into the head and brain, and then down and out to the heart.

There can be a loss of bodily desires and withdrawal of interest in the body so that physical survival may at times depend on input from people in one's surroundings. There can be a marked loss of appetite and interest in bodily sensations. Vision changes in that everything seems to be in slow motion. There is reliance primarily on peripheral vision rather than central vision. Time stops, which seems to be related to the loss of specific connection in space. There is also an unsteadiness of bodily movement.

When realization of the Self occurs, there is difficulty with pronouns and what to call what the world considers to be 'I' in terms that are understandable. It seems strange at first to watch people speaking to the physical body as though it were one's identity.

There is a loss of the fear and startle reflexes. It is more difficult to process linear thought and decipher ordinary human speech. This results in a delay in responding to verbal communication. This delay has to do with a process occurring in consciousness that translates linear processing of language into meaning in terms of essence. This delay does not occur with understanding animals or human body language. It seems to happen because consciousness focuses on essence and meaning rather than on the detail of form. It also has to shift from its natural attunement with silence to proximal detailed sound.

There is no separation between what appears to occur and the Self. 'Causes' are not sought externally, and so-called 'events' occur as a result of what is held in mind. There are no causes attributed to the world itself but only to consciousness.

People around one seem to be run by the irrelevant and inconsequential, with much wasted energy. These aspects of consciousness are experienced as though by separate individuals, but the inner experiencer is basically the same Self in everyone. The body is like a companion, a friendly pet that follows one around. It seems to be reliably present. It can also even have surgery without pain or anesthetics. One can continue to own the body and be responsible for it without identifying with it as one's identity.

CHAPTER 16

Karma, Guru, and Sage

Q: Would you explain your understanding of karma?

A: Every thought or action gives off a vibration or a track that is a high-frequency energy pattern associated with the person's energy body. This interacts with the sea of consciousness, which is filled with an infinite number of such energy patterns that emanate from other energy bodies. Within this complex sea of intricate patterns, selections are made that influence the decisions and directions of life. Persistent patterns become reinforced and are therefore more dominant. The interactions that could ensue might be likened to the structural form of a molecule that determines with which other molecules it is capable of interacting. Thus, it may be compatible with some molecular forms and incompatible with others.

Each person's energy body carries with it a historical track of patterns that persist over time and influence decisions, behavior, and the feelings of attraction or repulsion. This energy body, which is the locus of the sense of 'I', exists independently of the physical body, as anyone who has ever gone out of body will remember. This 'karmic body' is made up of the collected tracks of positionalities.

The field of consciousness is an infinite sea of interacting energy fields with various levels that can be calibrated. The fate of an energy body of an individual's soul is therefore similar to a floating object in space or a cork in the sea in that its innate buoyancy determines the level at which it will settle and float.

The nonmaterial realms of existence are composed of energy bodies at various levels in the frequencies of the sea of consciousness that tend to settle into realms. Each of these realms congregates about an attractor field. When the energy body or soul, with its historical collection of frequencies and patterns, separates from the physical body, it then gravitates to a compatible field or domain. These constitute the post-physical life potentialities or choices between the various levels, such as hells, purgatories, limbos, or heavens. Obviously, for some souls, there is also the opportunity, choice, or fate of choosing another physical lifetime. If we ask with muscle testing whether this is a fairly accurate depiction of spiritual reality, we get the answer "yes."

People have definite opinions about such matters, and the question of reincarnation is a favorite area for argument. All religions, however, agree that the energy body, after physical death, goes on to a fate determined by one's actions during the physical lifetime. Therefore, the fate is determined primarily by the spiritual decisions and actions that were made, with great importance given to intention, responsibility, and the assent of the Will.

Spiritually speaking, whether an actual physical reincarnation occurs or not is really quite academic. The same principles and fate of the energy body remain the same whether it would resume as a physical existence or continue on an energy plane. One's fate, obviously, will either be for the better or for the worse, depending on the choices made by the spiritual will. It would seem from studies of the spiritual nature of consciousness that the choice to resume another human physical life would be an option that is determined by the innate patterns of a specific soul. Of more importance is the inter-pretation and understanding of the factors that determine the fate of the soul/energy body and its destiny after physical death.

From the foregoing analysis and spiritual research, it appears that one's ultimate fate is the automatic and impersonal consequence of the energy patterns that have been set up in the aura of the spirit body, i.e., one's fate after physical death is merely the inevitable consequence of one's own choice and not a reward or a punishment meted out arbitrarily by some external figure, energy, or power. The self in the infinite sea of the Self gravi-tates to its fate solely by virtue of its own essence. This is the absolute justice of Almighty God that guarantees absolute fairness and impartiality. Judgment is therefore merely a semantic invention (like causality or heliotropism) that serves as a plau-sible 'explanation' derived from the anthropomor-phic presumptions of the human mind.

Inasmuch as one's spiritual destiny is sealed and determined by one's own hand and its actions, each person, with absolute fairness, determines their own fate. Thus, God's justice is indeed perfectly self-fulfilling. Mankind then needs to take responsibility for its own fate and stop blaming God, who has been much maligned. In reality, the love of God, like the sun, shines equally on all. With understanding, the spiritual domain makes sense, and there is no need for superstitious, anthropomorphic inventions, and fantasies to explain it.

Most of what has been said thus far is in agreement with most of mankind's accumulated spiritual information and experience. If, spiritually, everything happens as a consequence of Free Will, and there are no 'forces' to 'cause' anything that is not in accordance, then the question of physical reincarnation becomes clarified. If it occurs, it would have to be by choice and assent of the spiritual will, and it would then be determined by 'karmic' propensities.

The stronger one identifies with the physical body and earthly life, the stronger will be the pull or attraction of another earthly life. It is obvious that an attraction to reincarnating would be to undo or propitiate for past spiritual mistakes. Many souls apparently do decide that the only just propitiation is to suffer the same fate they have meted out to others. We certainly see that millions of souls choose lifetimes with disastrous endings. Even the chosen form of death is frequently so unique and specific that one intuits there must have been strong karmic determining factors involved in the specificity of the choice. Suicides also frequently take very specifically chosen forms and styles, with very specific meanings.

We can postulate that if lifetimes of the soul can be lived either in or out of the physical domain on either the physical or energy planes, then an almost infinite sequence of lifetimes is obviously quite possible. This formulation is in agreement with the ancient sages, the *Vedas*, and the teachings of Krishna, Buddha, and Hinduism, as well as other ancient religions.

At very advanced levels of consciousness, enlightened sages are able to recall prior lifetimes that are often described as having been very numerous. In the out-of-body experience, also, people remember that their energy body has inhabited prior physical bodies. Young children are also prone to recalling prior lifetimes, and studies show this to be a rather frequent occurrence. A sage was asked how real previous incarnations are and he replied that they are as real as this one—no more, no less.

The interest in whether one has had previous lifetimes is more than just a reflection of the ego's vanity or self-interest. Of more importance is that the understanding of how divine justice works out clarifies misunderstandings about the nature of the ego. It also clarifies Christian teachings that "As ye sow, so shall ye reap"; "People who live in glass houses shouldn't throw stones;""Those who live by the sword die by the sword"; "Not a hair on your head goes uncounted"; and "Every sparrow that falls is noted."

Jesus' comments about reincarnation are brief and appear in Mathew 11:7-14 and 17:10-13 where he states, "Elias (Elijah) has come back as John the Baptist."

Christianity is focused on the choosing of virtue over sin or good over evil as the importance of the fate of the soul takes precedence over the subject of reincarnation.

Q: **Spiritual destiny, or karma, then, is set by choice and personal responsibility?**

A: The most powerful determining factor is intention and decision of the spiritual will. The idea that contextualization and thought or action set up an energy pattern of a calibratable level of power versus force is the basis of the spiritual path called Karma Yoga, which means that all actions can be sanctified by their dedication to God.

Even the simplest action, such as peeling a potato, can be accompanied by resentment or by devotion to life out of joy, knowing that one is supporting life through life. In gratitude for the gift of life, one dedicates that life back as a gift to God through selfless service to His creation as all of life. With this dedication, one validates the sacredness of all life and treats it with respect. When we stop to assist a helpless beetle with a twig so it can turn over off its back and resume life, the entire universe knows it and responds.

To acknowledge and support the value of all life supports one's own, which is part of that life. What is generally meant by the term 'soul' is the capacity to experience life. The Self shines forth as awareness of existence in all that lives. The deer and all animals enjoy their lives to the same degree as people do. They derive joy from their existence and experience of life.

There is a documentary film about the lives of giant otters in the wilds of Peru. They are territorial. In the movie, a lone male who had a whole lake to himself was filmed. It stayed all alone for months and finally, the filmmaker's patience was rewarded when another otter discovered and appeared in the lake. The film showed the meeting of these two lonely otters and their joy of finding each other, which was overwhelming. They did endless summersaults and dances together out of their pleasure and happiness. Their joy was stunningly obvious even to the most ignorant person. Whether animals are capable or not of linear logic and its concomitant languaging is really irrelevant. What is significant is that on the level at which life is actually lived (the subjective), the experience of animals and their joy in life is equal to that of humans.

Q: In using the consciousness research method, is it true that any and all information is available to anyone?

A: That is true. One's inner life is actually a public document that can be accessed by anyone, anywhere, at any time. No secrets are possible; all stands revealed. This does not really seem so surprising in an age when modern technological software programs already exist that enable the individual Internet user to access and download any file in existence from any computer in the world. All information on the Internet is in the public domain; likewise, most public as well as private locations are under continuous video surveillance, including even the public streets. The surveillance and recording of all human activities go on continually via satellite. Every fingerprint leaves not only a unique identifying pattern but also a traceable DNA pattern as well. Computers track and analyze every purchase and transaction. Credit bureaus record all financial patterns in detail. It would seem that privacy is really a fantasy of a bygone era. An honest person finds all this rather reassuring because then honesty and innocence are documented. However, a dishonest or guilty person probably reacts to these realizations with fear. It is a certainty that in both this world and the next, all stands revealed and accountability is a certainty. For it to be otherwise, the universe would have to have been created as unjust, which is not possible as an expression of the nature of Divinity.

Q: **Is it necessary to have a guru? Some spiritual traditions say it is**.

A: Everyone already has a guru—the Self. The Presence of God is ever present. By Grace, the Holy Spirit is that aspect of divine consciousness available to all. Because one's ego blocks off awareness of the Self that is within, it is reconnected to Truth by contact with the spiritual master, the avatar, or spiritual teachings.

    The spiritual sage has, by means of greater spiritual evolution, closer contact and identification with the Self and so is able to speak, teach, and be of help and guidance. The hearing of spiritual experience is inspirational to others. All spiritual growth is by consent of one's free will. A true teacher does not impose their will on others but makes their understandings available to all. The enlightened teacher does not charge for information because that which was received as a gift is given out as a gift. The teaching that is shared is of a higher calibration and has by itself the capacity to catalyze spiritual advancement. To merely hear a great teaching is itself the consequence of spiritual merit. To act on it is of even greater benefit.

The Buddha is alleged to have said, "Rare it is in the universe to be born into a human lifetime; rarer still is it to hear of the dharma; rarer still is it to accept the teachings; rarer still is it to act on the teachings; and even rarer still is it to realize the truth of the teachings." To even hear of enlightenment is already the rarest of gifts. Anyone who has ever heard of enlightenment will never be satisfied with anything else.

Information itself thus becomes the teacher but requires assent by the individual's spiritual will to become activated. The spiritual teacher who has reached spiritual maturity remembers that the devotee is frequently enthusiastic but naïve. The naïve devotee is easily deceived by false teachers or teachings that are attractively packaged. Guidance is therefore another value of the guru who steers the student away from enticing pitfalls of spiritual seduction and glamour. The teacher's function is to inspire, to instruct, and to confirm by personal testimony the truth of teachings and to encourage students who are struggling with the path.

Another great service the teacher provides is explanation and clarification. Many ancient teachings are correct and valid but are merely 'bare bones' and insufficient, which leads to misinterpretation. The teacher is needed not only to speak the truth and light the way for the student's footsteps but also to give explanations. The true teacher, through enlightenment, is already total and complete and has no needs to be met by students, nor anything to be gained by having followers. The true teacher has no desire for control over others or any type of powers or symbols thereof. All pomp, wealth, and adornment are meaningless, and the sage is not attracted by the trinkets of the world or anything that is illusory and transient.

To the teacher, the body is relevant only to the degree that it is the means of communicating with others in the ordinary world. It is therefore a communication medium. The teacher is at all times the invisible Self. There is no 'person' present and, therefore, the Self is devoid of anthropomorphic traits. There remain about the teacher the vestiges of the persona, which is the collection of social learnings that facilitates interaction and verbalization with the ordinary world. There is neither attraction nor aversion to the world and its contents or values.

The mature teacher has passed beyond the incapacitating phase of initial bliss and exists in a domain of infinite peace. This is a nonemotional state of joy that consists of an all-knowingness and a certainty of the completeness of the absolute. The work of the teacher is to translate the ineffable into the comprehensible, the formless into form, and to try to anticipate misunderstandings that could arise. Although the teacher no longer 'thinks' in worldly terms, the knowledge of how to translate the infinitely subjective into meaningful terminology is his gift and is actually a function of the Holy Spirit.

The sage serves the followers in another nonverbal way in that the enlightened consciousness transmits that vibrational frequency to the human thought field of consciousness and awareness. This is an effect and consequence of that awareness. To teach it is a choice and the result of an agreement.

Q: You emphasize to always calibrate the level of truth of a teacher or a teaching. Can't teachers just be accepted on faith or reputation?

A: Absolutely not. The mind is very naïve and extremely gullible. It is easily impressed and vulnerable to persuasion and manipulation. Remember that the majority of people on the planet calibrate way below 400, the level of Reason and Intellect. They are easily swayed by logical sentimentality and absurd emotionalism and slogans. Juries convict the innocent, and voters pass absurd laws that are blatantly unconstitutional. These serious errors are occurring in an area of only ordinary matters. When it pertains to the spiritual, the mind is even less reliable. It has no experiential evidence to follow at all, and, therefore, it usually blindly follows social, ethnic, or family precedent. Most people's spiritual and religious beliefs are therefore determined by 'accident' of birth and cultural identification. The ego adopts the belief systems as 'mine' and then proceeds to defend them. Whether the beliefs have any validity cannot be ascertained by the mind and therefore have to be overly defended, and often to a fanatical degree, primarily because they are vulnerable to attack.

Truth that is experiential does not have to be defended. It is merely a matter of fact. Therefore, 'believers' are the most vociferous and militant in expressing their views. The true seeker of truth is therefore well forewarned to avoid the influence of believers, aggressive proselytizers, and religious fanatics of all persuasions.

Knowledge based on faith and true experience is calm. It invites rather than tries to convince. It attracts by virtue of its intrinsic merit and the innate power of the truth itself. Truth does not rely on force by persuasion or argument; it explains but does not try to convince.

Because of the mind's naïveté and vulnerability to error, plus a society that is dominated by 'non-truth', the discovery of a verifiable means of determining not only truth from falsehood, but also the actual degree of truth, is an amazing breakthrough and a practical boon to the spiritual seeker. We are now at a period in history comparable to the discovery of the compass or the telescope.

The evaluation of spiritual teachings basically requires only two calibrations, one of the teacher and one of the truth of the teachings themselves. These two figures then provide an extremely valuable guide to an understanding that previously has not been available to either teachers or students.

In the past, even the best sages were unaware of what level of truth they were experiencing or teaching. Each was really an explorer and discoverer of higher realms of awareness. Their memoirs and teachings are reports of rarely experienced and unfamiliar realms of possible awareness of Reality. To reach such levels also required greater-than-average courage and conviction to explore the stratospheres of consciousness without an altimeter or map. Each explorer had both an inner and outer sage but no 'global direction finder', such as the map of consciousness or muscle testing, to refer to for certainty.

In the world there are spiritual teachers whose knowledge comes from actual personal 'spiritual experience', and then there are the 'teachers about', whose information is via academic or intellectual means. A religious minister does not need to be enlightened personally at all but is educated in spiritual truth at a theological seminary. Then there are the spiritually 'realized' who are not formally educated in theology or comparative religion and who only give reference to established teachings as a point of information, orientation, or reference for interested students.

Of all the spiritual teachers in the world who are regarded as being 'gurus', approximately fifty-five percent are legitimate. Thus, in actual practice, the chances of finding a true teacher amongst the many are about fifty-fifty.

CHAPTER 17

Dialogues

Q: What is the best way to raise one's consciousness?

A: By interest, intention, and study, one develops a familiarity with spiritual subjects and teachings. Because the teachings themselves calibrate at a high level, they have a power beyond that of ordinary consciousness, and their inclusion into one's thoughts and reflections automatically energizes a progression of consciousness.

The Buddha said that once a person has heard of enlightenment and receives teachings, the end is certain, and they will never be satisfied with anything less. He also stated that this might proceed through a number of lifetimes but that eventually, enlightenment was certain as one's destiny. It is thus implied that anyone who is interested in material such as this is likely to be destined for enlightenment; otherwise, why would they be here? Why would they have any interest in the subject at all?

Q: What can you say about meditation?

A: It is both a large subject and yet a very simple one. The simplest practices are the best and can be continuous throughout the day's activities. Formally, if we sit still, close our eyes, and stay aware of the breathing, we can look at the patterns that appear to our vision behind closed eyelids. One simply observes the procession of the mind's activities without interference or comment. From there, one then moves on and focuses attention to what it is that is watching this procession. Identifying the watcher then leads into the witness, which in turn leads to the awareness of the experiencer that these are qualities of consciousness. One is aware of the witnessing, experiencing, and watching, and that these are happening by themselves. These are impersonal qualities of consciousness. They happen automatically. There is actually no personal entity that is 'doing' the watching, witnessing, or observing. It is also important to notice that this impersonal quality is unaffected by the content of that which is observed. The real, transcendent 'I' even witnesses sleep.

Q: **What is *satori*?**

A: It is a spiritual state of advanced awareness most often occurring during a course of meditation and which may remain for varying points of time. It may appear, disappear, change levels, and have permanent residuals or become a permanent state of awareness. Because it is a revelation, it cannot be controlled. Even if the state disappears, what was seen, realized, and understood remains permanently.

  For instance, one may suddenly 'transcend the opposites' and realize that the source of all experiencing is a positionality within. This may then lead to the awareness that there is no 'inner' or 'outer' in that they are the same, and that there is no possibility other than subjectivity.

Q: **Does not spiritual ambition lead to having a spiritual ego?**

A: Yes, if it remains only as ambition. By surrender and

humility, ambition is replaced by the motivation of love, inspiration, and devotion.

What is usually implied by the term 'spiritual pride' is the product of the illusion that there is a personal self that is doing the spiritual work. These tendencies are countered by humility, thankfulness, and gratitude, and it is merely the spiritual inspiration that emanates as a supportive energy from the Self. Spiritual intention attracts higher energy fields that are experienced as grace.

Q: How can meditation persist in one's daily existence?

A: By merely constantly posing the question to oneself of 'what' is doing the acting, talking, feeling, thinking, or observing. This is a focus of attention, with no languaging. The spiritual teacher Ramana Maharshi called that process 'self-inquiry', which he recommended as a technique that was suitable at all times in all activities. Continuous meditation could be likened to a mudra, or posture and attitude, in which every act is sanctified by its surrender as an act of service or worship. When one's attitude towards everything becomes a devotion, Divinity reveals itself.

Q: How can we stop judging others?

A: Through compassion arises the desire to understand rather than condemn. With understanding, we see that people cannot actually help being other than they are at any given moment. People are generally unaware that they are run by programs inherent in society and in the specific energy field that dominates their consciousness. The average mind is unwittingly brainwashed, and the people are dominated by a field of consciousness to which they are attracted.

As a typical example, although anyone who is relatively spiritually advanced is aware that the end does not justify the means, in our society, that is turned around as an operational dictum that the end does justify the means. (The proposition that the end justifies the means makes one go weak with muscle testing.)

Q: **What is meant by the Zen teaching of 'no mind'?**

A: Some spiritual teachings from the East use the term 'mind', ordinary mind, or ego, or in contrast, 'Mind', which paradoxically means 'no mind' or 'Self'. To complicate terminology further, some teachings use mind to mean Universal Mind, which is the same as Self, Oneness, or Allness. The doctrine of 'no mind' merely states that the eternal truth is self-awareness and is to be found in the silence and the presence beyond ordinary mind. Awareness of Self as Mind is blocked by focusing on the content-filled mind of the personal self.

Q: **Why did Buddha not speak of God?**

A: Because of religions, God has had many definitions and descriptions so that concepts about God would, paradoxically, actually be blocked to the awareness of the reality of God, and the seeker would end up seeking for a preconceived concept rather than surrendering it so that the reality could present itself.

Q: What is the state of 'no mind' like?

A: Initially, the awakening into a whole new realm is overwhelming. What is left of the former self is stunned by the massive revelation and the magnificence of the condition. Everything is brilliantly alive, and all is One and startlingly, massively divine. There is, however, also an infinite stillness and peace, a profound sense of having at last returned to one's real home. No fear is possible. What one really is, is beyond all form and always was beyond all time and space. These realities are self-evident. All thoughts, ideas, and mentations stop, and the stillness is everywhere present, all-pervading.

The Self is realized to be now everywhere instead of localized. All human activities and attitudes have ceased. There is no desire for anything. All is known and equally present so there is nothing left to know or know about. All questions are answered so there are none to ask. There is nothing to think about nor would there be a purpose to thinking. All feeling disappears and is replaced by absolute peace.

At the onset of this state, there is a short period of the agony of dying (death of the remainder of the ego), and it is the personal 'I' that feels itself dying. The personal will dissolves into the divine omniscience. Volition ceases. Everything moves, acts, and presents itself with equality of significance. Nothing is greater or lesser than anything else. There is neither cause nor change nor events, nor is anything 'happening'. All is as it is as a result of the ongoingness of the continuous evolution of Creation.

One witnesses potentiality emerging as actuality. The innermost essence of the universe reveals itself as a wondrous spectacle. It presents itself as a gift of love and trust, as though welcoming one home.

Q: How can one function in such a state?

A: At first, it is impossible. With the resumption of movement, there is a sensation like walking on land after one has lost their 'sea legs'. There is a problem with equilibrium in the exact whereabouts of the body and all its parts. There is no identification with the body nor is there a locus in space. The Self is invisible and nonlocal so that when people talk to the body as though it were 'you', it requires adjustment. The voice speaks on its own in response to questions. There is no mind or mentation to focus on or to perform worldly tasks. There is a loss of the sense of direction. The body and its actions or speech and activities occur without any inner direction or intention. What occurs does so spontaneously as a response to the will of the Presence. Everything occurs of its own as an expression of its essence and prevailing conditions. The body is a function of the universe and an accommodation to how the world operates.

All usual daily activities are stopped for a lengthy period of time. Speech is unnecessary. What people mean by their speech has to be translated in order to be understood. They speak in a linear sequence of thoughts, and an aspect of the Self/Divinity as the presence of the Holy Spirit acts as a translator, resulting in a delay between people's speech and the capacity to understand it. One seems to the world to be 'hard of hearing' or 'absentminded' (which paradoxically is actually the case). This translation takes the details of form and turns it into their understandable essence. Ordinary thinking is no longer a natural state or a spontaneous activity. It has to be willed to even occur at all. The world seems preoccupied with details and that which is irrelevant instead of essence. To focus on sequential form is tiring. It takes time and energy to shift one's focus from essence to form.

Q: What guides your day-to-day life now after so many years?

A: It goes on spontaneously. Its locus is within the field of consciousness. There was a necessity to leave the prior lifestyle and move to a quiet location in a simple setting with no worldly role for some ten years. It took, and still takes, effort to activate the intellect and mentation. It took months to retrain the mind to read and retain. The faculty that is called ordinary mind operates only when required to do so. It is not a natural state. The natural state is silence and repose. Even when the mind does reactivate, it is against the background of stillness and silence, which is not replaced. The analogy would be the stillness of the woods is not actually disturbed by a noise, which really has no effect on it, or just as a boat going across the ocean has no effect on the ocean.

Q: There still seems to be a personality present.

A: That is the automatic product of love, which inter-
faces between the Self and the people in the world.
Its function is to uplift, communicate, and heal, and
it frequently uses humor to interact with the world.
It uses laughter and humor to recontextualize
people's distorted viewpoints. Its main purpose is
to heal by recontextualization. The Self seeks to
make a healing contact with the Self of the person
in the world who is suffering. This same love, which
is equality of the Self, seeks to contact the Self in
everyone by its writing, speaking, or conveying of
information that could be useful.

Q: Who is it that speaks or writes?

A: The body and personality are like residual but necessary tools. The capacity to communicate is really
the function of the Holy Spirit, which is the translator between the Oneness and Allness of the Self
through consciousness to the many. Without the
intervention of the Holy Spirit, the body would
disintegrate from sheer neglect. The Self is not
subject to karma, but the body runs on its own like
a karmic windup toy.

**Q: Does spiritual progress or change stop? It is
complete or final?**

A: Absolute awareness is already complete and total.
Its capacity for expression increases and is increasing even now. In the past, with major increases in
awareness, the nervous system would feel a burning or a buzzing. Teaching reactivates the flow of
spiritual energy into the body.

Q: Are there two different states of consciousness?

A: No. Only the Infinite Self is actually present. Its all-present reality supersedes all appearances. It translates through the intervention of the Holy Spirit to the capacity for communication via the body, which is its servant. Whatever the body does is not really of great interest, nor is its survival. Although the perceived world is actually not real in the absolute sense, people think it is. It is therefore a means of reminding people of the availability of the Self and Reality, which are beyond all suffering and sorrow.

Q: What accounts for the functioning of the body?

A: It is consciousness itself that activates the body and its activities and responses. Its persistence is spontaneous and unintentional. The Self requires neither speech nor company nor activities and yet it experiences joy in all things. It delights in love in all its various expressions as existence. Because all that exists is aware, love is recognized by all of Nature, which responds in like. The essence of Reality shines forth as a luminescence. The Self unconditionally loves all that exists. All love benefits all life and all mankind. Even to love one's pet dog actually benefits all mankind and is noticed by the universe.

Q: Is any endeavor that is not 'spiritual' a waste of time?

A: It is not the action itself but the context of that

action which determines whether it is spiritual or not. Context is set by intention. Motive, though, is what makes the difference. One can earn money out of love for one's family, company, country, or all mankind, or one can make money out of fear, greed, or selfishness. If we view our work as a contribution to society, it then becomes a gift no matter how seemingly simple it may be. To peel potatoes out of love for one's family or for the benefit of those who need to eat is spiritually uplifting to the Self and the world.

One makes a gift of one's life and endeavors by sanctifying it with love, devotion, and selfless service. That is the way of the heart to God. In that way, domestic life becomes a form of worship and the source of joy to all. When we seek to uplift others, we are uplifted in the process. Giving is therefore self-rewarding for there is actually no 'other' that is being given to. Every kind thought or smile is therefore spiritual and benefits oneself as well as all the world.

Q: What is love? Often it seems to be unreachable.

A: Love is misunderstood to be an emotion; actually, it is a state of awareness, a way of being in the world, a way of seeing oneself and others. Love for God or nature or even one's pets opens the door to spiritual inspiration. The desire to make others happy overrides selfishness. The more we give love, the greater our capacity to do so. It is a good beginning practice to merely mentally wish others well in the course of the day. Love blossoms into lovingness,

which becomes progressively more intense, nonse-
lective, and joyful. There comes a time when one
'falls in love' with everything and everyone they
meet. This tendency to be intensely loving has to be
curtailed because love, curiously enough, frightens
many people. Many people cannot look fully into
another person's eyes for more than a brief second,
if at all. This is especially so if the one looking at
them radiates lovingness. Some people even panic
when exposed to love.

Some spiritual treatises teach that there are really
no stages of enlightenment, as though it were an
all-or-none phenomenon. This represents the
unexamined view or only a partial report that was
conveyed by some teacher for a specific purpose to
a specific audience at a specific time. To fully understand any statement, we need to know the context
within which it was made.

Study reveals that saintliness is a descriptive
term applied to people who have reached, usually,
the calibrated level of the high 500s. At this level,
joy leads many to become spiritual and inspirational teachers, healers, great artists, or even great
architects who create the great cathedrals, great
inspirational music, and the production of beauty in
all its forms.

Enlightenment proper, that is, the replacement
of duality with nonduality, calibrates at 600 or over.
We could say that any calibration of 600 or more
formally denotes enlightenment.

At about the calibrated level of 600, bliss intervenes and worldly activity stops, sometimes permanently. If the person is destined to remain in the

world, this state is said to 'ripen', and there is a slow return of the capacity to function. Some enlightened 'persons' retreat to spiritual practice and meditation and evolve into the 700s. At that level, the world as commonly described is no longer a self-existent reality. There are neither separate persons nor a world that needs saving. All is evolving according to Divine Will. The world is surrendered to God, and its destiny is self-fulfilling. No intervention is necessary. All life is the evolution of consciousness and the unfolding of Creation. The aura emanating from persons who calibrate in the 700s has an attraction and an effect on visitors. They like to be near its presence where they feel peace. In that energy field, so-called problems resolve spontaneously, and serenity replaces fear and anxiety. That energy field hastens the spiritual realizations and progress of visitors. The energy fields of 600 and up, especially in the 700s, recontextualizes positionalities that then resolve imaginary conflicts.

In the 700s, there is usually withdrawal from the ordinary world. There is a tendency to spontaneously teach. Many at that level develop groups of spiritual students and seekers, establish ashrams, yoga centers, monasteries, and spiritual orders. Some are called masters, gurus, sages, or various spiritual titles, depending on the culture.

Q: What of the 800s?

A: Much less is known. Whereas, in the 700s teachers address primarily individuals or groups, in the 800s and 900s, the concern is with the salvation of mankind as a whole. In *Power versus Force*, minimal data was reported on the 800s or 900s, although the various chapters in the book calibrate at 840 to 850. The concern in the 800s and 900s is with enlightenment and the spiritual inspiration of all humanity, along with the raising of the level of consciousness of all mankind. There is also the capacity to comprehend and delineate the nature of consciousness itself and to communicate that information in such a way as to support comprehension.

In the 700s, a typical statement might be, "There is no world to save; it is an illusion." This is not comprehensible nor information that is useful to many. In the 800s, however, there seems to be a concern with explanation by effective communication. The natural language in the 800s and 900s seems to be concerned with spiritual reality, essences, understandings, and clarifications. Form and its details are irrelevant except as a necessary style for communication.

Q: **The calibrated levels seem to have great significance.**

A: They are extremely useful and of great value. Each level denotes not only a level of power but also of content. It recontextualizes information in order to create a valid map that enables a meaningful approach and understanding, especially of spiritual information.

It is helpful to realize that truth is really a continuum of understandings and the capacity to comprehend. Much confusion in society as well as philosophy stems from not realizing the importance of defining the context of these levels. Each level has a different context of reality. What seems to be worth dying for at one level is seen as absurd or nonsensical at another. These levels define different sets of positionalities. At one level, right versus wrong is of primary concern and the basis for war and destruction. From another level, all such discussions are seen as arbitrary, naïve, and part of cultural conditioning or moralistic demagoguery. It is obvious that 'right' and 'wrong' positionalities have been the basis for genocide and the slaughter of multitudes throughout the centuries.

Q: **The centuries of slaughter have all been for nothing.**

A: We can calibrate the level of consciousness that underlies any aspect of human history to see what was the actual basis for conflict or failure as well as successes. All social problems are based on ignorance. The unforeseen consequences are often worse than the supposed cure. A society cannot solve a drug problem unless it realizes how it is the very source of it. Society is far more successful with mechanical problems that science can solve and is stymied by social problems whose resolution requires greater understanding of the nature of consciousness.

   The masses are easy to manipulate by religious or political slogans. The massive slaying of multitudes of innocents is dismissed as 'necessary' to the success of the revolution.

Q: Then what is the answer to the problems of society?

A: Other than an increase in awareness, there really is none. Problems cannot be solved at their own calibrated level of consciousness, but only by rising to the next higher level. Each solution has within itself a new set of limitations and issues to resolve. Our society is one of excesses; it swings like a pendulum too far in one direction and then too far in the opposite direction because it gets caught in the duality of either/or and this or that. Maturity results in a middle way that allows for both ends of the spectrum of human behavior.

The desire to control other people's behavior is a human failing with enormous cost. People's faith in coercion and the punitive approach is self-justifying and immune to logic or flexibility.

Q: Should we therefore be pessimistic about the future of society?

A: No. Although the level of consciousness of all mankind was only at 190 (a negative condition) for centuries, in the late 1980s, it suddenly crossed over the line of Truth at 200 and now stands at the current positive level of 207, which is within the realm of Integrity.

Q: What can we actually do to be helpful to the world?

A: Make a gift of your life and lift all mankind by being kind, considerate, forgiving, and compassionate at all times, in all places, and under all conditions, with everyone as well as yourself. That is the greatest gift anyone can give.

Q: What is the core essence of the spiritual search?

A: Consciousness advances itself when it is provided with essential information that then becomes activated by intention. This in turn prompts inspiration, humility, and surrender, and these tendencies become progressively more operative. When dominant, they lead to dedication and perseverance. In addition to these aspects of consciousness, progress is greatly aided by expert guidance and the usefulness of the calibrated levels of consciousness of the teachers and the teachings.

Spiritual endeavor in the past was really quite unreliable, and seekers were prone to falling into misleading error with no way of realizing what had happened or why. Sometimes high levels of truth are mixed in with serious spiritual error, and what could have led to real progress led instead to spiritual disaster. Often the error is outside the context of the reality of the seeker and thus escapes detection.

Through the mass media, great numbers of people are deceived, and millions of dollars flow in to pious-sounding spiritual leaders, quasi gurus, and ecclesiastic public figures. It is actually the talk that is glib. If the sound is turned off on the television set, simple observation reveals the truth. Happily, Krishna says in the *Bhagavad-Gita* that "Even if a devotee is misled and on the wrong path, if his heart is devoted to me, I will favor him as mine."

The impact on the devotee who has been misled is severe when the spiritual rape is uncovered. The disillusionment is more severe than that which follows deception or financial disaster in personal life. Some dejected former devotees never recover and go on to severe depression and total collapse. Some become like walking shells. Spiritual error and disillusionment can be grave and permanently damaging; therefore, the frequent admonition of *caveat emptor* recurs in these present teachings.

The loss of a monetary fortune is trivial compared to the major spiritual loss because the guru is often held in such high esteem and almost god-like adoration. This tendency on the part of the seeker is taken advantage of by the spiritual charlatan who is seductive, glib, and adept at the tricks of the trade that occur in areas least expected and unexamined. Often the spiritual error is so disguised and rationalized that it is all but undetectable. Even the teacher of false doctrine may be unaware.

With humility, one's vanity about spiritual choices is surrendered in favor of realistic and unprejudiced prior examination. In looking at the price of a mistake, there is also the loss of time to be considered. Often years, or even lifetimes, are spent in spiritual error and false teachings. Millions of people spend lifetimes or centuries pursuing teachings, texts, holy books, scriptures, and sacred writings supposedly from God that, with a single test of truth, check out as strongly false. Once one observes this test applied to some supposedly venerable ancient or traditional scriptures that reveal themselves to not be the truth but outright negative and destructive, the underlying faults of the teachings become obvious. Before that happens, however, the error cannot be detected because it is hidden by desire, love, one's cultural heritage, family, country, etc. It is through this misplaced loyalty and blind faith that error propagates and survives through the centuries, despite its black historical swath through the human race.

Q: How does spiritual 'knowing' come about?

A: The route of new information is quite different between spirit and mind. The ego/mind is inquisitive and aggressive in style. It grabs onto data and seeks to incorporate and master it. It categorizes, qualifies, evaluates, sorts, files, classifies, judges, and then colors with feelings and abstract meanings in an attempt to assimilate. All new data is also rated as to its potential usefulness or gain value. There is a never-ending hunger and greed of the mind to 'get'. People force the mind to concentrate, learn, memorize, accumulate, and master huge volumes of information with as many details as possible, including sophisticated statistical analysis and computer manipulation. All this endless detail is deemed to be even better if it can be depicted graphically and packaged attractively.

On inspection it will be seen that all the above is an impressive performance, and doubly so when one observes that all the complicated, multifaceted processing occurs in a fraction of a second. Not only is there the current instant of processing, but also simultaneously, the mind is comparing this split second with every other similar split second, contrasting that through the memory time file for comparison. In other words, this zebra is compared mentally with every other zebra one has read about, heard about, talked about, seen on television, and joked about, including evolutionary camouflage theory, etc. The mind tends to do all these complicated, multifactorial operations automatically as a result of its own nature.

By selection, one can choose available options to explore by focus. Although the possible functions are multitudinous, they are not unlimited. In summary, the mind views truth or enlightenment as something new to be acquired or achieved. At best, it is a destination to be arrived at through effort. All such endeavor is premised on the presumption that the functions of the mind serve as a learning model, and its processes are to be merely applied from the past to this new subject in the realm of duality where it will supposedly be equally useful. Thus it presumes that the applicability of that which is evolved for handling duality is useful in the search for nonduality. Such, however, is not the case; in fact, the very opposite of what has come to be viewed as the reliable, tried-and-true method of making progress now becomes the very obstacle to discovery.

Whereas ordinary mental functioning could be typified as a constant effort to 'get', spiritual realization is totally effortless, passive, and spontaneous. It is received rather than gotten. By analogy, when sound stops, the silence reveals itself. It cannot be gotten by effort or endeavor. With mentation, there is the capacity to control, but with revelation, there is no control at all. No control is possible where there is nothing to control and there is no means to apply control, even if it were possible. That which is formless cannot be manipulated.

Enlightened awareness is best described as a state or a condition, a realm or a dimension. It is self-revealing and all prevailing. It eclipses and displaces mentation, which becomes unnecessary and would, in fact, be an interference and intrusion. Revelation is subtle, powerful, soft, gentle, exquisite, and all embracing. The senses are bypassed, and all perception of 'this' or 'that' disappears. It is also apparent that the entire content of revelation has been there all along and simply not experienced or observed. The vision of what 'Is' in its totality is entirely 'Known' by virtue of the Self already being All That Is. Identity confers absolute authority of knowledge. The observer, that which is observed, and the process of observation are all identical.

In awe at the revelation, the mind is silent and becomes speechless at the wonder. Its silence is like a profound relief and peace. What was once prized is now seen to have been a nuisance and a troublesome distraction. People and their thoughts and words are like voice boxes connected to various energy fields. The mouths and minds parrot the thought forms that prevail at any given level of consciousness. As this occurs, the minds of individuals claim authorship and the prefix 'mine' is added to the thought. The content reflects the self-concept of the person speaking. There is an invisible, all-encompassing energy field of love that surrounds everyone. Therein resides the higher self or spirit through which the individuals, in varying degrees of consciousness, contact awareness or, unfortunately, may be cut off from it altogether. If quite unidentified with the Self, the individual can be afraid of or even repelled by love, which is seen as foreign, threatening, and to be resisted. All reminders of love or references to God have to be stricken from public awareness or acknowledgment. This is intrinsic to the success of totalitarianism or military dictatorships where only 'love' for the dictator is allowable. In our society, there are forces to make any reference to God 'politically incorrect'.

In true spiritual endeavor, no actual sacrifices are necessary or expected. Sacrifice in ordinary terminology means loss or even painful loss. True sacrifice really means the letting go of the lesser for the greater and is self-rewarding rather than depleting. Painful, reluctant 'giving up' is not really sacrifice but an attempt to purchase religious favor. With God, there is neither buy, sell, purchase, sacrifice, gain, favor, nor loss.

In the realm of the Divine, there are no rights to parade or proclaim. The world of rights and wrongs and political rights are all inventions of the ego to be used as bargaining pieces on life's game board. They are all based on seeking advantage and gain. In the Reality of nonduality, there is neither privilege nor gain nor loss nor rank. Just like a cork in the sea, each spirit rises or falls in the sea of consciousness to its own level by virtue of its own choices, and not by any external force or favor. Some are attracted by the light, and some seek the darkness, but it all occurs of its own nature by virtue of divine freedom and equality.

In a completely integrated universe, on all levels nothing accidental is possible. To be truly accidental, an 'event' would have to transpire completely outside the universe, which, by simple observation, is an impossibility. Chaos is only a perceptual concept. In reality, no chaos is possible. All in all, the mind of God is the ultimate attractor pattern that governs the totality of All That Is, down to the smallest iota.

Q: **The Buddha said there is really only one sin, that of ignorance. Christ also said to forgive people because they are ignorant. ("They know not what they do.") Is the problem with the ego just one of ignorance?**

A: In the context of these quotes, ignorance seems to signify lack of spiritual evolution or awareness. People lack insight into the consequences of their choices and the difference between goodness and negativity. Ordinary human consciousness cannot tell truth from falsehood. That was Eve's problem.

Q: **What is your understanding of the core of the ego?**

A: It is pride beyond all else. Pride in the form of the vanity of thought, mentation, concepts, and opinions is the basis of ignorance. The antidote is radical humility, which undoes the domination of perception. Ask for truth to be revealed instead of assuming that you already know it. The mind is not capable of actually knowing anything at all! It can only presume to know 'about'. The mind lacks the proper credentials to comprehend nonduality by virtue of its own structure. The mind is excluded from reality because of form. To enter the domain of reality is like going through a fine screen—only clear water can traverse through it, and all the fish, bugs, and debris are left outside. Only pure consciousness devoid of content can pass through the barriers of perception and become the clear water beyond the screen.

When it is said that no person can be enlightened, it means that personhood is filtered out by the screening and cannot pass beyond it. (This statement calibrates at 600.) Pure consciousness is awareness only, and therefore it alone passes through the screen and Knows what that state or condition of enlightenment absolutely is.

An analogy would be to say that the universal can comprehend the particular, but the reverse is not true. Realty is infinite, whereas thought is finite. Thus, the ego/mind/self can know about God but cannot, because of its finite, limited structure, realize God or even its own essence, which is unlimited and formless. The finite is born of the infinite and is never actually separated from it except by perception. The infinite potentiality of the unmanifest becomes the actuality of the manifest by the will of God as Creation.

Q: There are contrasting terms and concepts, such as form versus formless, unmanifest

versus manifest, linear versus nonlinear, and duality versus nonduality. How can these be resolved?

A: The resolution is by means of the awareness of the nature of thought. Perception itself is an illusion; it is like a mirror looking back at a mirror that is looking at a mirror reflecting a mirror. There are contrasting terms and concepts. God is both immanent and transcendent, both form and formless, both duality and nonduality, both manifest and unmanifest, both linear and nonlinear. All is God.

Q: **What is the essential difference between the teachings of Christ and the Buddha?**

A: The Buddha taught the way to Enlightenment; Jesus taught the way to Salvation.

CHAPTER 18

Truth and Error

Q: How do spiritual 'errors' come about?

A: What follows may sound abstract. The error occurs within consciousness itself before there is even any 'person' involved. Consciousness can experience itself either as singularity or as oneness. However, its awareness is misled by believing it has only the options of existence as singularity or nonexistence as voidness. The error is the belief that there is an opposite of truth. This may sound difficult unless we go back to the basic understanding that only Truth, Allness, God, and existence are actual possibilities. Nonexistence, nothingness, void, and falsehood are not possibilities in Reality. These exist only as concepts in mind.

If consciousness believes that these are actual possibilities, then the fear of nonexistence or voidness arises. The error is that consciousness confuses Allness with nothingness. This error is not abstract at all but pervades all human thought and is the very basis for the fear of death. It exists in our language as the terms 'true versus false'. In the muscle test, we see this phenomenon demonstrated. When the arm goes strong, we say in languaging that the response is 'positive', 'yes', or 'true'.

We language a weak response as 'negative', 'no', or 'false'. This perfectly represents the nature of the error. Actually, the weak response is not coming from a reality called 'falsehood', but is actually a *non-response*. It actually signifies the *absence of truth*, not the presence of falsehood.

We could say for clarification that only "yes" is a possible response. The analogy is to electricity in a wire; it is either present or not. When present, we say it is "on." When not present, we say "off ." Here the error is displayed for us in order to reveal the basic error—*no such thing as 'off-ness' exists!*

It is crucial to grasp this understanding for it is the basis of all illusion. No opposite to God exists. No opposite to existence has any possible reality. Only truth has the capacity to exist. Only Allness is a possibility. This is difficult to grasp, but it resolves all issues and errors.

Completing the understanding of this error is that belief can create experience. What is believed to be true within the mind is perceived to exist without because it is projected, and the mind is unaware of the mechanism of projection. This perception is self-reinforcing. Imagination becomes both the product and the source of error.

Let us compare this in a simple outline:

Reality	Impossibility
Life	Death
Existence	Nonexistence
Allness	Void
Truth	Falsehood
Good	Evil
Innocence	Sin
Yes	No

Any experiences of 'reality' to the list on the right, above, are coming only from belief systems with no independent, actual existence in Reality. They have no substantive, independent existence; they all depend solely on imagination and belief.

All these imaginings are fantasies and the product of fear and distortion. These are products of mind only.

Mind includes form, yet strangely enough, even voidness is imagination. It can only be thought to be experienced if all the attributes in realities of truth are negated.

Void is a state created solely by the mind's belief in it as an actual possibility. The only actual possibilities in Reality are Is-ness, Allness, and Beingness. It is obvious that theoretical opposites of these would then be conceived as non-God-ness, non-Allness, and that what is not even possible can 'exist'.

This dilemma of a seeming choice between existence as a body versus the illusion of nonexistence is believed to be a possibility. This was actually starkly experienced in this life at age three. Suddenly, out of nonawareness, there came into awareness and experience the presence of a 'me' as a body sitting in a little wagon. Before that instant, there had been oblivion. With the awareness that 'I exist' immediately arose the fear of nonexistence; the possibility arose in this mind that "It could have been that I wouldn't have come into existence." It was not a fear of death but of the possibility (to the imagination) of nonbeing and nothingness.

The mind then really feared the possibility, as it saw it, of voidness as a reality. The fear of nonexistence versus existence was behind the powerful, actual experience. The fear was not of having no body but of not experiencing an 'I'.

Existence is therefore experienced as the sense of 'I-ness'. Of course, had there been no 'I', the fact would have been unknown as there would have been no 'I' to know that it didn't exist! At age three, however, this was not apparent.

The state prior to the awareness of existence had actually been one of *oblivion*. Oblivion would be existence without the awareness of that existence. In ordinary life, we term that state 'unconsciousness', or 'sleep'. In sleep, we still 'are' but are unaware that we are. There seems, however, to be no possible suffering in that state of oblivion; in fact, we look forward to it every night and complain if we are not totally oblivious during the night.

Consciousness seems happy with periods of no recall as well as peace. The possibility of suffering does not arise until the recurrence of identification with singularity (me, the body) returns. Therefore, the basis of all suffering is the belief in separateness and singularity. In the state of Allness, no suffering is possible.

Reincarnation, then, is the rebirth of the sense of 'I' as a separate singularity. This is a recurrence that is independent of having a physical body at all. In the out-of-body and near-death experiences, only the sense of 'I' persists, with no necessity of a physical body at all. The sense of life, aliveness, and awareness of existence is a phenomenon that occurs within consciousness itself. This is equally apparent in meditative states where awareness of the body disappears, and one dissolves into consciousness, with no sensation of location, time, space, dimension, or even duration.

Enlightenment becomes an apparent state as a subjective realization of existence of awareness with no limiting identifications. Pure subjectivity is self-fulfilling, total and complete, radically identical only as knowingness of the Allness of existence beyond all time and space. It is inviolate, permanent, independent, omnipresent, omniscient and omnipotent, all-fulfilling, and without any opposite. It completes in absoluteness the totality of all possibility and depletes all possible potentiality to its ultimate.

The Self is the awareness, its source, its completion, its totality, its fulfillment, and its essence. It is the Reality of Reality, the Oneness and Allness of Identity. It is the ultimate 'I-ness' of consciousness itself as the manifestation of the unmanifest. Thus only can the indescribable be described. Amen.

Q: Is enlightenment truly a possibility in this lifetime?

A: It is if essential information is available, and certain guidelines are strictly followed. The purpose of these chapters is to provide that necessary information. The goal must preclude all others. Time cannot be wasted in investigating all the astral diversions. The educated spiritual student of today has very decisive and critical advantages over the students of the past. Just as before navigational instruments were perfected, generations of seafarers and explorers lost their lives; likewise, not only multitudes but actually the vast majority of mankind throughout the ages has lost its way and lacks the necessary information for major spiritual development.

As we are aware from our studies, the consciousness level of mankind stood for many centuries at 190, and for the last thousand years, the consciousness of mankind was within the realm of nonintegrity. Only very recently has it crossed over the crucial line of 200 to its current level of 207, which implies a whole new era for the future of mankind.

There are traditionally two general contrasting spiritual pathways—that of gradual enlightenment and that of sudden enlightenment. The gradual path is that of traditional religion by which one seeks spiritual purification with the aid of a spiritual master, great teacher, or avatar as the guiding light and savior. The way of sudden enlightenment is through strict adherence to spiritual awareness and specifics of consciousness so that the personality (or ego) is transcended rather than perfected. In practice, the path of gradual perfection is occasioned by sudden leaps in awareness, and the path to sudden enlightenment (such as Zen) is accompanied by progressive perfection of the personality.

Q: **In Asia and India, enlightenment as a goal and respected state has a long history. In the West, the historical recognition is that of sainthood. What is the relationship between the two conditions? Are they different?**

A: The culture of Asia is much older than that of the Western world. In the ancient cultures, great importance was given to spiritual realization, and spiritual knowledge of great authenticity was available from ancient times, as evidenced by the *Vedas* and the *Bhagavad-Gita*. Inquiry into spiritual truth, therefore, had a long tradition. In Eastern cultures, the awareness that Divinity was innately present within all mankind is evidenced by the custom, even to the present day, of people putting their hands in a prayerful position when they meet and bowing to each other.

In those cultures, the spiritual traditions and teachings were revalidated throughout the ages by a succession of gurus who reaffirmed that the ultimate fulfillment of man's spiritual potential was that of enlightenment. It was also accepted by the culture that divinity accounted for and was the source of all life.

In those cultures, individuals who had a propensity for spiritual dedication had a traditional role and lifestyle to follow. Their endeavors were seen as fulfilling and revitalizing the truth that the existence of the Self as the divine source in its absoluteness and infinite expression is the totality of all Creation. Thus, the goal of the spiritual devotee and that implied by society were not in conflict, and the enlightened masters validated the very basis of the Eastern culture. Society then tended to support those of advanced spiritual awareness and granted them the privilege of being excused from the ordinary duties associated with material survival or worldly success. Those designated as holy men were revered and thus had a special niche in society as teachers.

When Buddha appeared in approximately 500

BC, he was supported by a culture that was capable of recognizing enlightenment so he was not in conflict with the then-existent culture. Although he may perhaps have been considered a new great teacher, the teachings and accepted treasures of wisdom and truth already existed.

By contrast, the Western world was far behind in the advancement of consciousness. The culture was pagan and preoccupied with nature deities, magic, and nature worship. The Greek, Roman, Germanic, and Hebraic traditions included pantheons of gods who were given anthropomorphic characteristics so that, in the end, they actually had the same feelings as humans but merely on a broader scale. In all these primitive versions, God was always seen as 'elsewhere'. The anthropomorphic God, however, was seen as taking direct action, for better or worse, in human affairs.

Whether greater wisdom existed before recorded history was information probably lost in the great fire at the library of Alexandria that had included all the recorded wisdom of the ancient world. In native cultures around the world, spiritualism prevailed, but there was no tradition of enlightenment. There was, however, the shared truth of the omnipresence and divinity of the Great Spirit as God. Thus, both the Native American cultures and the pre-Sumerian culture, as well as that of the Hebrews, were monotheistic as was the belief in Mazda, the god of Mesopotamian culture as expressed through Zoroaster.

Into this preexistent culture outside the Far East appeared Jesus Christ, whose coming had been foretold by prophecy. Unlike Buddha and Krishna, his teachings were in conflict with the then-prevailing culture, and the ensuing conflict with the religious establishment resulted in his untimely death at an early age.

Although not well received by the culture of his birthplace, Jesus' teachings, via the disciples and Greeks, spread rapidly to the Greco-Roman world and then across the cultures of Europe. The purity of the teachings remained relatively undefiled for the first four hundred years but then progressively declined, especially after the Nicene Council.

In the meantime, the Arab world had embraced Islam, and a power struggle between Islam and Christianity ensued, with major political consequences for all society. The focus of organized religion, however, became diverted into rivalry between the different cultures. The religious goals of the individual were focused primarily on that of avoiding sin, penance for sin, and the possibility of reaching heaven in an afterlife. These were in accord with the branch of Buddhism called 'Pureland', which also had the more modest goal of reaching heaven rather than the likelihood of becoming enlightened in this lifetime. Sainthood resulted from purification of the personality in Islam, Christianity, and Pureland Buddhism. This was in accord with the perception that enlightenment itself was a more advanced stage and reachable only from the higher levels of spirituality, such as those that existed in heaven. There was thus the agreement that the worldly life and its intrinsic negativity precluded the likelihood of reaching enlightenment during an earthly lifetime.

This consideration is also expressed in the *Bhagavad-Gita* where Krishna says that enlightenment is rare because it is chosen as a goal only by a few out of many thousands, and even of those who choose it as a goal, very few accomplish the goal. Consequently, in Eastern religions, the attainment of enlightenment was said to take many life cycles, and the best the average seeker could accomplish was the accumulation of good karma that ripened into the final earthly lifetime when enlightenment occurred, bringing with it the finality and cessation of rebirth.

The spiritual seekers who made major progress during this lifetime were often viewed as saints in all religions, and some of advanced consciousness were termed mystics by Christianity. The mystics, however, were often suspect by the Church and were considered as possibly heretical by the establishment. This view prevails today, even in certain fundamentalist Christian sects that view the Buddha, for example, as 'possessed by a demon'. (All demons calibrate below consciousness level 200, whereas Buddha, like Krishna, Brahman, Christ, and Zoroaster, calibrate at the maximum possible consciousness level of 1,000.)

Q: What differentiates these seemingly different spiritual goals?

A: The difference is very basic and critical for the seeker of enlightenment to know. A religion primarily addresses the realm of duality, whereas enlightenment addresses nonduality. This strict path to enlightenment says that inasmuch as duality is illusion, there is no point in trying to perfect it. Therefore, the ego is to be transcended and seen for the illusion that it is. 'Good personhood' is laudable, but it does not of itself result in enlightenment. The possibility of reaching enlightenment is based on advanced understanding of the nature of consciousness itself.

Q: Is there an observable difference between the saint and the sage?

A: Yes, that may be so. The way of spiritual purification and perfection will lead to a personality that is seen as more 'saintly' or pure. In contrast, the enlightened sage has no interest in either the body or the personality and may therefore seem to the ordinary person to be more gruff or even unkempt.

Nisargadatta Maharaj (consciousness level over 700), for example, smoked endless Indian cigarettes, pounded on the table when he got excited, and exhibited his ordinary personality. A Zen master can be very abrupt and brisk; however, the love is the same in all but is merely expressed differently.

Q: Is perfecting the body and personality then a waste of time?

A: It is a diversion and an error of emphasis. The body is a product of nature, and what it does is really of no interest. The mind and personality are products of social milieu, family influence, and cultural programming. A refined and cultured person is an agreeable and valuable social asset, but it is not the Self. As one approaches enlightenment, it becomes apparent that the self is not the Self, although included in it.

Q: Is one spiritual path better than another?

A: There are two ways to travel—either a direct route to one's destination, or the leisurely trip that investigates the countryside and visits all the tourist attractions. Most spiritual seekers are on the leisurely path, even if they do not realize it. This, however, is undoubtedly the best way for many people. It is neither wrong nor a waste of time but merely the path that works best for them.

In reality, time is merely an illusion and an appearance. No 'time' is really wasted once one has chosen the spiritual goal. Actually, it makes no difference whether enlightenment takes a thousand lifetimes or one; in the end, it is all the same.

Q: Are you saying, then, that the way through traditional religion is a slow path, and the one through the understanding of consciousness is faster?

A: Again, it is a matter of choice, practicality, and inspiration.

CHAPTER 19

Commentaries and Examples

Q: What are the basic realizations that make enlightenment in this lifetime possible?

A: To understand the nature of consciousness makes enlightenment possible. This essentially entails the realization of the difference between duality and nonduality and how to transcend the realm of duality.

Q: Practically speaking, how is this possible?

A: Duality is the product of perception, which itself is limited. Intellection and perception can be refined and perfected to the level of genius but will still be a limitation that restricts the level of consciousness to the 400s. Consciousness level 499 is the level of scientific genius, whereas spiritual genius becomes evident at 600 and goes up as far as 1,000.

Q: How can one undo the limitation of perception?

A: By understanding its nature. Perception is appearance and an artifact of mentation. It is useful in dealing with the world of ideas, concepts, and physicality, but its usefulness ceases when the goal is spiritual evolution.

Q: How is perception overcome?

A: It is not overcome but instead is transcended. This is made possible by an understanding of its structure and function. Realize, to begin with, that perception has to do with form. Duality is quantifiable.

Let us try to unravel its function by means of examples.

Example 1: Picture a wall that is pure white (or pure black, if you wish). Now choose to see an imaginary dot on that wall. This dot will now be a point of focus. It is obvious that the spot can be anywhere on the wall that one chooses for it to be. The position one finally selects can be marked with a crayon or chalk. In common thinking (which is therefore dualistic), the point will be said to 'exist', in fact, to be exactly 'there'.

With some reflection, it is obvious that there is, in actuality, no such thing as a 'point' anywhere, much less a point that is 'there'. The idea is altogether only in the mind. There is no point anywhere at all except in the imagination. The point is therefore not a self-existent reality and its definition is totally dependent on the human mind for it even to be said to exist. If attention is removed from establishing such a point, it instantly disappears. This is possible because it never did actually exist as a reality.

It is obvious that languaging is about mentation itself and leads to the confusion of mentalizing as opposed to external reality.

Example 2: A 'point' was created by *selective attention of focus*. To be effective, this requires its corollary function of *inattention* to everything else except the point of focus. To 'see' a spot means to blot out the awareness of all that is 'not a spot', that is, the rest of the wall.

Example 3: Imagine a second dot on the wall that then becomes point number 2. Realize now that both points are really in the imagination and exist only in the mind of the observer. Now, imagine a line drawn between the two points that one can now call 'distance'. We can now see that inasmuch as both points are strictly imaginary and exist only in the mind, the same applies to any imaginary distance between them.

Example 4: We can now imagine our third point is existing at a distance in front of the wall. Again, if we connect all three points in our imagination, we thereby create a 'plane'. Like the three points, the plane exists only in our imagination. There is not a plane 'out there'. Also note that the lines between the points have no innate 'direction.'

Example 5: If we add a fourth imaginary spot in contrast to the imaginary triangle, we now have an imaginary 'third dimension'. We can now also say that the interval between the points constitutes 'space'. However, as we do this, we realize that all this exists only in our imagination.

Example 6: At this point, we realize that imaginary points result in imaginary locations, directions, planes, space, and dimensions. The next expectation conjured up by the mind is to describe the duration or 'time' that it would take to go from one point to another. You can see that the time to traverse an imaginary distance between imaginary points would have to be in the imagination.

Example 7: We look up at the night sky and see innumerable points of light. We can arbitrarily select and connect any number of these into imaginary figures and create our own constellations. Like a child with a crayon, we can create the constellation of the cat, the dog, the mouse, or whatever. However, if we board a spaceship and travel out to a constellation, we will find that Orion, as well as all the rest, have no such existence.

From the foregoing, it can be understood how the mind perceives the 'many' in what is really 'the one'. To transcend the mind is to see that the many and the one are the same. Without the contrasting mental dualistic terms of 'many' or 'one', neither would be said to exist. Instead, there could only be the realization that 'All Is'.

There is no subject and object possible in the sentence, "All Is." Reality is neither the one nor the many but is only itself beyond description, dimension, time, locality, beginning, or end. To describe it, even the term 'now' is subtly fallacious for it implies the possibility of a 'not now'. No 'not' is possible in Reality, which includes the totality of all that exists and therefore 'is'. All error arises from the 'is not' and therefore has no reality or need for it to be explained or answered. No error is possible in what actually 'is'.

Q: What then is the value of perception?
A: Perception is of value to animal life in dealing with physicality. It deals with form. Spiritual awareness is

beyond form. Once we reach consciousness level 500, form becomes progressively less useful, a hindrance. The spiritual qualities of love, compassion, joy, and beauty are already beyond the perceptual world of form. They cannot be measured, quantified, or even aptly described because they are subjective, experiential realities beyond language. They are subjective states of knowing that are beyond perception.

To be correct, Love really emerges at consciousness level 200 and intensifies until, at 500, it becomes the predominant energy field. As the levels of consciousness go up, form is progressively transcended.

On the calibrated scale of the levels of consciousness, Love prevails at level 500 but does not become unconditional until level 540. This means that some form persists from 500 to 540, so that Love is conditional. The full flowering of Love emerges only when it becomes unselective. It is characterized by lovingness, which is unconditional, because it is what one has become. This leap is accomplished by the 'letting go of the polarity of the opposites', which is an intrinsic error of mentation. After this happens, there are no longer 'good trees' or 'bad trees'. Instead, all trees are seen as perfect and beautiful just as they are. Each living thing is a perfect sculpture in its expression of its essence.

Q: How is it that the world sees as it does?
A: The limitation of perception imputes to events in the world an invisible, magical force called

'causality'. It confuses necessary conditions as being causes. It also confuses temporal sequence with causality.

'Events' do not really 'happen' in Reality. These are arbitrary abstractions that are the result of selective, sequential focusing. In Reality, no 'events' are occurring; therefore, no explanations are necessary. In Reality, creation is continuous. The unmanifest becomes manifest. Each observation, however, is couched in mentalizations of time and location and therefore ostensible sequence. These are only mentations.

In the examples given, we see how the observable comes about. It is created out of consciousness. From the mind of the architect springs the cathedral. Nothing in the world can cause a cathedral. The seed does not 'cause' the plant to be born. With favorable conditions, it assumes visible existence by virtue of its essence manifesting its potentiality.

Nothing in the world 'causes' anything else. All is intertwined in a holographic dance wherein each element influences every other element but does not cause it. 'Cause' is an epistemological invention and is only that of a mentation. The artifact of mentation creates spurious conundrums that then require the spurious explanation of causality to 'explain'. In reality, the absoluteness and totality of Creation leave no vacancy to be filled with any explanatory thought form such as cause. Totality is complete and requires no causes. Cause is force; creation is power.

Q: **What then of karma as the supposed cause of destiny?**

A: In the universe, each thing becomes positioned by its essential qualities becoming manifest. It is like a cork in water that rises, depending on its innate buoyancy. The 'universes of consciousness' can be described in terms of calibrated levels of power. Each entity rises within that sea of consciousness to its own level in this life or after. The soul ascends or descends, depending on its own nature, and is not caused to do so by some external force.

God is power, not force. God doesn't force anything or anybody anywhere. A hot air balloon rises and falls in the sky, depending on wind, weather, temperature, and humidity, and the underlying choices of the operator to add hot air or not. To let go of the attachments of the ego is like shedding ballast.

The belief in 'cause' as a substantive reality has profoundly limiting and injurious consequences. It divides all life into arbitrary divisions of Perpetrator and Victim. This is the lament of seventy-eight percent of the population that calibrates below the level of integrity (at 200). Personal responsibility evolves in the mind of those who believe in causes. Some plausible explanation as 'cause' can be manufactured to explain or excuse any human event or action. In our current society, the courts and trial lawyers have stretched the concept to the point of absurdity. Even if somebody gets burned by touching something that has a large sign in red letters that says, 'Do Not Touch', inventiveness can find an imaginary perpetrator with deep pockets, and it could be said that the sign was not large enough, it was in a foreign language, it was not illuminated at night, or some other excuse.

Since cause exists only as a mentation of imagination, it can be conjured up and manufactured at one's convenience. When taken to extremes, the concepts of perpetrator and victim merge. The criminal now becomes the victim, and the police are the perpetrators. One can see by analysis at depth that who is the victim and who is the perpetrator is really an arbitrary selection or positionality. The victim seduces the perpetrator to act via the predator/prey response. The policeman or prison guard is required by the extremism of the victim's behavior to use force or extreme measures, and thus the roles of perpetrator and victim blur into each other in a cognitive confusion.

Q: Why do actions have consequences?

A: They are linked, but not by cause and effect. Conditions affect occurrences but do not 'cause' them. All potentiality is limited by essence. A bee cannot become a flower. The caterpillar does not 'cause' the butterfly to happen but is a necessary precondition.

Q: How does this apply to spiritual life?

A: The essence of man includes the potentiality for enlightenment. Readiness implies that one has evolved through the lower levels of consciousness so that spiritual inspiration now becomes the spark that ignites the quest.

Q: Perception, then, is merely sensory appearance?

A: That is correct. Even Creation itself is merely an appearance. 'Creation' or 'destruction' merely describes a point of view. Materials are merely converted to another form. If the form is desirable, we call it 'creation'. If it is not desirable, we call it 'destruction'. Converting a tree into 2-x-4 lumber is 'creative' to the carpenter but 'destructive' to the conservationist. The classic 'Dance of Shiva' is the shift of appearance from creation to destruction. In reality, neither is occurring; likewise, whether a turkey dinner is good or bad or creative or destructive depends on whether you are the turkey or the diner.

Recontextualization

Q: What of practical considerations, such as financial pressures? How does recontextualization help?

A: The perception of 'financial pressures' is due to expanding one's life at too rapid a pace. This creates the illusion of a monetary shortage. The answer is not a financial one but merely one of patience. Are there too many sheep in a pasture, or is there a grass shortage? Wanting things impatiently results in moving ahead too fast for comfort. Learn to differentiate wants from needs. Learn to value having credit rather than cash. Fortunes both large and small can be wiped out overnight but credit lasts a lifetime. The cost of living on credit is interest; living on cash costs principle. Cash is convenience; credit is security.

Q: What about so-called 'problems'?

A: Partial and limited positionalities create the illusions called 'problems'. In reality, no such thing as a problem is possible; there is merely what we want and what we do not want. Suffering is due to resistance. This applies to physical pain as well. For instance, by intensely focusing on the pain and being persistent and not resisting it, pain actually disappears. Pain and suffering are two distinctly different things. The mind assumes that they are inseparable, which they are not. It is possible to experience pain but not suffer from it. Suffering is due to resisting the pain. If one is willing to surrender to it, accept it, and completely stop resisting it continuously, the suffering, and even frequently the pain itself, will cease.

By using this technique, it was possible for this writer to go through major surgery on two different occasions without anesthesia. Also, healing then takes place more rapidly. It is possible, for instance, to walk on a severely twisted ankle within minutes, and the relief is very similar to the effect of a narcotic that relieves the suffering. The pain itself may remain but one is indifferent to it.

Q: What about anger?

A: As one progresses spiritually, anger becomes less frequent, but when it does occur, it is increasingly unwelcome. Most frequently, it is usually impatience. Therefore, it is resolvable by realizing that one is not really angry but just in a hurry. To know that in itself relieves guilt. Anger stems from a positionality, and taking a different viewpoint resolves it.

It is helpful to realize that the anger is not at what 'is', but at what 'is not'. We are angry not because someone is selfish or stingy, as we think, but actually because they are not considerate, generous, or loving. If recontextualization is done in this way, then people are seen as being limited rather than being bad or wrong. Each person has developed only up to a specific point in their evolution, and therefore, it is easier to see and accept limitation rather than fault.

Another prevalent cause of anger is desire, or not getting what one wants. This is the anger of infancy that persists in the adult as the so-called self-centered, narcissistic core of the ego called self-ishness. The ego confuses wants and needs and is impatient. It is constantly demanding and wanting. At this focal point, surrendering craving, wanting, and desiring to God brings about great and rapid spiritual progress.

The surrender of this core of the ego triggers rapid spiritual advancement. This is the very focal point and source of the ego, which is focused on survival. Its desires and wants are deemed to be essential because of the ego's beliefs about survival. The ego therefore has to 'get' or 'keep' and acquire because it views itself as separate and therefore dependent on external sources of supply. These may take the form of energy, attention, possessions, status, security, protection, image, money, gain, advantage, and power. Its primary view is lack, and with lack come fear, need, greed, and even homicidal rage and threats. Fear is its motor.

From the viewpoint of consciousness and enlightenment, the reign of fear does not cease until the desire for existence itself is surrendered to God. In the silence that ensues comes a great realization that one's existence has always been due to the presence of the Self that has attracted from the Universe whatever is necessary for survival. Karmic destination for survival then ensures that survival is provided by virtue of the power of the Self to martial the necessities, such as physicality, breath, strength, hunger, curiosity, and intelligence.

The ego is the imaginary doer behind thought and action. Its presence is firmly believed to be necessary and essential for survival. The reason is that the ego's primary quality is perception, and as such, it is limited by the paradigm of supposed causality. In this limited paradigm of duality, the 'I', or ego, sees itself as cause, and actions and events as effects. In Reality, actions and survival are taking place automatically and are actually autonomous. They are activated by the life energy emanating from the Self, and the qualities of the universe supply the forms. Notice, for instance, that in clinical states of amnesia, human life continues even when the source of imagined identity is lost. Notice then that all fear is fear of loss of identity—existence/survival.

This is connected to identifying the self and the source of existence in life as form (thoughts, feelings, body). The resolution of fear is therefore the willingness to surrender one's existence in all its expressions to God. With that total surrender arises the awareness that the Self is formless, and that it is not form but the formless within form that is the Source and the experiencer of life. It then becomes obvious that death, as commonly believed, is not even a possibility.

There is no opposite or alternative to God. It is the spirit within the body that says 'I Am'. The body of itself does not even know that it exists.

Q: What of simplicity?

A: All spiritual truth is contained in every spiritual concept. It is only necessary to completely and totally understand *one single concept* to understand all of them in order to arrive at the realization of the Real. The secret of success is to choose one concept or spiritual tool and pursue it with intensity, nonstop, to its ultimate end. It could be forgiveness or kindness carried to the absolute, or it could be the third step from a '12-step' program. It then gets applied to every single thought, feeling, action, or behavior, without exception. It takes only a single scalpel to dissect the entire human body, and it only takes a single spiritual scalpel to dissect oneself free of the ego.

In the beginning, it takes effort because of resistance, but when willingness becomes perfected due to progressive surrender, the tool takes on a life of its own. There is no longer a 'me' to do it. One eventually realizes the tool is being guided by something other than the personal self. One does not 'find' the truth, so it is futile to 'seek' it. Divinity reveals itself effortlessly.

There is the sudden agony of dying, and then a

profound awe as the Truth of All Creation reveals itself as the everlasting Self, beyond all time, before all worlds, before all universes, in all its Absolute Perfection and Beauty in which and by which all form is merely perception, with no independent existence. All is One; there is no 'here' or 'there', no subject or no object, no 'me' or 'you'. The mind is stilled forever. There is no individual self. All Is by virtue of its own essence and shines forth spontaneously in absolute perfection. There is no causality; everything already is. The body is mainly an 'it', a karmic wind-up toy that goes about its destiny on its own. It never needed a 'me' to run it at all. How could such a thought have arisen and held sway? There is nothing more wonderful than arriving back home again to one's Source.

Q: How does one resolve the identification with body and mind?

A: The ego identifies itself as the doer and the experiencer and, therefore, the core of the body and mind. This is reinforced constantly in thought and language in which all actions are prefixed by the word 'I'. With practice, one can retrain the mind to think in a language according to the facts of Reality. This is done by using the term 'the' instead of 'I'. Thus, in actuality, it is 'the' body or 'the' mind, not 'my' body or 'my' mind. 'The' mind has feelings and thoughts, and 'the' body acts. Possessions can also be referred to as 'the' car instead of 'my' car, rug, house, etc. Although the forms of the body/mind/ego are actually included within the Allness of the Self, the ego uses the term 'I' in its illusory sense. Both the body and the mind are actually 'its'.

Q: How can one detach from possessions?

A: The very word 'possessions' is illusory. Relationship in the world of form is expressed in words and concepts, the existence of which is merely operational and linguistic. Because of the ego's tendency toward concreteness, it goes on to believe that the term must therefore have some independent, objective existence.

All relationships are merely conventional social understandings and arrangements. Because they have no independent reality, they can also be extinguished or canceled by changes in agreements. For instance, to 'own' anything is really an impossibility. What we mean is that, in actuality, there is a legal right to use or possess something, but that is external to the actual relationship between an object and its supposed owner. The 'right' to own is merely a social contract. One can grasp an object, use it, and put it somewhere for safekeeping, but to 'own' is merely an abstract concept. To own in radical Reality would mean that one actually would have to be the object.

In native cultures, the land belongs to everyone, and nobody claims to personally own any part of it. Tribal lands are held by the tribe for all, and use of a particular area is by mutual agreement. To be able to actually own, one would have to have absolute, unconditional control, whereas, in fact, we merely have temporary domain.

These same conditions apply to so-called

'rights'. They are all merely political, contractual, or legal arrangements that rest on the shifting sands of popular opinion and court decisions. Many so-called rights are merely arbitrary conventions that are nothing but passing popularities. At best, society grants only temporary stewardship.

Q: What do you mean by 'the Radical Now'?

A: Like the notes of music that fade away as soon as they are sounded, the experiences of life are fleeting and ephemeral. Each moment is already in the process of ceasing at the very instant it arises. The focus of awareness is like a moving flashlight in the night that briefly illuminates each object and then quickly moves on. They appear and disappear. To the observer, life is therefore merely a procession of appearances and disappearances. Therefore, nothing can be said to be happening because of this constant sequencing of attention. Focus is therefore an arbitrary positionality and accounts for the so-called Dance of Shiva.

Like all of time, even the 'now' is an evanescent illusion. To merely notice something does not create some self-existent, objective reality called 'now'. There is neither 'now' nor 'then', 'past' nor future'. For example, a road is already complete from beginning to end. The traveler does not create some special place in space that becomes 'here'.

Q: If the 'now' disappears, then the infinity of Always takes its place. If the 'now' is an illusion, then when does one supposedly have existence?

A: Even to think 'exist' is to grab at a passing split second in consciousness. The absolute Reality is beyond even existence. To 'exist' is again a passing notion. There is a presumption that some independent, objective reality is depicted by that statement. All such statements are merely products of consciousness. Reality is beyond even existence itself. Existence is only possible as an evanescent experience in consciousness within consciousness itself, with no independent beingness or independent reality.

Q: **If there is no actual 'now' or 'past' or 'present' and Reality is completely outside of time, then when does the 'I' exist?**

A: The answer now is obvious; it does not. The absolute Reality is forever, always. Note that the words 'is', 'was', 'exists', and 'beingness' are all denotations of time. All these statements are merely mental categories of thought.

Q: **Can you please explain more about identity?**

A: The ego fears dissolution and therefore resists giving up the illusion of a separate existence in an imaginary 'here' and an imaginary 'now'. It fears it will dissolve into being nothing, and, therefore, the conscious awareness will also cease. With examination, it will become clear that one's reality is not a 'who' at all but instead is an intensely loving Allness that is realized and known to be much closer and more comforting and fulfilling than the prior sense of 'I'.

In the evolution of consciousness, the sense of

the small 'I' is replaced by a more profound, invulnerable, and nontransitory sense of Universal Presence. The sense of 'I' is now infinite, grander, gentler, more aware, and more gratifying than the sense of the little 'I' had been. The small 'I' is like a penny whistle compared to the full symphony of the Self.

Q: What does the Self feel like?

A: It is like the ultimate completion of being home. There is a knowingness of finality, conclusion, completion, fulfillment, satisfaction, perfection, and beauty. The quality of Love dissolves all possibility of suffering or wanting. No mentation occurs, nor is it necessary. A profound sense of certainty prevails. Divinity is unmistakable.

There is absolutely nothing in ordinary human experience to compare with the joy of the presence of the Love of God. No sacrifice is too great nor effort too much in order to realize that Presence.

Q: What is the ultimate truth of one's reality?

A: One's absolute reality is beyond consciousness itself. It is the substrate of consciousness; it is beyond Allness or Voidness. It is prior to Creation, beyond the manifest and the unmanifest. It is prior to existence, beingness, or is-ness. It is beyond identity, yet out of it arises the Self. It is neither transcendent nor imminent, yet both. It is the infinite potentiality out of which the All and the One arise. The Self is the Presence expressed as existence, and out of that consciousness arises the sense of Existence.

Q: **Where or when could enlightenment occur? If there is no reality such as time, or here or now, or a real 'me' to become enlightened, how can it be possible?**

A: If it were a phenomenon that had to occur at a certain time or place, then indeed it would not be a possibility. The only explanation is that the state or condition termed enlightenment already is a reality and therefore needs only to be allowed to be realized in order to prevail. What already 'is' requires no future. Acceptance is an ever-present option. Complete surrender to God unveils the Truth. Nothing is hidden; only the ego is blind. Reality lies just beyond the mind. Out of the fear of becoming nothing, consciousness denies its only reality that it is everything—the infinite, everlasting Allness out of which existence itself arises.

Truth prevails when falsity is surrendered. To do this, however, requires great dedication, courage, and faith, which are supplied by divine inspiration in response to surrender. The trigger is the consent of the will.

Q: **Can you say more about where and when God is realizable?**

A: The doorway to Divinity is located and available as a direct experience in the exact split second of 'now', which is discernible between two thoughts. To the mind, this instant arises and passes. Between the arising and the passing away is the aperture that allows consciousness to become aware of the ever-present, infinite, timeless Reality. The arising of this instant is the unfolding of God as Creation. The universe is the historical record of God's creation. Remember that the 'is' of 'now' becomes the 'was' of the next instant.

There is no separation between Creator and created, no subject or object; they are one and the same. Such terms as 'new' or 'old' are only nonexistent points of view, like 'now' or 'then'. We are the constant witness to Creation at the very moment of Creation itself. What we witness is the Hand of God as experience. Awareness is the 'Eye' or witness, and Creation is the handiwork of the infinite Self.

The truth of the ongoingness of the unfoldment of Creation is hidden behind the beliefs, perceptions, and illusions of causality. The miracle of Creation is continuous, and its appearance is the scintillation of appearance.

Q: **What of the duality of ego versus spirit?**

A: This is one of the prime sets of opposites that have to be transcended. It is helpful to look at the two concepts operationally. In the state of being at One with the Spirit, the Self, by virtue of one of its innate qualities, knows at all times. In the world of form, the ego is hard set to duplicate this effortless, instantaneous performance, and over time, it has thus evolved an extremely complex set of operations. The ego could be called the central processing and planning center, the integrative, executive strategic and tactical focus that orchestrates, copes, sorts, stores, and retrieves. In addition, it chooses among options and evaluates, weighs, compares, and categorizes those options. To do this, it requires abstractions, symbols, hierarchies of meanings and values, prioritization, and selection.

This is made more effective by constant acquisition of facts and their realignment into modified strata of meaning and significance in order to effect endless detail, and at the same time, overall, to seek pleasure and survival and avoid that which lacks pleasure or is painful. This complex performance requires extreme degrees of education, training, and development of tools of cognition and mentation, called intelligence and logic. Another overriding function of the ego is to analyze, correlate, integrate, synthesize, memorize, subordinate, arrange, and develop complex programs of faculties, skills, and behavioral patterns.

Behind this dazzling performance is 'the great Oz', called the 'I'. The existence of this 'I' is hypothecated because the performance of the ego has to do with form, and it integrates all its experience under the belief system called 'causality'. Therefore, the great Oz is the central focus of this causality and, as in sentence structure, the 'I' becomes the imputed subject and the 'me' the imputed object of actions and experience.

Q: As one advances in consciousness, the question arises, is the great Oz the 'I', a 'who', or a 'what'?

A: Because the ego deals in form and definition, it cannot comprehend the Self, which is beyond all form but without which form would not appear to exist. In Reality, there is neither subject nor object; therefore, there is no relationship to be explained.

No causality is necessary, which then precludes time and space, or doer versus experiencer.

In a peculiar way, the ego is caught in the famous dyad of perpetrator versus victim. As the subject, it imputes itself as cause and therefore perpetrator. If it disowns that definition, it then becomes the object and therefore the martyr or victim. The ego thinks, "If I'm not causing something, then something out there is doing it to me." This is the primary concept of today's construction of social interaction in which society is seen as the alteration between victim and victimizer.

Q: How can one get out of this trap?

A: Although various methods have been described, one that is helpful is to cease having opinions about anything. Because all opinions are vanities, they are based on duality and tend to reinforce it. It is observable, for instance, that spiritual organizations that have a very high calibrated rating have 'no opinions on outside matters'.

Q: After what has been called Enlightenment, what remains of the former personal self?

A: The inner state is similar to sleep in that there is silence, peace, and stillness. There are no volition, movement, or form. There is an absence of thoughts or mental activity.

It takes volition and energy to focus attention from the formlessness of the Self to the processing of information. Consciousness in its higher states merely notes the interaction of essences, presences, and significances as they are prevailingly held by the world. To pay attention to detail and form takes more energy and is accomplished only by an act of the will as a response to the value of life. What is left of what the world would consider the personal self is a shadow of the former persona, but it has no desires, wishes, or needs. It has no desire to control events, circumstances, or people. It lacks nothing within itself; therefore, it does not seek gain inasmuch as all is complete at every moment. There is not even a desire for continuance. There is nothing one needs or wants to experience.

The Presence is all fulfilling. Because one already is the All, there is nothing left to desire as there is no separation. There is no future to anticipate. There is no interest in acquisition or physicality. Eating or maintaining the body arises primarily from the interest of others in the world, whose love sustains the ongoingness of the physicality. There is a delay in processing speech, events, or details of form into a level that is more formless and meaningful. This translation is performed by an aspect of the Self called the Holy Spirit that replaces what was formerly volition, selection, or mentation. The activation of the Holy Spirit seems to occur as a result of volition and will, which are associated with choice.

The central focus of the ego, which was relinquished, was replaced by the more pervasive and powerful effect of the presence of the Holy Spirit that effortlessly orchestrates simultaneity and synchronicity as it automatically sorts out the irrelevant from the relevant because it interacts only with Reality. Thus, what appears to be a miracle is merely the action of the Holy Spirit sorting out the false from the true so that what appeared to be imperfection is revealed as perfection. To the ego, which deals in causality, no such occurrence is logical or possible, but to the Spirit, this quality is automatic and inherent to Reality.

Q: **We often hear the rationalization that a person needs some form of ego in order to survive. What is the truth about that?**

A: This is an understandable question and rises from the belief in causality. The ego as we know it has a large number of complex operations. It imagines that there is an 'I' behind these operations. In actuality, these operations are autonomous and do not require an 'I'. The main transition occurs when one no longer identifies with these operations and no longer assumes there is a volitional, independent entity behind them.

   This is easy to understand if one looks at one's relationship to the body. Although people loosely call it 'me', they do not refer to their knee as 'me'; they call it 'mine'. The knee is a physicality that operates without thinking. The operations of the body are extremely complex, similar to those of the ego, and occur autonomously. When one stops identifying with either the body or the mind, the functions continue autonomously but merely without an identification as 'myself'. The sense of authorship disappears. Ongoing survival is autonomous, and continuance is an expression of consciousness in its alliance with the Holy Spirit. The prevailing conditions are related to karma and operate impersonally. Karma then becomes part of the impersonal conditions that are in accord as appearance.

By analogy, one can enjoy beautiful music without the ego's claiming authorship for the origination of the music itself. The enjoyment is spontaneous. If one claims authorship for the music, then many anxieties and feelings arise that have to do with belief systems about perfection, approval, desirability, and acceptance.

CHAPTER 20

Duality versus Nonduality
Science versus Spirit

Q: How can one clarify the relationship between science and spirituality?

A: It entails simply being aware that all life can be described from two different approaches or categories of thought: linear versus nonlinear.

The domain of ordinary consciousness (linear) is concerned with form, logical sequence, and perception, which separate, define, and categorize. The scientific world is thus contained within the Newtonian paradigm of reality and its languaging and expressions as mathematics, science, and technology. Explanations in the Newtonian paradigm are based upon the presumption of the hypothecated process called 'causality'. It deals with forces and measurements, such as time, duration, distance, speed, weight, and dimension. This mode of perception and its languaging allow for relatively accurate prediction. When events fall outside the predictable and comprehensible or that which is explicable by differential calculus or measurement, the data have been traditionally ignored or discarded as noise or chaos. The Newtonian universe is therefore definable, logical, predictable, and coincides with linguistics, conventional semantics, and explanations by reason of causality.

This is also the realm of the ego where perception sets up the categories of the 'opposites'. The underlying weakness of this paradigm is that it projects the mental mechanisms of cognition onto a presumed and purportedly self-existent 'objective' universe that exists independently of the observer. This paradigm fails to recognize the crucial and ever-present substratum of subjectivity that is the basis of all experience and observation or so-called scientific description. Therefore, this deficiency reveals an underlying epistemological flaw in that all purported objectivity rests solely upon subjectivity that is present as a necessary substrate of all that is 'objectively' possible.

To merely state that objectivity exists is already a subjective statement. All information, knowledge, and the totality of all experience are the product of subjectivity, which is an absolute requirement intrinsic to life, awareness, existence, and thought.

It is not possible to make any statement that is not inherently subjective as its substratum. Based on perception are the animal world, sensation, and the human emotions and motivations of like and dislike. These subsequently elaborate into psychological mechanisms, attitudes, and individuality. In the world of perception, differences are all-important, all-defining, and spell out value, desirability, and pleasure/displeasure within the contrasting sets of opposites of attraction and aversion. This leads to either seeking or avoidance and the determination of value and desirability that then become the mainspring of society.

In contrast to the tangible and visible linear, sequential world of cause, effect, and form based on perception, there is the infinite, all-encompassing domain described as 'nonlinear'. It has only recently been addressed by science in the fields now labeled 'chaos theory' and 'nonlinear dynamics'. The study of nonlinear dynamics was only recently occasioned by the advent of rapid modern computers which could detect ultra-minute events that had previously been ignored as stochastic (meaningless), indefinable, and outside the world of predictable order.

In order to be 'objective', science excluded the essentially human elements of experience other than intellections. In contrast, psychiatry and psychoanalysis dealt with the unseen domain of feelings, options, meaning, value, significance, and the very essence of life itself. All life in its essence is nonlinear, nonmeasurable, and nondefinable. It is purely subjective.

All that is really meaningful and significant in human life is nonlinear, invisible, and unmeasurable. It is the domain of spirituality, life, consciousness, awareness, and existence itself. It is the domain of the subjective and the capacity for experiencing without which knowledge would have no value. This profound substrate has been ignored by science, which relegated it to the 'lesser' significance or importance of philosophy, metaphysics, and mysticism.

Qualities of experience that are of crucial importance to human life, such as love, inspiration, respect, joy, happiness, peace, satisfaction, completion, and fulfillment, have been relegated by science to the 'warm and fuzzy' questionable realities. It was therefore thought that such subjects were 'unscientific' and thereby consigned to philosophy and literature. Even psychology was downsized to experimental data and the Skinner and Pavlovian theories where white mice and levers produced comforting data of reasonable statistical significance of stimulus and response in the pristine atmosphere of the academic laboratory.

The nonlinear domain is invisible, without form, and beyond time, dimension, or measurement. It includes qualities and meanings, and power emanates from its intrinsic essence. The source of power and creation is in the invisible, nonlinear domain and by the exercise of will can result in form. The visible world is therefore the world of effects and the interaction of forces. It is out of inspiration and volition that action arises by assent of the will, which has the capacity to activate possibilities or options.

For simplification, the characteristics of linear as compared to nonlinear can be listed. It is to be realized, however, that they are not separate but mutually inclusive, and that the linear is contained within the nonlinear, just as all form is included within the formless. These are, therefore, not two different realms but are the same viewed from two different points. In common parlance, we speak of digital versus analog, left brain versus right brain, holistic versus specific, or limited versus unlimited to imply that there are two different, contrasting approaches to reality.

Newtonian Linear	Nonlinear	Newtonian Linear	Nonlinear
Duality	Nonduality	Ego	Spirit
Form	Formless	Material	Nonmaterial

Newtonian Linear	Nonlinear	Newtonian Linear	Nonlinear
Visible	Invisible	Controllable	Useable
Force	Power	Exhaustible	Inexhaustible
Time	Timeless	Depleted	Ever Present
Location	Nonlocal	Observe	Know
Limited	Unlimited	Content	Context
Duration	Eternal	Material	Life
Perception	Vision	Object	Subject
Quality	Essence	Without	Within
Know about	Be	Exclusive	Inclusive
Dimension	Immeasurable	Physical	Metaphysical
Tangible	Intangible	Thing	Witness
Desire	Inspire	Object	Observer
Material	Spiritual	Either - Or	Both
Local	Diffuse	Here - There	Everywhere
Motion	Immobile	Divided	United
Move	Still	Part	Whole
Audible	Silent	Forcing	Facilitating
Mathematical	Unpredictable	Adrenaline	Endorphin
Travel	Stationery	Desire	Fulfill
Fact	Meaning	Tension	Relaxation
Difference	Sameness	Incomplete	Complete
Separate	Oneness	Caesar	God
Distinct	Diffuse	Cost	Value
Start - Stop	Continuous	It	I
Finite	Infinite	Dependent	Independent
Duration	Timeless	Illusion	Reality
Structure	Quality	Temporal	Infinite
Effect	Source	Secular	Spiritual
Sequential	Simultaneous	Describable	Ineffable
Precise	General	Deplete	Sustain

Newtonian Linear	Nonlinear	Newtonian Linear	Nonlinear
Observed	Awareness	Price	Value
Desire	Motivate	Impulsive	Spontaneous
Change	Unchanging	Relative	Absolute
Vulnerable	Invulnerable	Past – Future	Now
Thought	Consciousness	Limited	Transcendent
Want	Satisfaction	Scientific	Mystical
Conflict	Peace	Object	Field
Stress	Ease	Receive	Give
Proof	Self-evident	Definition	Meaning

Q: How does one transcend the opposites?

A: Consciousness does so automatically when understanding occurs through reflection, familiarity, prayer, meditation, or inspiration. It is also facilitated by the words or level of consciousness of the teacher. What is impossible at one level of consciousness becomes obvious and simple at a higher one. A human being is both spirit and body; therefore, it is at all times actually existing in both the linear and the nonlinear domains. The body, unless imbued with consciousness and subjective awareness, is not aware of its own existence. It takes action only when it is motivated and presented with value, such as the desire for enjoyment in the experience of life.

When a person or animal becomes 'dispirited', it dies. When the life force or spirit no longer energizes the body, the spirit then leaves and goes to a different dimension. Although it is in a different dimension, the consciousness level of the spirit can still be calibrated by the simple muscle test. Some spirits leave the body in a state of joy, ecstasy, or bliss. Others do so in the lower states of despondency, such as anger, guilt, or hatred. These states will then obviously affect the destination of the spirit, which has been traditionally called the soul or nonmaterial aspect of life. When the spirit leaves the body, its destination correlates with its specific level of consciousness as determined by its calibrated frequency, which one can presume leads to the different levels of hell, purgatory, limbo, heavens, and celestial realms as well as astral levels ('inner planes') or discarnate states.

Like a cork in water or a balloon in the atmosphere, each spirit rises to its own level of buoyancy within the infinite realms of energy fields of consciousness. No external 'judgment' or divine coercion is involved. Each being radiates forth its essence and so determines its own destiny. Thus is divine justice perfect. By choice, each spirit becomes what it has chosen. Within all realms there exists the moment-to-moment choice of the absolute reality that is ever present and whose absolute choice results in liberation.

By analogy we could say that the soul, united with a physical body or not, is somewhat like a small particle within an electromagnetic field. The attractions and repulsions of the particle depend on its size, charge, polarity, and position within a larger field that includes gradations of energy, power, and different qualities to which the particle would be attracted or repelled. All possibilities and eventualities are therefore a reflection of the state

THE EYE OF THE I

of consciousness or level of evolution of the individual within the All. It is inescapable because the individual is an essential 'part' of the All. One could say that each level of consciousness is represented in the field as an 'attractor', as in *chaos theory*.

This design is observable in everyday life in human interaction with its likes and dislikes, along with its attractions and repulsions as expressed in lifestyles, occupational choice, social behaviors, habits, frailties, strengths, and group identifications.

Q: Are there simple devices or techniques that facilitate this progression?

A: Differentiate the 'this' from the 'that', the 'who' from the 'what', the 'volitional' from the 'automatic', and the 'observer from the 'observed'. The bridge is afforded by delineating the observer/witness/awareness of consciousness. It is like differentiating the capacity for hearing and seeing from what is seen and heard.

The Eye of the I is the Self that gives the self its capacity for awareness. Without the sun shining forth, nothing would be visible. Without the light of the Self, the self would not even know of its own existence. Were it not for the awareness of consciousness, neither the body nor the ego would know that the other exists. Holiness reflects that Divinity is the source of existence of All That Is, including the Self.

The infinite, timeless, nondualistic Self shines forth in the world of duality and perception as self. It is characteristic of self to be unaware of its actual source. The ego, in fact, primarily refutes its source and instead claims it to be separate, autonomous, self-activating, and independent. Once the ego has advanced to the level of reason and intellectual capacity, it reaches its limit and seeks beyond itself for answers. At the lower levels of intellectual evolution, however, the intellect tends to be prideful, it tends to claim credit for all capacities or actions, and it claims authorship and sees itself as the pinnacle of evolution.

The mature intellect, at some point, discerns spiritual information, which it then pursues. Again, it may be blinded by pride and positionalities. With further experience and serious spiritual work, humility lessens the grip of the intellectual ego and allows for the more profound experiencing of progressively higher states of spiritual awareness. This threshold is a gift that accompanies the willingness to love, and the inspiration that ensues leads to emergence into the realms of peace and joy. Compassion then becomes dominant and transforms perception into vision. With completion of the process, the self dissolves into the Self. This level, which calibrates at 600, marks the level of consciousness that the world has traditionally referred to as Enlightenment. At this point, bliss may bring about incapacitation as far as further functioning; however, if the bliss itself is then surrendered to God, the state of the Sage ensues. As this stage ripens, there may or may not be a return to the world where the Will of God determines all that follows.

Q: Does the sense of self disappear? After all, the ego fears death.

A: When the self dissolves into the Self, it is experienced as a great expansion from limited, transitory, and vulnerable to immortal, infinite Allness that transcends all worlds and universes. As such, the Self is not subject to death or birth, as it exists beyond temporality. The obscurity of the Self was the result of merely misidentifying perception as representing all Reality.

Q: What of physical death?

A: It may sound surprising, but no one actually experiences their own death. There is, of course, the experience of the conditions that precede death, but when actual physical 'death' occurs, one instantly leaves the body effortlessly and merely witnesses the body's death. With separation from the body, the former experiencer or inhabitant becomes aware that it is a spirit. Sometimes at this point, denial sets in. The spirit is then attracted to its destination by the actions of attraction or repulsion, which are the automatic consequences of the soul's evolution.

Again, the freedom to choose is present. Salvation is assisted by devotion to spiritual truth and its teachers. The mercy of God is infinite and unconditional. The soul alone has the power to determine its own fate. Each soul is attracted to the appropriate level, with absolute precision. That which is omniscient is incapable of injustice or caprice. Thus it is that 'every hair on one's head is counted' by virtue of the infinite knowingness of the field. Nothing escapes detection or consequence.

Q: Whither science?

A: The understanding of the basic structure of the material world has reached a major state of advancement with the demonstration and discovery of the last remaining elusive 'tau neutrino'. Science will probably move its interest to epistemology since a continuation of the function of science would be the study of consciousness itself. In order to proceed, it will be necessary to be very clear on how does one know and how does one know that one knows.

The universe will be discovered to be an extrapolation of man's categories of concept formation and processing. Eventually, the limits of the Newtonian paradigm of reality (a consciousness level of 499) will be transcended, which opens for study the processes of Nature and life itself, which are beyond logic, form, perception, and duality.

Spiritual inquiry will become legitimate and investigation will look within instead of without. The search for objective reality will be discovered to be purely subjective, which discovery is in itself the road to Enlightenment. Mankind will be lifted to greater and greater heights and eventually to a unity in which each lives for the All.

This evolution has only become an actual possibility in very recent years. The total field of consciousness of humanity is rising. Of major importance is that it finally crossed over the critical consciousness level of Integrity (Truth) at 200, and rose to the present level of 207. Every act of kindness, consideration, forgiveness, or love affects everyone. Even in the physical world, there are yet more dimensions to be discovered, e.g., the speed of light can be exceeded (as reported by Lijun Wang in *Nature*, July 20, 2000). The universe is expanding at an ever-increasing rate. To know the nature of consciousness catapults understanding to ever-expanding capacities and discoveries. The journey is from knowing to Knowing, from perception to omniscience. The true scientist sees everything as equally important. As a result, today's real scientists will become the mystics of the future. The dedication to truth is the only requirement.

Developments in genetics and bionics will make ethics and consciousness increasingly important. We will indeed need to know what it is that makes a human being a human being.

Q: How does transcending these apparent opposites relate to self-realization or enlightenment?

A: Simply put, realization or enlightenment is the condition where the sense of self moves from the limited linear material to the nonlinear infinite and formless. The 'me' moves from the visible to the invisible. This occurs as a shift of awareness and identification from perception of form as objective and real to the realization of the purely subjective as the ultimate reality.

That which is the ultimate and eternal transcends both objectivity and subjectivity and is beyond awareness. It is referred to in the ancient spiritual literature as the Supreme Spirit. Out of the

Supreme arises all that is manifest and unmanifest; all consciousness and awareness; all existence; All That Is, either form or nonform; all that is linear and all that is nonlinear; all that arises out of creation; all possibility and actuality. The Supreme is beyond existence or nonexistence; beyond beingness or is-ness; beyond all gods, heavens, and spiritual forms; beyond all names or definitions; beyond all divinities and spiritual denotations. It is out of the Godhead that Divinity arises, and out of the Supreme arises the Godhead.

CHAPTER 21

Genesis: Creation and Evolution

Q: How does life itself originate as we know it?
A: It is obvious that life originates from the Infinite
Potentiality of the Unmanifest, which alone has
sufficient power to create life. The material world
of form is an effect and without intrinsic power,
much less the power of Creation. Power emanates
from the Supreme Reality that is itself without form
yet intrinsic to it.

When the Radiance of the Infinite Spirit/
God/Light falls upon inert matter, there originates
within that substance an organizational influence, a
potentiality, that is an effect of the attractor field of
life within consciousness. Thus, life is spawned by
the light of Divinity, which is the Ultimate Source of
all existence. In this unfoldment, consciousness is
the agent.

Form arises in appearance as the 'this' and the
'that' of substance/matter. Life, however, is not
dyadic but triadic because between the 'this' and
the 'that', an agent is necessary for growth and
action. This third aspect arises as an attractor
pattern in Consciousness and manifests as basic,
alive protoplasm.

It is because of the requirement of the presence
of the Radiance of Divinity that life cannot arise
from substance alone. For life to continue, propagation and sustenance are necessary. The attractor
patterns of Creation are triune in that the presence
of God activates the potentialities wherever conditions are favorable (i.e., 'the Breath of God').

In the beginning, there was God as Light, which is the energy of Creation and all life. In the beginning, there were only infinite energy and potential, and this energy then manifested as materiality and substance. Activation of the basic dyadic of structure of matter was enabled by the addition of an agent that enlivened them so that life could unfold.

The first life forms were extremely simple and basic, and their first task was that of survival and duplication. Consciousness was the activating agent of evolution, and within it, attractor fields gave pattern to form; thus, feedback and learning were made possible. Evolution occurred within the attractor fields of consciousness that manifested as more complex life forms with basic intrinsic intelligence and the capacity for data storage. Motility arose along with other adaptive learning. The requirement for data storage and communication resulted in the creation of the nervous system and eventually the brain.

Creation includes the esthetics of intelligence and the emergence of life into endless displays of beauty and grace. Evolution is therefore the Grace of God made manifest as continuous creation that is patterned by the intelligence of consciousness itself.

Life is the radiance of God made manifest as the universe expressed through evolution. We are both the product and the witness of Creation as a continuous, eternal process.

Science addresses solely the mechanisms of form, but life is comprehensible only from the viewpoint of the nonlinear domain of consciousness.

This is why there is now such interest by science in consciousness itself as a legitimate subject of study. It is considered that the science of consciousness is the most fruitful area for investigation to further man's evolution.

Q: Why is the evolution of consciousness so important?

A: To mankind, this expansion of awareness is crucial, for without it, humanity has been at an impasse. The main area in which man has evolved in the last thousand years has been in technology. The quality of life improved but remained at an impasse for the majority of the world's population. Humanity's most basic problems, such as poverty, crime, addiction, emotional and psychiatric disorders, war, and conflict, have predominated continuously for thousands of years. In just this lifetime, there have been two world wars, the Great Depression, disease epidemics, burgeoning populations, and increasing problems with crime, drugs, and poverty. Primarily in the area of medicine has real progress been made, with the elimination of disease and help for mental illness.

Until 1986, the consciousness of mankind, as we have pointed out, remained in the destructive, negative range below 200. While it stood at 190, humanity was trapped in the level of suffering. Popular proposed solutions for social problems, such as fascism, communism, dictatorships, and utopian schemes, all turned out to be worse than the original conditions for which they were proposed to solve. Even religion became a great oppressor and was embroiled in and supportive of slaughter and cruelties of immense proportion.

The corruption of power invaded every area of human activity. The progress that did occur in society originated from and was sustained by the minority of the population that calculated at over level 200. Thus, we could suspect that medicine and science, which are both in the 400s, would be a major contributor of positive benefits. Industry, in the 300s, has also been a benefactor to society. In contrast, even now, it is significant that the majority of the world's population still calibrates below the level of Integrity at 200.

This mass negativity has continued to be counterbalanced by the small minority of the population that is in the very high positive range. It is sufficient to counterbalance the gross negativity of the masses that, if not counterbalanced, would result in the destruction of mankind.

With an overall consciousness level of 190, nuclear annihilation of mankind was not only a possibility but also a likelihood. Bombs that could annihilate all human life on the planet were actually under consideration and planning by militaristic nations to use as a vindictive retaliation in case of a military defeat. The prophesied 'end times' came very close to manifesting. The prophecy signal was to be whether the great bear of the north, that is, Russia (the USSR), remained atheist or turned back to God. The fall of monolithic, atheistic communism signaled a shift in balance from 190 to 207 for all mankind, which precluded the destruction of humanity.

Although, historically, the tendency is to blame specific leaders for any catastrophes, in actuality, they do not succeed without the support of the masses who, if below 200, are vulnerable to distorted concepts, slogans, propaganda, and mass programming by hatred, revenge, pride, anger, and greed. Therefore, it is crucial to the evolution of mankind that its overall consciousness level be kept above 200.

In contrast, in a recent opinion poll in the United States, seventy-nine percent of the respondents favored capital punishment. This is so even though it is blatantly a violation of all major spiritual teachings. In addition, current publicly reported studies show that the homicide rate is highest in the states that still use capital punishment and lowest in the states that have stopped it. All of this opinion occurs in a society that has increasingly been made aware of the frequency with which innocent people have been put to death to such a degree that governors have been declaring a moratorium on the death penalty. The consciousness level of America is currently at 425.

The consciousness level that supports the death penalty is below 200 and is historically associated with the 'spleen', considered the seed of hatred, vindictiveness, cruelty, and revenge, which are, interestingly, the same level as that of murder itself. Therefore, the consequences in consciousness of murder are apparently the same whether the accused is deemed innocent or guilty.

Q: Why is there such limited understanding and

confusion about Creation?

A: The problem is merely that of paradigms. In the linear Newtonian dimension with its limitations of belief in linear causality, the 'cause' of the universe is sought in time and place. This, of course, begs the question, and actually is an insolvable riddle, as it would lead to an infinite regression of what would be the cause of the cause of the primary cause.

Understanding of the totality requires inclusion of understanding from both the linear and the nonlinear dimensions. Creation bursts forth from the nonlinear infinite source of Creation as a continuous process outside time and space. In this unfoldment, the unmanifest 'Transcendent' becomes the manifest 'Immanent'. The immanent then powers transformation via evolution, which is merely the unfolding of the forms of Creation to appearance. Thus, the universe does not have a 'cause' but instead has its Source in the unmanifest.

With a little reflection, it is quite apparent that Creation could not possibly be a stationary 'event' in time or the Creator would also have to be limited in time and place. By that limitation alone, the Creator would be unable to create because of limitation. Infinite power is beyond form. Only the formless has the power to create form.

The unenlightened human mind is incapable of comprehending infinite power. It tries to capture an understanding but uses the wrong tools to do so. The answers cannot be found in the paradigm of linear causality, which is a paradigm of force based on the notion of 'causality' as an explanation.

Q: **In the ongoing, endless social arguments between the religious creationists and the evolutionists, both sides are incorrect?**

A: That is apparently the reason for the lack of resolution of the conflict. Biblical creationists make the same error as scientists and skeptics in assuming there was a 'roll of the dice' creator who created the whole universe in time and place and then withdrew elsewhere to 'heaven'. Evolutionists also miss the whole point as well. Creation is ongoing and continuous due to the omnipresence of God. Evolution is merely the style of expression and unfolding of the ongoingness of Creation. It is obvious that that which is the Infinite God does not 'start' and 'stop'. That which is beyond all dimensions is not subject to limitation.

According to current science, the potential energy in one cubic centimeter of 'empty' space is greater than the mass of the entire universe. What has not yet been noted is that the potential energy in every cubic centimeter of space increases continuously at an infinite rate. (The power of the unmanifest would be equal to or greater than that of the manifest.)

The infinite glory, greatness, and power of God has been severely and grossly underestimated and not comprehended by man. With the replacement of the self by the Self, the power of omnipotence is known by virtue of the fact that the Infinite is one's source and reality. There is no limitation to God.

An allegorical approximation of reality would be to state that the entire duration of all time of infinity takes less than an instant. At this point, it becomes apparent that one paradigm cannot be stretched to include another.

Q: What is the truth inherent in Genesis?

A: Interestingly, Genesis is one of the three books of the Old Testament that test strong with muscle testing (the others are Psalms and Proverbs). It states that Creation arose out of the darkness, the formless void of the unmanifest as light and form by the agency of the Godhead, the spirit of God. The light created matter or form and then spawned life in the progressive forms of vegetation, fish, then birds, and other animals.

The source of the power of Creation was reiterated as 'light'. Each animal appearance is stated to be an expression in form of its essence 'according to its kind'. Lastly, man was created to have greater power than all the rest of living creatures and, therefore, dominion. Then came the fateful admonition to avoid duality and the nonreality of good and evil, which are linked with perception and create belief in the unreal. This admonition was necessary because man was a limited creature, and unlike an enlightened deity, was unable to differentiate between truth and falsehood.

Man came into existence in form (he named all the animals of the earth). Man, however, had sufficient power of consciousness to create belief. After falling into the pit of duality, the human mind gave reality to falsity and then believed that the fallacious had an independent existence. By creating belief in the pseudoreality of that which is false, man became subject to suffering in the forms of shame, guilt, pride, fratricide, and the dread of punishment and fear. This condition brought forth from the heavens the appearance of Avatars and the Buddhas of enlightenment who revealed that only by transcending duality (in this case, good and evil) could the realization of innate innocence be retrieved.

The limitation of man's consciousness to a level that is vulnerable to error is historically ascribed to the vanity of the desire for power as knowledge. Thus, man, shortly after his creation, became unenlightened and subject to error.

Actions that arise from consciousness levels below 200 are historically labeled as sin. All the great spiritual teachers admonished the populace to avoid sin because of its karmic consequences in the form of hells. It appeared that man could not arise above the consciousness level of 200 without help; thus the need for saviors whose level of consciousness was so high that mere alignment with them brought one over the 200 level.

Consciousness levels below 200 lack power and therefore substitute force. But to ascend spiritually requires power, which resides in the invisible level of the spirit. The saviors therefore rescue the lower levels by virtue of the power of Divine Love and Truth that radiate as an energy field. The value then of a religious or spiritual commitment by prayer, devotion, or worship is that the allegiance qualifies and enables the follower to benefit by the grace of God as it radiates through the divine teachers.

All the above can be verified by muscle testing.

To merely think or image a divine figure makes anyone go strong. Therefore, prayer and religious or spiritual devotions have a very quickly demonstrable positive effect. Actually, a savior is necessary for all people who calibrate below 600, which means that mankind as a whole does indeed need the contribution of great spiritual teachers.

In accordance with the above, we can make several observations. A universal observation made by thousands of clinicians over the years is that certain stimuli make everyone go weak with muscle testing. Thus, to demonstrate this research method to large audiences, it is common to have the test subjects look at a fluorescent light or hold a pesticide over their solar plexus. These stimuli dependably make everyone in the audience go weak. Even to look at a pesticide-contaminated apple at the front of the lecture hall makes large audiences go weak. (In contrast, imaging a divine figure makes everyone go strong.)

There was a group of people who came at one time to the clinic to learn about muscle testing and, surprisingly, none of the reliable negative stimuli had any affect on them, and they were found to be immune to external negativity. Upon questioning, it was revealed that they were all spiritual aspirants and students who, in this particular case, had studied a spiritual course of instruction called A Course in Miracles®. This discovery was important and led to a further investigation in which students who intended to do the one-year *A Course in Miracles* workbook were tested before starting the course and serially thereafter. By the time the students were up to about Lesson 75, they had lost their vulnerability to negative stimuli. (A Course in Miracles is based on the power of forgiveness.) This enables the replacement of the ego's perception and its dualistic positionality with truth that replaces falsehood. The critical lesson in *A Course in Miracles* where the student showed this shift is 'I am only subject to what I hold in mind'. However, for this lesson to become absorbed, the preceding seventy-four lessons had to be taken daily and sequentially as prescribed. (*A Course in Miracles* calibrates at 600.)

Another interesting observation of spiritual power is accorded by a study of the spiritual organization of Alcoholics Anonymous (AA), which has an overall organizational energy field of 540 (Unconditional Love). It is a common observation that so long as the recovering person remains within the influence of that powerful energy field, they remain sober, and when they decide they are going to 'go it on their own' and leave AA, they relapse quickly. Thus, unless a participant's personal level of consciousness rises to 540 or above, their recovery depends on the spiritual power of the group itself. It is comparable to iron filings being held within a powerful electromagnetic field.

Q: How do you explain the miraculous?

A: The term 'miraculous' stems from the Newtonian paradigm, which is limited to the confines of logic in material form and the assumption of causality. Miracles are only comprehensible from the nonlinear domain. When spiritual power becomes focused on faulty perception, it is replaced by vision of the underlying reality, which is not within the realm of logic.

In mankind's experience, forgiveness is probably the most frequent trigger of this phenomenon because it brings about healing and the return of positive spiritual attributes such as love. We see this demonstrated widely by the veterans of World War II and subsequent wars where former fierce enemies have long since forgiven each other, and their hatred has been replaced by respect and brotherhood.

Q: Carl Jung introduced the concept of synchronicity. Is that concept now more understandable?

A: The consciousness level of the genius of Freud calibrates at 499 and that of Jung at 540. Therefore, Jung could see and comprehend beyond the limitation of conventional logic. This leap in consciousness allowed Jung to intuit that the visible is subject to the invisible where true power resides.

Attractor fields in consciousness can therefore simultaneously influence multiple events that are widely separated to observation with no apparent mechanism or purported cause to explain the phenomenon. This synchronicity cannot be explained within the linear dimension. To those who have evolved past consciousness level 600, the miraculous and synchronicity are the prevailing patterns of life. They also demonstrate the validity of the often spoken characteristic of consciousness that "energy follows thought," or that "what is held in mind tends to materialize."

With this understanding as a basis, the usefulness of visualization has become well known. Synchronicity signifies a 'quantum' correlation but not a causality. The correlation is a pattern in the unobservable domain that simultaneously manifests in an apparently divergent time and place. Thus, thousands of iron filings can be affected by a single electromagnetic field in which a slight change would then bring about simultaneous shifts in observable events.

Spiritual power has the capacity in its expression as consciousness to influence a great multitude of individual minds and therefore events. In everyday life, although sequences are ascribed to logic and intention, in truth, everyone realizes that they come about as a result of the intangibles of attitude, viewpoint, sentiment, appeal, and inspiration.

Life as we observe and experience it, is the result of the intangibles in the invisible domain finding arrangement and form to facilitate intention as well as attraction and aversion. It is not the tangibles but what they mean to us that determine the quality of life.

Happily, a loving thought is enormously more powerful than a negative one. Were it not so, there would be no one left on this planet to tell the tale.

Section Five

Appendices

APPENDIX A

CALIBRATION OF LEVELS OF TRUTH OF THE CHAPTERS

APPENDIX B

MAP OF THE SCALE OF CONSCIOUSNESS®

God-view	Life-view	Level		Log	Emotion	Process
Self	Is	Enlightenment	⇑	700-1000	Ineffable	Pure Consciousness
All-Being	Perfect	Peace	⇑	600	Bliss	Illumination
One	Complete	Joy	⇑	540	Serenity	Transfiguration
Loving	Benign	Love	⇑	500	Reverence	Revelation
Wise	Meaningful	Reason	⇑	400	Understanding	Abstraction
Merciful	Harmonious	Acceptance	⇑	350	Forgiveness	Transcendence
Inspiring	Hopeful	Willingness	⇑	310	Optimism	Intention
Enabling	Satisfactory	Neutrality	⇑	250	Trust	Release
Permitting	Feasible	Courage	⇕	200	Affirmation	Empowerment
Indifferent	Demanding	Pride	⇓	175	Scorn	Inflation
Vengeful	Antagonistic	Anger	⇓	150	Hate	Aggression
Denying	Disappointing	Desire	⇓	125	Craving	Enslavement
Punitive	Frightening	Fear	⇓	100	Anxiety	Withdrawal
Disdainful	Tragic	Grief	⇓	75	Regret	Despondency
Condemning	Hopeless	Apathy	⇓	50	Despair	Abdication
Vindictive	Evil	Guilt	⇓	30	Blame	Destruction
Despising	Miserable	Shame	⇓	20	Humiliation	Elimination

APPENDIX C

HOW TO CALIBRATE
THE LEVELS OF CONSCIOUSNESS

General Information

The energy field of consciousness is infinite in dimension. Specific levels correlate with human consciousness, and these have been calibrated from "1" to "1,000." (See Appendix B: Map of the Scale of Consciousness.) These energy fields reflect and dominate human consciousness.

Everything in the universe radiates a specific frequency or minute energy field that remains in the field of consciousness permanently. Thus, every person or being whoever lived and anything about them, including any event, thought, deed, feeling, or attitude, is recorded forever and can be retrieved at any time in the present or the future.

Technique

The muscle-testing response is a simple "yes" or "not yes" (no) response to a specific stimulus. It is usually done by the subject's holding out an extended arm and the tester pressing down on the wrist of the extended arm, using two fingers and light pressure. Usually the subject holds a substance to be tested over their solar plexus with the other hand. The tester says to the test subject, "Resist," and if the substance being tested is beneficial to the subject, the arm will be strong. If it is not beneficial or has an adverse effect, the arm will go weak. The response is *very quick and brief.*

It is important to note that the intention, as well as both the tester and the one being tested, must calibrate over 200 in order to obtain accurate responses.

The higher the levels of consciousness of the test team, the more accurate are the results. The best attitude is one of clinical detachment, posing a statement with the prefix statement, "In the name of the highest good, _____ calibrates as true. Over 100. Over 200," etc. The contextualization "in the highest good" increases accuracy because it transcends self-serving personal interest and motives.

For many years, the test was thought to be a local response of the body's acupuncture or immune system. Later research, however, has revealed that the response is not a local response to the body at all, but instead is a general response of consciousness itself to the energy of a substance or a statement. That which is true, beneficial, or pro-life gives a positive response that stems from the impersonal field of consciousness, which is present in everyone living. This positive response is indicated by the body's musculature going strong. For convenience, the deltoid muscle is usually the one best used as an indicator muscle; however, any of the muscles of the body can be used, such as the gastrocnemias, which are often used by practitioners such as chiropractors.

Before a question (in the form of a statement) is presented, it is necessary to qualify 'permission'; that is, state "I have permission to ask about what I am holding in mind." (Yes/No) Or, "This calibration serves the highest good."

If a statement is false or a substance is injurious, the muscles go weak quickly in response to the command "Resist." This indicates the stimulus is negative, untrue, anti-life, or the answer is "no." The response is fast and brief in duration. The body will then rapidly recover and return to normal muscle tension.

There are three ways of doing the testing. The one that is used in research and also most generally used requires two people: the tester and the test subject. A quiet setting is preferred, with no background music. The test subject closes their eyes. *The tester must phrase the 'question' to be asked in the form of a statement.* The statement can then be answered as "yes" or "not yes" (no) by the muscle-testing response. For instance, the *incorrect* form would be to ask, "Is this a healthy horse?" rather than make the statement, "This horse is healthy," or its corollary, "This horse is sick."

After making the statement, the tester says "Resist" to the test subject who is holding the extended arm parallel to the ground. The tester presses down with two fingers on the wrist of the extended arm sharply, with mild force. The test subject's arm will either stay strong, indicating a "yes," or go weak, indicating a "not yes" (no). The response is *very short and immediate*.

A second method is the "O-ring" method, which can be done alone. The thumb and middle finger of the same hand are held tightly in an "O" configuration, and the hooked forefinger of the opposite hand is used to try to pull them apart. There is a noticeable difference of the strength between a "yes" and a "no" response.

(Rose, 2001).

The third method is the simplest, yet, like the others, requires some practice. Simply lift a heavy object, such as a large dictionary or merely a couple of bricks, from a table about waist high. Hold in mind an image or true statement to be calibrated and lift. Then, for contrast, hold in mind that which is known to be false. Note the ease of lifting when truth is held in mind and the greater effort necessary to lift the load when the issue is false (not true). The results can be verified using the other two methods

Calibration of Specific Levels

The critical point between positive and negative, between true and false, or between that which is constructive or destructive, is at the calibrated level of 200 (see Map). Anything above 200, or true, makes the subject go strong; anything below 200, or false, allows the arm to go weak.

Anything past or present, including images or statements, historical events, or personages, can be tested. They need not be verbalized.

Numerical Calibration

Example: "Ramana Maharshi's teachings calibrate over 700." (Y/N)

Or, "Hitler calibrated over 200." (Y/N) "When he was in his 20s." (Y/N) "His 30s." (Y/N) "His 40s." (Y/N) "At the time of his death." (Y/N)

Applications

Muscle testing cannot be used to foretell the future;

otherwise, there are no limits as to what can be asked. Consciousness has no limits in time or space; however, permission may be denied. All current or historical events are available for questioning. The answers are impersonal and do not depend on the belief systems of either the tester or the test subject. For example, protoplasm recoils to noxious stimuli and flesh bleeds. Those are the qualities of these test materials and are impersonal. Consciousness actually knows only truth because only truth has actual existence. It does not respond to falsehood because falsehood does not have existence in Reality. It will also not respond accurately to nonintegrous or egoistic questions, such as should one buy a certain stock.

Accurately speaking, the muscle-testing response is either an "on" response or it is merely "not on." Like the electrical switch, we say the electricity is "on," and when we use the term "off," we just mean that it is not there. In reality, there is no such thing as "off-ness." This is a subtle statement but crucial to the understanding of the nature of consciousness. Consciousness is capable of recognizing only Truth. It merely fails to respond to falsehood. Similarly, a mirror reflects an image only if there is an object to reflect. If no object is present to the mirror, there is no reflected image.

To Calibrate A Level

Calibrated levels are relative to a specific reference scale. To arrive at the same figures as in the chart in Appendix A, reference must be made to that table or by a statement such as, "On a scale of human consciousness from 1 to 1,000, where 600 indicates

Enlightenment, this _____ calibrates over _____ (a number)." Or, "On a scale of consciousness where 200 is the level of Truth and 500 is the level of Love, this statement calibrates over _____." (State a specific number.)

General Information

People generally want to determine truth from falsehood. Therefore, the statement has to be made very specifically. Avoid using general terms such as a "good" job to apply for. "Good" in what way? Pay scale? Working conditions? Promotional opportunities? Fairness of the boss?

Expertise

Familiarity with the test brings progressive expertise. The "right" questions to ask begin to spring forth and can become almost uncannily accurate. If the same tester and test subject work together for a period of time, one or both of them will develop what can become an amazing accuracy and capability of pinpointing just what specific questions to ask, even though the subject is totally unknown by either one. For instance, the tester has lost an object and begins by saying, "I left it in my office." (Answer: No.) "I left it in the car." (Answer: No.) All of a sudden, the test subject almost 'sees' the object and says, "Ask, 'On the back of the bathroom door.'" The test subject says, "The object is hanging on the back of the bathroom door." (Answer: Yes.) In this actual case, the test subject did not even know that the tester had stopped for gas and left the jacket in the restroom of a gasoline station.

Any information can be obtained about anything anywhere in current or past time or space, depending on receiving prior permission. (Sometimes one gets a 'no', perhaps for karmic or other unknown reasons.) By cross-checking, accuracy can be easily confirmed. For anyone who learns the technique, more information is available instantaneously than can be held in all the computers and libraries of the world. The possibilities are therefore obviously unlimited, and the prospects breathtaking.

Limitations

Approximately ten percent of the population is not able to use the muscle-testing technique for as yet unknown reasons. The test is accurate only if the test subjects themselves calibrate over 200 and the intention of the use of the test is integrous and also calibrates over 200. The requirement is one of detached objectivity and alignment with truth rather than subjective opinion. Thus, to try to 'prove a point' negates accuracy. Sometimes married couples, also for reasons as yet undiscovered, are unable to use each other as test subjects and may have to find a third person to be a test partner.

A suitable test subject is a person whose arm goes strong when a love object or person is held in mind, and it goes weak if that which is negative (fear, hate, guilt, etc.) is held in mind (e.g., Winston Churchill makes one go strong and bin Laden makes one go weak).

Occasionally, a suitable test subject gives para-doxical responses. This can usually be cleared by doing the "thymic thump," as was discovered by Dr. John

Diamond. (With a closed fist, thump three times over the upper breastbone, smile, and say "ha-ha-ha" with each thump and mentally picture someone or something that is loved.)

The imbalance may be the result of recently having been with negative people, listening to heavy metal rock music, watching violent television programs, playing violent video games, etc. Negative music energy has a deleterious effect on the energy system of the body for up to one-half hour after it is turned off. Television commercials or background are also a common source of negative energy.

As previously noted, the muscle-testing method of discerning truth from falsehood and the calibrated levels of truth has strict requirements. Because of the limitations, calibrated levels are supplied for ready reference in prior books, and extensively in *Truth vs. Falsehood*.

Explanation

The muscle-testing technique is independent of personal opinion or beliefs and is an impersonal response of the field of consciousness, just as protoplasm is impersonal in its responses. This can be demonstrated by the observation that the test responses are the same whether verbalized or held silently in mind. Thus, the test subject is not influenced by the question, as they do not even know what it is. To demonstrate this, do the following exercise:

The tester holds in mind an image unknown to the test subject and states, "The image I am holding in mind is positive" (or "true," or "calibrates over 200," etc.). On direction, the test subject then resists the downward pressure on the wrist. If the tester holds a positive image in mind (e.g., Abraham Lincoln, Jesus, Mother Teresa, etc.), the test subject's arm muscle will go strong. If the tester holds a false statement or negative image in mind (e.g., bin Laden, Hitler, etc.), the arm will go weak. Inasmuch as the test subject does not know what the tester has in mind, the results are not influenced by personal beliefs.

Correct Muscle-Testing Technique

Just as Galileo's interest was in astronomy and not in making telescopes, the Institute for Advanced Spiritual Research is devoted to Consciousness research and not specifically to muscle testing. The DVD, *Power vs. Force* (Veritas Publishing, [1995], 2006), demonstrates the basic technique. More detailed information about muscle testing can be found on the Internet by searching for 'kinesiology'. Numerous references are provided, such as the College of Applied Kinesiology (www.icak.com), and other educational institutions.

Disqualification

Both skepticism (cal. 160) and cynicism calibrate below 200 because they reflect negative prejudgment. In contrast, true inquiry requires an open mind and honesty devoid of intellectual vanity. Negative studies of behavioral kinesiology (mscle testing) *all* calibrate below 200 (usually at 160), as do the investigators themselves.

That even famous professors can and do calibrate

below 200 may seem surprising to the average person. Thus, negative studies are a consequence of negative bias. As an example, Francis Crick's research design that led to the discovery of the double helix pattern of DNA calibrated at 440. His last research design, which was intended to prove that consciousness was just a product of neuronal activity, calibrated at only 135.

The failure of investigators who themselves, or by faulty research design, calibrate below 200 (all calibrate at approximately 160), confirms the truth of the very methodology they claim to disprove. They 'should' get negative results, and so they do, which paradoxically proves the accuracy of the test to detect the difference between unbiased integrity and nonintegrity.

Any new discovery may upset the apple cart and be viewed as a threat to the status quo of prevailing belief systems. That a clinical science of consciousness has emerged which validates spiritual Reality is, of course, going to precipitate resistance, as it is actually a direct confrontation to the dominion of the narcissistic core of the ego itself, which is innately presumptuous and opinionated.

Below consciousness level 200, comprehension is limited by the dominance of Lower Mind, which is capable of recognizing facts but not yet able to grasp what is meant by the term 'truth' (it confuses *res interna* with *res externa*), and that truth has physiological accompaniments which are different from falsehood. Additionally, truth is intuited as evidenced by the use of voice analysis, the study of body language, papillary-response EEG changes in the brain, fluctuations in breathing and blood pressure, galvanic skin response, dowsing, and even the Huna technique of measuring the distance that the aura radiates from the body. Some people have a very simple technique that utilizes the standing body like a pendulum (fall forward with truth and backward with falsehood).

From a more advanced contextualization, the principles that prevail are that Truth cannot be disproved by falsehood any more than light can be disproved by darkness. The nonlinear is not subject to the limitations of the linear. Truth is of a different paradigm from logic and thus is not 'provable', as that which is provable calibrates only in the 400s. Consciousness research muscle testing operates at level 600, which is at the interface of the linear and the nonlinear dimensions.

Discrepancies

Differing calibrations may be obtained over time or by different investigators for a variety of reasons:

1. Situations, people, politics, policies, and attitudes change over time.

2. People tend to use different sensory modalities when they hold something in mind, i.e., visual, sensory, auditory, or feeling. "Your mother" could therefore be how she looked, felt, sounded, etc., or Henry Ford could be calibrated as a father, as an industrialist, for his impact on America, his anti-Semitism, etc.

One can specify context and stick to a prevailing modality. The same team using the same technique will get results that are internally consistent. Expertise develops with practice. There are some people, however, who are incapable of a scientific, detached attitude and unable to be objective, and for whom the muscle-testing method will therefore not be accurate. Dedication and intention to the truth have to be given priority over personal opinions and trying to prove them as being "right."

APPENDIX D

REFERENCES

A Course in Miracles, 1975. Foundation for Inner Peace. Amityville, NY: Coleman Graphics.

"Applied Kinesiology." *Time*. April 16, 2001.

Barnes, T. 1999. *The Kingfisher Book of Religions*. Kingfisher, New York.

——. 1980. *Wholeness and the Implicate Order*. London: Routledge & Kegan Paul.

Briggs, J. And Peat, F. D. 1989. *Turbulent Mirror: An Illustrated Guide to Chaos Theory and the Science of Wholeness*. New York: Harper & Row.

Brinkley, D. 1994. *Saved by the Light*. New York: Villard Books/Random House.

Diamond, J. 1979. *Behavioral Kinesiology*. New York: Harper & Row.

Eadie, B. J. 1992. *Embraced by the Light*. Placerville, California: Gold Leaf Press.

Glerck, J. 1987. *Chaos: Making a New Science*. New York: Viking Penguin.

Hawkins, David R. 1986. "Consciousness and Addiction." (Videotape) Sedona, Arizona: Veritas Publishing.

——. 1986. Sedona Lecture Series: "Map of Consciousness"; "Death and Dying"; "Hypertension and Heart Disease"; "Cancer'; and "Alcohol and Drug Addiction." (Videotapes) Sedona, Arizona: Veritas Publishing.

——. 1986. Twelve Lectures: "Weight"; "Alcoholism"; "Illness"; "Health"; "Spiritual First Aid"; "Pain and Suffering"; "Sex"; "Worry, Fear, and Anxiety"; "The Aging Process", and "Handling Major Crises". (Videotapes) Sedona, Arizona: Veritas Publishing.

——. 1995. *Power vs. Force: An Anatomy of Consciousness*. Sedona, Arizona: Veritas Publishing.

——. 1995. "Power vs. Force." (Videotape) Sedona, Arizona: Veritas Publishing.

——. 1995. *Quantitative and Qualitative Analysis and Calibration of the Levels of Human Consciousness*. Sedona, Arizona: Veritas Publishing.

——. 1996. "Realization of the Presence of God." Concepts. July 1996, 17-18.

——. 1997. "Consciousness and Spirituality." (Videotape) Sedona, Arizona: Veritas Publishing.

——. 1997. "Dialogues on Consciousness and Spirituality." Sedona, Arizona: Veritas Publishing.

——. 2001. "The Nature of Consciousness: How to Tell the Truth About Anything." Sedona, Arizona: Veritas Publishing.

Henon, J. 1976. "Mapping with a Strange Attractor." *Com. Math. Physics*: 50, 69-77.

History and Culture of Buddhism in Korea, 1993. Korean Buddhist Research Institute. Seoul Korea: Dongguk University Press.

Huang Po. 1958. *The Zen Teaching of Huang Po: On Transmission of the Mind*. John Blofield, trans. New York: Grove Press.

Judge, W. O. 1969. *Bhagavad-Gita – Essays*. Pasadena, California: Theosophical University Press.

Jung, C. G. 1973. *Synchronicity as a Causal Connecting Principle*. R. F. Hull.

Korean Buddhism, Chogye Order, 1996. Seoul, Korea: Ven. Song Wol-Ju, Kum Sok Publishing Co.

Lamsa, G. M. 1933. *Holy Bible from Ancient Eastern Manuscripts (Aramaic, Peshotta)*. Philadelphia: A. J. Holmes & Co.

Lamsa, G. M. 1957. *Holy Bible from Ancient Eastern Manuscripts*. Philadelphia: A. J. Holmes & Co.

Lee, Yang Hee. 1999. *Omniology "Secret of Cosmos."* Koyang City, Korea: Wisdom Publishing Co.

Maharaj, Nisargadatta. 1973. *I Am That*. Bombay, India: Chetana.

Maharshi, Ramana. 1958. *Collected Works*. Madras, India: Jupiter Press.

Maharshi, Ramana. 1972. *Spiritual Teachings*. Boulder, Colorado: Shambala.

Monroe, R. 1971. *Journeys Out of the Body*. New York: Anchor/Doubleday.

Pelmen, M., and Ramsay, J. 1995. *Juan Yiu*. San Francisco: Thorsons.

Rahula, Walpola. 1959. *What the Buddha Taught*. New York: Grove Press.

Rodriguez, M. 1995. "Quest for Spiritual Rapid Change," in *Rediscovering the Soul of Business*. Defeore, B., and Renalch, J. (Eds.). San Francisco: New Leaders Press, Sterling and Stone, Inc.

Rosband, S. N. 1990. *Chaotic Dynamics of Non-Linear Systems*. New York: John Wiley & Sons.

Ruelle, D. 1989. *Chaotic Evolution and Strange Attractors: Statistical Analysis of Time Series for Deterministic and Nonlinear Systems*. New York: Cambridge University Press.

Stewart, H. B. and Thompson, J. M. 1986. *Nonlinear Dynamics and Chaos*. New York: John Wiley & Sons.

The Teachings of Buddha. 1966. Tokyo: Bukkyo Dendo Kyokai, Kosardo Printing Company.

Varvoglis, M. 1994. "Nonlocality on a Human Scale...Consciousness Research." *Toward a Scientific Basis for Consciousness; an Interdisciplinary Conference*. University of Arizona, Health Sciences Center, Tucson, Arizona, April 12-17, 1994.

Wang, L., et al. 2001. *Nature*, July 20.

Yorke, J. A., and Tien-Yien, L. 1975. "Period Three Implies Chaos." *American Math Monthly* 82, 985-992.

ABOUT THE AUTHOR

Biographical and Autobiographical Notes

Dr. Hawkins is an internationally known spiritual teacher, author, and speaker on the subject of advanced spiritual states, consciousness research, and the Realization of the Presence of God as Self.

His published works, as well as recorded lectures, have been widely recognized as unique in that a very advanced state of spiritual awareness occurred in an individual with a scientific and clinical background who was later able to verbalize and explain the unusual phenomenon in a manner that is clear and comprehensible.

The transition from the normal ego-state of mind to its elimination by the Presence is described in the trilogy *Power vs. Force* (1995) which won praise even from Mother Teresa, *The Eye of the I* (2001), and *I: Reality and Subjectivity* (2003), which have been translated into the major languages of the world. *Truth vs. Falsehood: How to Tell the Difference* (2005) and *Transcending the Levels of Consciousness* (2006) continue the exploration of the ego's expressions and inherent limitations and how to transcend them.

The trilogy was preceded by research on the Nature of Consciousness and published as the doctoral dissertation, *Qualitative and Quantitative Analysis and Calibration of the Levels of Human Consciousness* (1995), which correlated the seemingly disparate domains of science and spirituality. This was accomplished by the major discovery of a technique that, for the first time in human history, demonstrated a means to discern truth from falsehood.

The importance of the initial work was given recognition by its very favorable and extensive review in *Brain/Mind Bulletin* and at later presentations such as the International Conference on Science and Consciousness. Many presentations were given to a variety of organizations, spiritual conferences, church groups, nuns, and monks, both nationally and in foreign countries, including the Oxford Forum. In the Far East, Dr. Hawkins is a recognized "Teacher of the Way to Enlightenment" (Tae Ryoung Sun Kak Dosa).

In response to his observation that much spiritual truth has been misunderstood over the ages due to lack of explanation, Dr. Hawkins presented monthly seminars that provided detailed explanations which are too lengthy to describe in book format. Recordings are available, along with questions and answers that provide additional clarification.

The overall design of this lifetime work is to recontextualize the human experience in terms of the evolution of consciousness and to integrate a comprehension of both mind and spirit as expressions of the innate Divinity that is the substrate and ongoing source of life and Existence. This dedication is signified by the statement "Gloria in Excelsis Deo!" with which his published works begin and end.

Biographic Summary

Dr. Hawkins has practiced psychiatry since 1952 and is a life member of the American Psychiatric

Association and numerous other professional organizations. His national television appearance schedule has included *The McNeil/Leher News Hour, The Barbara Walters Show, The Today Show,* science documentaries, and many others.

He is the author of numerous scientific and spiritual publications, books, videotapes, and lecture series. Nobelist Linus Pauling coauthored his landmark book, *Orthomolecular Psychiatry.* Dr. Hawkins's diverse background as researcher and teacher is noted in his biographical listings in *Who's Who in America* and *Who's Who in the World.* He was a consultant for many years to Episcopal and Catholic Dioceses, The Monastery, monastic orders, and the Zen Monastery.

Dr. Hawkins has lectured widely, with appearances at Westminster Abbey; the Universities of Argentina, Notre Dame, and Michigan; Fordham and Harvard Universities; and the Oxford Forum. He gave the annual Landsberg Lecture at the University of California Medical School at San Francisco. He is also a consultant to foreign governments on international diplomacy and was instrumental in resolving long-standing conflicts that were major threats to world peace.

In recognition of his contributions to humanity, in 1995 Dr. Hawkins became a knight of the Sovereign Order of the Hospitaliers of St. John of Jerusalem, which was founded in 1077.

NOTES

NOTES

Hay House Titles of Related Interest

YOU CAN HEAL YOUR LIFE, the movie,
starring Louise Hay & Friends
(available as a 1-DVD program, an expanded
2-DVD set, and an online streaming video)
Learn more at **www.hayhouse.com/louise-movie**

THE SHIFT, the movie, starring Dr. Wayne W. Dyer
(available as a 1-DVD program, an expanded
2-DVD set, and an online streaming video)
Learn more at **www.hayhouse.com/the-shift-movie**
✸✸

*BEYOND HAPPINESS: Finding and Fulfilling
Your Deepest Desire,* by Dr. Frank J. Kinslow

*CHOICES AND ILLUSIONS: How Did I Get Where I Am,
and How Do I Get Where I Want to Be?,* by Eldon Taylor

*THE HONEYMOON EFFECT: The Science of
Creating Heaven on Earth,* by Bruce H. Lipton, Ph.D.

*MIND OVER MEDICINE: Scientific Proof That You Can
Heal Yourself,* by Lissa Rankin, M.D.

*THE TAPPING SOLUTION: A Revolutionary System
for Stress-Free Living,* by Nick Ortner

All of the above are available at your local bookstore,
or may be ordered by contacting Hay House (see next page).
✸✸

We hope you enjoyed this Hay House book. If you'd like to receive our online catalog featuring additional information on Hay House books and products, or if you'd like to find out more about the Hay Foundation, please contact:

Hay House, Inc., P.O. Box 5100, Carlsbad, CA 92018-5100
(760) 431-7695 or (800) 654-5126
(760) 431-6948 (fax) or (800) 650-5115 (fax)
www.hayhouse.com® • www.hayfoundation.org

———

Published in Australia by: Hay House Australia Pty. Ltd.,
18/36 Ralph St., Alexandria NSW 2015
Phone: 612-9669-4299 • *Fax:* 612-9669-4144
www.hayhouse.com.au

Published in the United Kingdom by: Hay House UK, Ltd.,
The Sixth Floor, Watson House, 54 Baker Street, London W1U 7BU
Phone: +44 (0)20 3927 7290 • *Fax:* +44 (0)20 3927 7291
www.hayhouse.co.uk

Published in India by: Hay House Publishers India,
Muskaan Complex, Plot No. 3, B-2, Vasant Kunj, New Delhi 110 070
Phone: 91-11-4176-1620 • *Fax:* 91-11-4176-1630
www.hayhouse.co.in

———

Access New Knowledge.
Anytime. Anywhere.

Learn and evolve at your own pace
with the world's leading experts.

www.hayhouseU.com